EMPIRE *WITH* IMPERIALISM

EMPIRE *WITH* IMPERIALISM
The Globalizing Dynamics of Neo-liberal Capitalism

by James Petras
and Henry Veltmeyer
with Luciano Vasapollo and Mauro Casadio

FERNWOOD PUBLISHING • ZED BOOKS

Editing by Douglas Beall, Brenda Conroy
Printed and bound in Canada by Hignell Printing Limited

Published in Canada by Fernwood Publishing
Site 2A, Box 5, 32 Oceanvista Lane
Black Point, Nova Scotia, B0J 1B0
and 324 Clare Avenue, Winnipeg, Manitoba, R3L 1S3
www.fernwoodbooks.ca

Published in the rest of the world by Zed Books Ltd.
7 Cynthia Street, London NI 9JF, UK
and Room 400, 175 Fifth Avenue,
New York, 10010, USA
Distributed in the USA exclusively by Palgrave Macmillan,
a division of St. Martins Press, LLC, 175 Fifth Ave., New York, 10010, USA.

Zed Books ISBN 1 84277 668 1 hb; 1 84277 669 X pb

British CIP available from the British Library.
American CIP has been applied for.

Fernwood Publishing Company Limited gratefully acknowledges
the financial support of the Department of Canadian Heritage,
the Nova Scotia Department of Tourism and Culture
and the Canada Council for the Arts for our publishing program.

Library and Archives Canada Cataloguing in Publication

Empire with imperialism: the globalizing dynamics of neo-liberal capitalism /
James Petras ... [et al.].

Includes index.
ISBN 1-55266-174-1

1.Imperialism—Economic aspects. 2.Capitalism.
3.Globalization. I.Petras, James F., 1937-

JC359.E45 2005a   325'.32'09051   C2005-904237-0

CONTENTS

ACKNOWLEDGEMENTS

THE AUTHORS WOULD LIKE TO ACKNOWLEDGE THE EXCELLENT WORK on our text by Fernwood Publishing, as relates to copyediting (Douglas Beall, Brenda Conroy) and production (Beverley Rach). And then there is the irrepressible Errol Sharpe, who supported the project from the outset.

We would also like to gratefully acknowledge the contributions to the book by Mark Rushton, who prepared the index and designed the cover of the book. Mark's numerous skills and excellent judgement were at our full disposal, for which we would like to express our deepest appreciation.

And of course we would be remiss if we did not acknowledge the unstinting support of our life partners, Robin Eastman Abaya and Annette Wright. In addition Robin wordprocessed and edited all of the text prepared for the book by James Petras. Much appreciated.

PREFACE
The State of the United States

GEORGE W. BUSH'S "STATE OF THE UNION" SPEECH OF 2004 WAS NOT IN praise of "America" as claimed; it was about imperialism abroad — what President Putin in the context of the political crisis in the Ukraine describes as "the United States seeking to establish an international dictatorship of international affairs" — and quasi-fascism at home. It was a speech in praise of conquests of failed or rogue states in the Third World (Afghanistan and Iraq), a celebration of force as an instrument of political blackmail (Libya) and a declaration of new imperial impositions in the entire Middle East. The speech reiterated the most retrograde elements of the Bush doctrine: unilateral use of force, preventive war and the supremacy of US imperial dictates over the national sovereignty of enemies and allies. The smiling president glorifying US imperial conquests while his sycophants and partisans packing the Congress cheered was a kind of "Nuremberg lite" — a choreographed scenario to exalt the accomplishments of the imperial president.

The emperor denied any imperial intentions even as he defended imperial conquests and projected new military expeditions. His speech went beyond "triumphalism" and mendacity. It was based on a surreal vision that places the US at the centre of a divine universe in which the "Chosen People" of the US will exterminate their enemies and forcibly enlighten their reluctant allies.

Bush spoke as a millenarian, slaying devils ("terrorists") with a righteous sword (or cluster bombs), as an ordained and anointed disciple of God. Between triumphalism and celebration, however, the emperor sowed fear of enemy violence to justify the imperialist mission. This mission is complemented by paranoia: "terrorism" is everywhere, hidden and disguised, an evil force which at any moment could reproduce September 11.

The imperial ideology of triumphalism was juxtaposed with permanent vulnerability — celebration with fear. However, the illogical, contradictory and totally dissembling nature of the "State of the Union" discourse does not matter. We are all too familiar with ideology in its various guises, especially one so transparent as a discourse on freedom and peace brought about by smart bombs, missiles and the military apparatus of an imperial power seeking world domination. What matters is power. Triumphalist rhetoric was used to capture domestic resources (inflated military budgets and soldiers) to continue a vicious colonial war, and paranoia was used to justify the concentration of freedom-restricting dictatorial powers (via the Patriot Act) to repress, silence and cower the anti-war opposition. (Under Section 501 of Patriot II, a US citizen engaging in lawful activity can be picked off the streets or from home and taken to a secret military tribunal with no access to or notification of a lawyer, the press or family. This would be considered justified if an agent "inferred from the conduct" suspicious intentions of that citizen.)

Nothing mundane or factual was allowed to interfere with the construction of this glorious vision of world empire. There was no mention of the hundreds of US soldiers killed, the thousands maimed or dismembered, the scores of suicides or the thousands of mentally disturbed. Bush did not mention the US dead and wounded, not merely because it wouldn't have served the purpose of exalting empire, but because it would have demonstrated that US soldiers are vulnerable (and not God's chosen and protected "supermen") and that the colonized people were effectively resisting the "invincible military machine."

Bush and his inner circle know full well, in their less exalted moments, that each victory for the Iraqi resistance and each US casualty erodes his electoral support and undermines Rumsfeld's "will to power." Defeats in Iraq make a mockery of the Pentagon-Zionist-militarist vision of unlimited wars in the Middle East. The militarist-Zionist millenarian vision of successive military conquests (after Iraq, Syria, Iran and others) has been shattered by the battles in the suburbs of Baghdad, the hundreds of thousands of demonstrators in Basra and the landmines planted everywhere.

The Iraqi resistance has put the lie to the racist image held by Arab haters in the Pentagon and their colleagues in Israel: Arabs are neither cowed by US military power nor incapable of organizing resistance; it is the US soldiers in the hundreds who are resigning from the military, and it is the US government that is desperately begging for mercenaries from Central America to replace demoralized US forces.

Bush's report on the "State of the Empire" necessarily included a sweeping panegyric about the domestic social and economic successes of his regime. The empire was built of "guns and butter," or so his message was supposed to convey. But here the story was less credible, even to the most backward and chauvinistic sector of the US public.

Most people knew that three million US workers had lost their jobs over the previous three years. Most Americans know full well that private health and pharmaceutical plans are failing and that Bush's policies have increased the vulnerability of everyone but the very rich. It is precisely because Bush knew that over 60 percent of the US public rejected his social policies that he emphasized the need to extend the fascistic and repressive Patriot Act, with its clauses enabling the president to suspend all democratic rights.

Like the fascists of the 1930s and the fundamentalist religious right of more recent years, Bush declared war on non-traditional families, same-sex marriage, homosexuals and illegal immigrants (no amnesty for 10 million Mexicans) in order to mobilize his mass base of fundamentalist Christians.

Cloaked in the rhetoric of national security, Bush emphasized in his speech the central role of the police, (repressive) legislation and the military: no mention of the close to 80 percent unemployed in Iraq (or the 98 percent of Iraqis opposed to the war and US occupation), the bombing of villages in Afghanistan, the daily slaughter of Palestinians or the abusive police-state treatment of non-Europeans visiting the US who are presumed guilty (and are photographed and fingerprinted) and must prove their innocence.

Like emperors of bygone years, Bush is in total denial of the fragile domestic foundations of the empire, or of the massive transfer of state funds from the "republic" (domestic economy) to finance the empire, resulting in massive budget deficits which in 2004 climbed to over half a trillion dollars. Blinded by hubris or stupidity, or both, and by the dream of imperial economic expansion and world domination, he cannot see that the outflows of capital and the exports of overseas subsidiaries of US companies are creating a monstrous trade deficit and undermining the US currency.

Like his imperial predecessors, Bush believes that the "American people" must sacrifice for the greater good of his virtuous empire of freedom and peace. With the total support of the quasi-state, subservient and "self-censored" mass media, this message is spread in the US and throughout the world, but its reception in the rest of the world is rather different from that in the US. *Le Monde* reports that after Bush's speech, 67 percent of its readers felt that the US represents a grave threat to world peace. The same opinions were expressed in other parts of the world (with the exception of Israel). In the United States fewer than 15 percent of the people actually listened to the speech, and apart from the convinced, few voiced any outward support. The day after the speech there was more interest in the Super Bowl football championship game two weeks away than in Bush's oratory.

The US version of what historians have described as "fascism" is in some ways quite distinct from its antecedents. It buys votes with hundreds of millions of dollars of mass media propaganda; it does not coerce approval or overtly terrorize the population, but instead it sows paranoia and fear of "others" — the enemy within, without, anywhere and everywhere. There are no mass organizations and mass spectaculars to mesmerize the population; instead there is frivolity and banal lies to alienate voters and produce an abstention rate of over 50 percent. The US President was to be elected in 2004 by less than a quarter of the potential electorate, given a roughly one-half abstention rate and the exclusion of (10 million) "illegal" immigrants and the (four million) former prisoners. If this exclusionary electoral process is not sufficient to ensure an appropriate outcome, there can be voter fraud, exclusion and judicial interference.

Some might see this as "fascism lite," but it holds the potential for the heavier version known to us through the history of the twentieth century. The former commander of the US invasion force in Iraq, General Tommy Franks (a close adviser to Bush) recently declared that if there is another "major attack" in the US, the Constitution should be suspended, martial law should be declared and military tribunals should be established to try suspects. Bush's repeated defence of the Patriot Act echoes General Franks' quaisi-fascist pronouncements. In other words, any regime-instigated provocation could shift the fragile balance towards fascism as we know it.

Authoritarianism in pursuit of imperialism faces three fundamental obstacles at the moment: the forces of popular democracy, armed resistance, and the decline of the US republic. Members of the new world ruling class, the agents of transnational capitalism, who assemble and meet each year at the Swiss resort in Davos, Switzerland, are clearly troubled by the continuing decline of the dollar, the outcomes of inter-imperialist rivalry and "excessive" competition, the destabilizing effects of social inequality and poverty, the clash of civilizations, terrorism and other threats to the global order, and threats to the US and the global order. But the US and diverse national contingents of the world ruling class, assembling at Davos and at other such policy forums and summits, supported the US invasion of Iraq and refuse to recognize the connection between imperialist expansion and republican decay in the US.

The dilemma of the self-appointed neo-conservative guardians of the neo-liberal world order is the left's opportunity. The greater the solidarity with the forces of resistance in Iraq and elsewhere that challenge and weaken the forces of imperialism, the greater the likelihood of success in refounding the democratic republic, building and strengthening mass revolutionary movements, and bringing about another world.

1. THE FRAGRANCE OF IMPERIALISM

The past is never dead. It's not even past. — William Faulkner

THE NAME OF THIS BOOK DERIVES FROM AN ANALYSIS OF THE GLOBAL political economy made by Michael Hardt and Antonio Negri in a volume published in 2000 that bore the title *Empire* and an implied subtitle of "Without Imperialism." Hardt and Negri's book purported to be an analysis of the dynamics of global development, but, according to the authors, as a result of the forces of science and technology, global capitalism now functions as an autonomous "empire" ruled only by the market and multinational corporations. In direct opposition to this thesis, we maintain that the role of the imperial state in determining the form taken by capitalist development, preserving the system and adapting it to changing conditions has been seriously underestimated or ignored by Hardt and Negri. We also argue that the economic impact of innovation, science and technology on capitalist productivity has been overestimated. Not only is the imperial state still important to an understanding of the global dynamics of change and development today, but it also plays a central role in the contested terrain of global politics where the forces supportive of and opposed to capitalism, neo-liberalism, globalization and imperialism confront each other.

There are three basic ways of understanding the dynamics of transformative change and global development today. One is with reference to the notion of "international development," described most often as a process of modernization, industrialization and economic growth, and as a means of bringing about an improvement in the lives of most people in the so-called "Third World" — many of whom (up to 1.4 billion, it is estimated), despite their best efforts and because of their situation (separation from any ownership of the means of production, lack of access to productive resources or secure livelihoods) are mired in poverty and unable to meet their basic needs. A second popular interpretation of the sweeping changes and deteriorating conditions that have characterized recent decades is based on the concept of "globalization," defined as a multi-faceted and multi-dimensional process of sweeping changes resulting in a growing interconnectedness among people and nations at the level of economics, society, politics and culture. However, there is also a third approach, which we employ in this volume. In the view of this approach, both development and globalization are ideological masks thrown over an entirely different project and agenda: "imperialism," which can be minimally defined as a project of world domination, as a subjection of people and countries across the world to the interests and dominant power of an imperial state. Imperialism so defined has taken — and is taking — diverse forms and entails the projection of economic and ideological as well as political and military power.

This book is about the dynamics of imperialism in the current era. It is about the US imperial state and its efforts to establish a new world order of US hegemony over the entire system. At issue in these efforts is not only what Hardt and Negri term "Empire," but also what an increasing number of analysts and observers, even inside the "neo-conservative right," understand as imperialism. Given the misguided and possibly less than innocent efforts of Hardt and Negri to deny the reality of imperialism and to purge imperialism, economic crisis, the state, class and class struggle from the dynamics of global capitalist development, we begin our exploration of the terrain of imperialism with a critical review of *Empire*. We focus this critique on the implications of Hardt and Negri's analysis for understanding the situation of workers (the working class in its multitudinous forms) and peasant farmers, another component of what they choose to term "the multitude."[1]

Empire: With or without Imperialism?

Like so many others of the same postmodern ilk, Hardt and Negri seek to persuade the reader (yet again) that we all live in "new" times. In this regard their book represents what can only be termed the intellectual synthesis and political nadir of postmodern theoretical "analysis." It does for international relations and global capitalism what previous postmodern texts have done for national, local, regional or village relations and conflicts.[2] Just as the latter analyses have expelled class and class struggle from an understanding of the dynamics of the agrarian grassroots, Hardt and Negri attempt to expunge imperialism from the way the world economy works, banishing this important concept to the epistemological black hole of "post-history." As such, the book has profound implications for the study of peasants and workers, the dynamics of their struggle and the whole issue of capitalist transition in the Third World.

These implications can be stated simply. If there is no imperialism, then capitalism itself cannot be said to give rise to contradictions (which manifest in imperial rivalries). Nor can it be said to carry within itself the seeds of its own demise (and thus possess an alternative to its historically specific forms of property, production and exchange). The concept of systemic transition is thus swept off the political agenda, and with it emancipation of various kinds, not least that of peasants and workers operating at the margins of existence.

Although the subject of imperialism, and whether or not this concept continues to be applicable to the global capitalist system, seems to be far removed from the everyday reality of a peasant in a Third World village, the opposite is in fact the case: not only is the debate about the presence or absence of imperialism still relevant to the study of agrarian grassroots transformation, but the impact/effects on the latter context of imperialism could be said to form an epistemological dimension missing from much recent discussion about the peasantry, Marxist and non-Marxist alike. This has not always been the case: the imperialism/agriculture/peasantry link has a long history in the political debates of the left, and it is only necessary to mention the work of Rosa Luxemburg, Nicolai Bukharin and Lenin for this to be clear.

For all these reasons, and also because their book will assuredly become fashionable as an "analysis" of globalization, the arguments put forward by Hardt and Negri merit close scrutiny.

Our critique of *Empire* is in five parts. First, we raise several questions about the authors' general, rather *philosophical* (as opposed to political economy) approach. Second, we dispute the book's argument that the imperial state has been superseded by the global expansion of corporate capital. We argue to the contrary that the imperial states have grown and become essential components of the world political economy. The concept of "Empire" used by Hardt and Negri mystifies the role of the imperial state — thus undermining an essential adversary — in defence of the privileges and power of the multinational corporations. The next section challenges the authors' claim about the existence of a "new capitalist epoch" based on a purported information revolution. *Pace* Hardt and Negri, it is clear that the innovations of the early and middle twentieth century were far more significant sources of productivity improvement than the computerized information systems of the late twentieth century. The forth section suggests that, instead of "empire," the current situation corresponds to a new imperialism. The final section considers related questions concerning micro-level structure, and the kind of agency to which this empire gives rise. The analysis informing *Empire*, it is argued, follows what is now the well-worn path of postmodern theory. Not only do Hardt and Negri replace "class" with the "subaltern," but they also then conflate the latter with what they term a "new proletariat," and this resulting category exhibits all the characteristics that Negri in his earlier autonomist phase attributed to the marginal subject that then formed a "sub-proletariat."

The Empire as a Non-place

Empire is an odd book, to say the least. At a time when the US is the only superpower, a hegemon, when almost 50 percent of the 500 biggest multinational corporations (MNCs) are US-owned and headquartered, and Washington is leading a war of intervention against the peasants and workers of Afghanistan and Iraq — after previous wars of intervention against peasants and workers in the Balkans, Central America (Panama), the Caribbean (Grenada) and proxy wars in Colombia (Plan Colombia) and earlier Angola, Mozambique Nicaragua — the authors of this widely praised book tell us that imperialism is a thing of the past. They argue that the new empire is a post-imperialist phenomenon in which power is dispersed, and over which no single nation has control. More than this, their view is that this empire is a positive advance in world history.

After 413 pages of text and 57 pages of notes, the best the authors can do is to tell us that: "In this smooth space [?] of Empire there is no place of power — it is everywhere and nowhere. Empire is an *ou-Topia* or really a *non-place*" (p. 190). Without providing us with a clear notion of the agents of "Empire," or of its dynamic in the real imperial states and their corporations of our world, we are told that Empire is "imperial" but not imperialist, and that the US Constitution is imperial and not imperialist. From this they deduce (and we learn) that the US Constitution is imperial because — in contrast to imperialism's project always to spread its power linearly in closed spaces and invade, destroy and subsume subject countries within its sovereignty — the US constitutional project is constructed on the model of re-articulating an open space and reinventing incessantly diverse and singular networks across an unbounded terrain.

"The contemporary idea of Empire is born through the global expansion of the internal US constitutional project" (p. 182). In other words, this celebration of Empire is also a celebration of US constitutionalism (the idea, to be exact), which is a model for "democratizing" the Empire. The study disposes of classes and class conflict (and with them peasants and labourers) as outdated and imprecise concepts, and substitutes the notion of "biopolitical production multitudes," a term that is never clearly delineated and lacks historical or empirical specificity. Apart from the "multitudes" there are no designated agencies for the announced but unspecified "revolution." The program of this novel revolution is not very different from that embraced by welfare-state social democrats.

Much has been written about the "sweep of the book, its theoretical grandeur." Not surprisingly, the postmodern theorist Frederic Jameson (Hardt's colleague at Duke University) calls it "the first great new theoretical synthesis of the new Millennium." Hyperbole aside, few literary reviewers have commented on the book's lack of historical and empirical evidence to buttress its innumerable and unsubstantiated assertions. Hardt and Negri argue early on that the intellectual origins of the US revolution can be traced to Spinoza and Machiavelli, while Rousseau and Locke are given short shrift, despite their greater immediate relevance. Extended and tendentious discussions of sovereignty are interspersed with reductionist assertions, which either collapse or omit numerous variations. For example, in their discussion of totalitarianism and the nation-state, Hardt and Negri argue: "If Nazi Germany is the ideal type of the transformation of modern sovereignty into national sovereignty and of the articulation in its capitalist form, Stalinist Russia is the ideal type of the transmission of popular interest and the cruel logics that follow from it into a project of national modernization, mobilizing for its own purposes the productive forces that yearn for liberation from capitalism" (p. 110). These quotes illustrate the confused, illogical and unhistorical nature of the authors' broad and vacuous generalizations. What empirical or historical basis is there for claiming Nazi Germany is "the" ideal type? National sovereignty predated the Nazis and continued in non-totalitarian settings after their demise. If Stalin's Russia embodied "popular interest," why would anyone have sought to be liberated from it? The "cruel logic" of "popular interests" is stuff from the *ancien régime* — hardly the basis for orienting the "multitudes," whom the writers describe as being the new agents for democratizing the world. Where, precisely, workers and peasants feature in all this (except as part of the socio-economically amorphous "multitudes"), and what kind of agency they will undertake and with what aims, remain unclear.

The authors engage in what George Saboul once referred to as the "vacuum cleaner" approach to history, providing a little bit of ancient history, a smattering of the exegesis of elementary political theory, a plus and minus evaluation of postmodernism, a celebration of US constitutionalism and a brief synopsis of colonialism and post-colonialism. These discursive forays provide an intellectual gloss for the core argument dealing with the contemporary world: the disappearance of imperialism; the obsolescence of imperial states, nation-states (and boundaries) and the ascendancy of an ill-defined Empire; globalization; and supranational governing bodies apparently resembling the United Nations. Drawn into a conceptual black hole along with imperialism and class is the role of peasants and workers as agents of historical transformation.

Imperialism-is-US

Let us examine the assertion made by Hardt and Negri regarding the decline of the nation, or imperial state. Their argument for a stateless Empire exaggerates the autonomy of capital vis-à-vis the state, and parrots the false propositions of free market ideologues who argue that the "world market" is supreme and politically acceptable precisely because it operates independently of any specific national interest. Contrary to the view of Hardt and Negri, however, in the contemporary world, the national state, in both its imperial and neo-colonial forms, has expanded its activity. Far from being an anachronism, the state has become a central element in the world economy and within nation-states. However, the activities of states vary according to their class character and whether they are imperial or neo-colonial. In recent years the centrality of the imperial state has been evident in all the fundamental political-economic, cultural and economic activities that buttress the position of the imperial powers, particularly that of the US.

Over recent decades major financial and economic crises have occurred in various regions of the world. In each instance, the imperial states, particularly the US, have intervened to save multinational corporations and avoid a collapse of the financial system. For example, in 1994, when Mexican finances were on the verge of collapse, President Clinton intervened to dispatch \$20 billion[3] to the Mexican state to bail out US investors and stabilize the peso. Similarly, during the Asian crisis of 1998 the US and European governments approved an International Monetary Fund (IMF) and World Bank multi-billion-dollar bailout in exchange for an opening of Asian economies, particularly that of South Korea, to foreign takeovers of basic industries. In the Brazilian crisis of 1999 and the present Argentine crisis, Washington has pressured the IMF to bail out the regimes. Within the US itself, the threatened bankruptcy of a major international investment bank led to Federal Reserve (US central bank) intervention, leading to a private bank bailout. With greater frequency and with greater resources, therefore, the imperial state has played a dominant role in crisis management, saving major investors from bankruptcy, propping up insolvent multinational corporations and preventing the collapse of currencies. More than ever, the multinational corporations and the so-called global economy depend on constant and massive intervention by imperial states to manage crises and secure benefits through buyouts of local enterprises.

Much of the same is true of national debt in general, and that of the US farming and agribusiness sector in particular. The 1970s and 1980s were boom times for US farmers, as the then-USSR made large grain purchases. This was a period when markets were relatively secure, and US farmers who had guaranteed outlets expanded production, bought more land and machinery, and borrowed heavily. US banks were happy to lend money, since markets were buoyant and land prices were high. In the 1980s, however, agricultural commodity prices fell as President Carter embargoed further grain sales to the USSR following its invasion of Afghanistan. Bank collateral declined in value, and farmers, together with banks that had lent them money, were technically bankrupt. To avert this domestic debt crisis, and help the US agribusiness enterprises affected, the US state turned increasingly to export subsidies.

Historically and currently, competition among rival economic enterprises and multinational corporations has been spearheaded essentially by rival imperial states. This is particularly true where agriculture is concerned. For example, in 1989 the European states threatened to ban meat imports from the US on the grounds that growth-inducing hormone treatment of livestock constituted a health risk. This would have blocked $140 million worth of US exports, and the US government threatened to retaliate by preventing imports of European meat worth $100 million. A common feature of this inter-imperialist rivalry surfaces in the form of disputes over what are regarded as trade-distorting price supports. During the late 1980s, for example, the US operated an Export Enhancement Program (EEP) in an attempt to dispose of grain surpluses and win new markets or recapture old ones. Both the Canadian and European states responded, not by reducing grain production but by matching US subsidies. Currently, the US imperial state is leading the fight to open European markets to US beef and US exports of bananas from South and Central America, while the Japanese and the European states negotiate with the US to increase the "quota" on a series of exports (including steel and textiles). Trade and markets are largely defined by state-to-state agreements, and the supposedly autonomous and spontaneous process of "globalization" is not only a product of the growth of the multinational corporations, but also largely an artifice of these state-to-state agreements. Accordingly, competition between national forms of capital is mediated, influenced and directed by the state; markets do not transcend the state, but operate within state-defined boundaries.

The state plays a pervasive and profound role in the conquest of overseas markets and the protection of local markets. To begin with, the state provides indirect and direct subsidies to export sectors. In the US, agricultural exports receive both indirect subvention, in the form of subsidized water and electrical power, and direct subsidies in the form of tax relief. Second, the imperial state, via the international financial institutions (IFIs), pressures loan recipient states in the Third World through conditionality agreements to lower or eliminate trade barriers and privatize and denationalize enterprises, thus permitting US, European and Japanese multinational corporations to penetrate markets and buy into or purchase local enterprises. In short, so-called globalization would not exist were it not for state intervention, nor would markets remain open were it not for imperial state military and electoral intervention, politico-economic pressure and threats, and recruitment of local clients.

Imperialism takes many forms but pursues similar goals: conquest of markets, penetration of competitors and protection of home markets. The US has an elaborate set of trade barriers in a wide range of product areas of strategic importance: auto imports are limited by quotas, as are sugar, textiles and steel. A multiplicity of non-traditional constraints and informal agreements limit export countries from entering US markets — all negotiated on a state-to-state basis. In many cases, in its dealings with neo-colonial regimes like Brazil under Cardoso, the US state rejects reciprocity, instead demanding and securing the liberalization of the information industry while restricting Brazilian steel exports on the bogus pretext of "anti-dumping" charges.

All major internationally binding trade agreements, liberalizing trade and establishing new trade regulations, are negotiated by the states, enforced by the states and subject to state modification. Thus, for example, the General Agreement on Tariffs and Trade (GATT), the World Trade Organization (WTO) that succeeded it, and the Lomé Convention, which established the trade rules and framework for global trading networks, were all formulated by states. In addition, bilateral as well as regional multilateral trade pacts, such as the European Union (EU), the North American Free Trade Area (NAFTA) and the Latin American Free Trade Area (LAFTA), are initiated by states to open new markets for multinationals. The imperial state operates in synergy with its multinational corporations. The "expansion in markets," which Hardt and Negri perceive as spontaneous and unguided, has nothing to do with MNCs superseding anachronistic states. On the contrary, most movements of capital to new markets depend on state intervention to eliminate barriers and, in some cases, destabilize nationalist regimes.

The same is true of investment agreements, protection, subsidies and adjudication. New multilateral as well as bilateral investment agreements are formulated at the state level, with the agreement and active participation of multinational corporations. The reason is clear: the multinational corporations want state participation to guarantee that their capital will not be expropriated, subject to "discriminatory" taxes or restricted in remitting profits. The state is, to put it bluntly, the enforcer of investment guarantees, a crucial element in corporate investment expansion. In many cases the imperial states use their representatives in the IFIs to impose new investment codes as conditions for "stabilization" or development loans. The imperial states within the European Union impose powerful protection barriers for their agricultural products. Both the US and European states subsidize agriculture heavily, with low rates for electricity and water use. Research and development of new technology are heavily financed by the state, and the results are then turned over to the multinationals for marketing. At each stage prior to, during and after the expansion of an MNC into the international market overseas, the state is deeply involved. Moreover, where national enterprises are non-competitive, the imperial states invent pretexts to protect them from more efficient producers. Thus, for example, Japan protects its rice producers, even though their production is ten times more costly for consumers to purchase. The US provides huge subsidies to agro-business exporters in the form of research, cheap water rates and loans tied to the purchase of US grain exports, while the European Union subsidizes the formation of its high-tech industries.

What might be termed "statism" or "neo-statism" is central to the "global expansion" of multinational corporations based in the imperial states. The state has grown, its reach has extended and its activities have expanded: in short, its role in the international economy is essential to the reproduction of the capitalist system. Given this, it is unfortunately the case that the empty rhetoric of "free markets" promoted by conservative ideologues has been consumed and parroted by those who should know better, the "globalist left." While Hardt and Negri write about the declining role of the state, the political right worldwide has been active in promoting state activity to further the interests of the MNCs. Similarly, while Hardt and Negri write about the "globalization" of markets, the multinational corporations from the imperial countries carve up these markets, enlarging their spheres of influence, domination and control. Above all, the imperial state is not simply an economic institution; the overseas expansion of the multinational corporations is heavily dependent on the military and political role of the imperial state.

The overseas expansion of the multinational corporations has been made possible by the military and political expansion of Euro-American imperialism via the North Atlantic Treaty Organization (NATO) and surrogate armies in southern Africa, Latin America and Asia. In Russia, the former USSR and Eastern Europe, client regimes have been sponsored and supported by the imperial states, laying the groundwork for the takeover of a vast array of strategic industries, energy sources, etc. The US imperial state's triumph over the USSR provided the impetus for dismantling the welfare states in Europe and what pretended to be a welfare state in the US. The Euro-American wars in the Gulf and the Balkans consolidated the imperial states' dominance and extended their influence over dissident states. The destabilization of former communist regimes, and the destructive wars against nationalist and socialist regimes in southern Africa, Latin America and elsewhere, opened their countries to neo-liberal policy prescriptions. Military expansion was organized by state apparatuses, which accompanied and promoted the overseas expansion of the MNCs.

So-called globalization grew out of the barrel of a gun — a gun wielded, pointed and fired by the imperial state. To protect overseas capital further, the US and the European Union created a new NATO doctrine that legitimates offensive wars, outside of Europe against any country that threatens vital economic interests (i.e., their MNCs). NATO has been expanded to incorporate new client states in Eastern Europe and new "peace associates" among the Baltic states and the former republics of the USSR (Georgia, Kazakstan, etc.). In other words, the imperial state military alliances have incorporated more states, involving more state apparatuses than before, to ensure the safe passage of European and US multinational corporations into these countries and an easy flow of profits back to headquarters in the US and Western Europe. The argument made by Hardt and Negri about a stateless, classless empire without imperialism is based, in short, on the notion of a world market dominated by capital (MNCs), which, they argue, "must eventually overcome imperialism and destroy the barriers between inside and outside" (p. 234). According to them, these "global" corporations have turned the nations and imperial states into anachronisms.

Hardt and Negri provide no data whatsoever on the internal organization of the MNCs, no analysis of the decision-making structure and no discussion of their relations with states. Theorizing by fiat is a convenient way of evading inconvenient empirical studies. In essence, their argument is based on a number of unsubstantiated assumptions, of which the first is that MNCs are global enterprises that have no specific location in any particular nation-state. According to Hardt and Negri, such enterprises form the core of a new world economy divorced from national controls, and they are part of a new world ruling class. This assumption is based in turn on the fact that large corporations operate in a number of countries, are mobile and have the power to evade both taxes and regulations — particularly those protecting the workers or peasants they employ — in many national jurisdictions. There are several conceptual and empirical problems with this assumption.

First, the fact that MNCs operate in many countries does not detract from the fact that the headquarters, where most of the strategic decisions, directors and profits are concentrated, are located in the US, the EU and Japan. Second, mobility is based on strategic decisions taken by these directors in the imperial centres and these decisions depend on the political and economic conditions created by the imperial state and its representatives in the IFIs. Mobility is contingent on inter-state relations. Third, evasion of taxes and regulations is possible because of the deliberate policies of the imperial states and their multinational banks. Non-enforcement of laws against transfers of illicit earnings from the neo-colonial countries to the imperial countries is a form of state activity favouring large transfers of wealth that strengthen external accounts. The flouting of neo-colonial state regulations on the part of multinational corporations is part of a broader set of power relations between imperial and neo-colonial states.

The second assumption informing the analysis of Hardt and Negri is that the old nation-state governments have been superseded by a new world government, made up of the heads of the IFIs, the WTO and the heads of the MNCs (p. 336). This is an argument based on a superficial discussion of epiphenomena, rather than a deeper analytical view of the structure of power. While it is true that in a great many geographical locations the IFIs make many important decisions affecting significant economic and social sectors, these decisions and the decision-makers are closely linked to the imperial states and the multinational corporations that influence them. All top IFI officials are appointed by their national/ imperial governments, and all the crucial policy guidelines that dictate their loans and conditions for lending are set by the finance, treasury and economy ministers of the imperial states. The vast majority of funds for the IFIs themselves come from the imperial states, and representation on the executive boards of the IFIs is based on the proportion of funding provided by the imperial states. The CEOs of the IMF and the World Bank, the executive manager of the first and the president of the latter, are always European or American. The vision Hardt and Negri have of IFI power is based on a perception of derived power and not its source. Thus what they fail to see is the degree to which global power is located in the imperial states, not in supranational entities, which are but adjuncts of the most powerful states grouped in the G-8. Their view grossly exaggerates the autonomy of the IFIs and consequently underestimates their subordination to the imperial states. The real significance of the IFIs is how they magnify, extend and deepen the power of the imperial states, and how — because of this — they become a terrain for competition among rival states. Far from superseding the old states, the IFIs have strengthened these states' positions.

Globalization theorists like Hardt and Negri like to write of an "imperial system" as opposed to imperialist states, as if one could exist without the other. The "system" has no "centre," since all states have lost their special significance before the all-powerful MNCs that dominate markets. Their "system approach" fails to recognize the class-based and institutionally derived power of nationally owned and directed banks and industries. Even more worrying, world system theorists like Hardt and Negri fail to connect the structures, operations, legal codes and linkages that exist among imperial states, the MNCs and their offspring in the IFIs with the vast reach of their power and the concentration of profits, interest, rents and royalties in the imperialist countries. The "system" is, in fact, sustained by the combined forces of the imperial state and its MNCs. To abstract from the specificities of ownership and state power in order to ascribe an imperial system is to lose sight of basic contradictions and conflicts, inter-state imperial rivalries and class struggles for state power (to be discussed in Chapter 8).

The Sweet Smell of (Scientific/Technological) Success?

One of the more common arguments made by globalization theorists like Hardt and Negri is that an information revolution has taken place and eliminated state borders and transformed capitalism (i.e., creating a "new epoch") by providing new impetus to the development of productive forces. The claims that information technologies have revolutionized economies and thus created a new global economy in which nation states and national economies have become superfluous are extremely dubious. Moreover, the US population census provides another explanation for the higher productivity figures: the five million or more illegal immigrants who have flooded the US labour market since the 1990s. Since productivity is measured by output per estimated worker, these five million uncounted workers inflate the productivity data. If they were included, the productivity figures would deflate.

According to Hardt and Negri, we are living in a new "world order" that has superseded the "old economy" of manufacturing, mining, agriculture and social services (pp. 285ff.) with indirect reference (via Castells) to a third scientific technological revolution. Hardt and Negri maintain that we are living in a totally new epoch, nothing less than a completely new form of capitalism. According to globalization theorists, the "market" creates new efficiencies produced by the new technologies and ensures high growth. If nothing else, the recession of late 2000–2002 certainly refutes the claims of the "new economy" ideologues: the business cycle continues to operate and, moreover, it is particularly accentuated by the highly speculative nature of the "new economy." As it turns out, the "new economy" demonstrates all the features of a volatile speculative economy driven by exorbitant claims of high returns. In the absence of profits, or even revenues, it turns out that much of what was touted as a "new economy" was a colossal financial swindle, where high returns for early investors led to financial ruin for later investors.

Unfortunately for Hardt and Negri, detailed empirical studies of the 1990s economy have effectively refuted the argument that information technology (IT), fibre optics and biotechnology inaugurated a "new epoch of capitalism" via a revolutionizing of the forces of production. Japan, which early on robotized its factories and engineered and applied many of the new IT products, has been stagnant (with an average annual growth of about one percent since the early 1990s) and in 2001 entered a deep recession. The US manufacturing sector was in negative growth at the end of August 2000, a situation that continued for twelve consecutive months — the longest period of negative growth on record since the end of World War II. This recession was expected to continue for an uncertain period — estimates ran from one to three years — although in 2004 there was much relief and jubilation in government circles after a first quarter posting of the highest rate of economic growth (7 percent) in years. However, by November 2004 this growth had yet to translate into jobs — another "jobless recovery."

The IT growth rates were negative throughout 2001 and have been very sluggish ever since, reflected in dramatic declines in related stock values. Prospects for recovery are poor, as negative savings rates, huge deficits exceeding half a trillion dollars, and a strong dollar propped up by foreign investors inhibit domestic or export-powered growth. As structural and cyclical crises coincide, it is likely that the recession will continue for some time ahead. The recession, and the collapse of the stock market bubble in technology stocks, totally undermines the position of IT ideologues who declared that the "new economy" has made the "business cycle" (the "normal" ups and downs in business, not to speak of the longer-term "structural" cycles and the "long downturn" of 1973 to 1995) obsolete. In fact, the IT companies have been the hardest hit in the current downturn, and over 80 percent of the dot.coms have failed to show a profit — ever.

With the decline of the information economy and its stock valuations, it becomes clear that the "information revolution" is not the transcendent force defining the economies of the major imperial states, let alone defining a new world order. The facts that most people have computers and browse, and that some firms have better control over their inventories and sell online, do not mean that power has shifted beyond the nation-state. Claims made by publicists about an "information revolution" accordingly ring hollow, particularly as investors in the world stock markets move funds toward the real economy and away from the high tech-firms which show no profits and increasing losses.

A study by Paul Strassman (1999), a leading critic of IT ideologues, that was based on a study of three thousand European companies demonstrates no relationship between investment in computers and profitability. Thus the three basic claims of the IT revolution, that it has put the business cycle to rest, has generated a sustained-productivity revolution and produces high profits are not in accordance with reality. In fact, the systemic irrationalities of capitalism have been amplified by the IT bubble: the business cycle operates in full force, productivity tends to stagnation and there is a tendency for the rate of profit to decline. Robert Gordon (1999) analyzes the increase in productivity over the 1995–99 period and raises serious doubts about the claims made by Hardt and Negri concerning the existence of a "new epoch." He argues that almost 70 percent of the improvement in productivity can be accounted for by improved measurements of inflation (lower estimates of inflation necessarily mean higher growth of real output, and thus productivity) and the response of productivity to the exceptionally rapid output growth of that period. Thus, only 30 percent of the one percent increase in productivity (or 0.3 percent) during the 1995–99 period can be attributed to computerization, the so-called information revolution — hardly a revolution. According to Gordon's longitudinal study of technical progress from 1950 to 1996, the period of maximum technical progress as manifested in annual multi-factor productivity growth was in the period between 1950 and 1964, when it reached approximately 1.8 percent. The period of lowest multi-factor productivity growth in this century was during 1988–96, approximately a half of one percent!

The "new efficiencies" promised did not overcome the logic of the capitalist business cycle. What was optimistically categorized as "just-in-time production" was premised on a stable and continuous growth of demand. The recession of 2000–2002, and the sudden decline in demand, led to an accumulation of inventories among producers and sellers, and to layoffs. Cash-flow problems, increased indebtedness and bankruptcies characteristic of the "old economy" reappeared with a vengeance. It is clear that the so-called new economy does not transcend capitalist crisis. On the contrary, it is in fact more vulnerable and has fewer resources to fall back on since most of its cash flow depends on speculative expectations of continuous high returns. Sharp declines in commercial advertising earnings on websites, and the saturation of the computer market, have led to a structural crisis for producers of hardware and software, leading to a giant shakedown in the industry. The exorbitant paper value of its stocks have tumbled to a fraction of their value, and the major internet companies are struggling to survive, let along define the nature of a "new capitalist epoch."

The New Imperialism: An Alternative to "Empire"

The current "global supremacy" of the US and Europe is built on three unstable and increasingly unsustainable supports. One of these is a highly vulnerable and speculative sector prone to great volatility and entering into deep recession. The second is the large transfers of profits, interest payments and royalties from neo-colonized areas. In the case of Latin America alone, over $700 billion was transferred as payments to European and US banks and multinationals from 1990 to 1998. The third support underpinning the "empire" is political power (including the power to print money to cover deficits) and the security that European-US states provide to foreign nationals who transfer funds, including billions illicitly secured from their home countries. Political power and the security of the imperial states depend on the acquiescence or consent of strategic economic sectors that are vulnerable to free market competition by rival imperial and non-imperial countries. The problem for European and US rulers, in short, is how to manage their empires in the face of recession, a deflated IT sector and rising unemployment in economic sectors which are not competitive in the world market.

As many have pointed out, neo-liberalism was always a myth: the imperial states have never completely opened their markets, eliminated all subsidies or failed to intervene to prop up or protect strategic economic sectors, either for political or social reasons. Neo-liberal imperialism always meant selective openness to selective countries over specified time periods in selective product areas. Markets were opened by the US government to products produced by US affiliates in overseas countries. "Free trade" in the imperial country was not based on economic but political criteria. On the other hand, European and US policymakers and their employees in the IMF and World Bank preached "market fundamentalism" to the Third World: elimination of all trade barriers, subsidies and regulations for all products and services in all sectors. Imperial states' selective free market practices allowed their multinationals to capitalize on market opportunities in target countries practising market fundamentalism while protecting domestic economic sectors that included important political constituencies. Conflict erupted when the two imperial rivals, the US and European governments (both selective free marketers), attempted to pry open the others' markets while protecting the economic interests of their own political supporters.

With the advent of the triple crises of recession, speculative collapse and intensified competition, the imperial countries have resorted to greater state intervention in a multiplicity of sectors: increased agricultural and other state subsidies ($30 billion in the US in 2001); increased interference in trade to impose "quotas" on imports (e.g., Bush's commitment to the US steel industry); and intensified exploitation of Third World regions to increase the flow of profits, interests and trading advantages (the US "Free Trade of the Americas" proposal); and war (military Keynesianism), as in the US attacks on Afghanistan and Iraq. State-managed trade that combines protection of home markets and aggressive intervention to secure monopoly market advantages and investment profits defines the content of neo-mercantilist imperialism. Neo-liberal imperialism, with its free market rhetoric and selective opening of markets, is being replaced by a neo-mercantilism that looks toward greater monopolization of regional trading zones, greater unilateral political decisions to maximize trade advantages and protect domestic producers, and a greater reliance on military strategies, all to deepen control over crisis-ridden neo-liberal economies run by discredited clients, and to increase military Keynesianism. Just as the US was the leader in developing its neo-liberal empire and Europe was a follower, so with regard to the transition to a neo-mercantilist empire the US plays a leading role. Equally important is the fact that the US state will dictate the rules and regulations that govern trade, investment and patent laws that will reign throughout the Americas. This will enable the US government to be in a position to combine protectionism at home, European exclusion from Latin America and free markets within the Americas.

Mercantilist imperialism, in which the imperial state combines protectionism at home, monopolies abroad and free trade within the empire, is thus the chosen strategy for maintaining empire and sustaining domestic political support, at a terrible cost to Latin America and to the dismay of its European competitors. In pursuit of the neo-mercantilist empire,

Washington must increasingly rely on unilateral decisions and policymaking. By its monopolistic nature, neo-mercantilism depends on excluding competitor allies and maximizing trade advantages via unilateral state decisions. Hardt and Negri notwithstanding, the terrorist attacks in New York and Washington have led to the bombing Afghanistan by the US in the best (or worst) imperialist tradition, even as conditions in world markets deteriorated. The alliance-building strategy, particularly with the European Union, has not modified Washington's pursuit of hegemony. On the contrary, the alliance is built on European Union subordination to US military command and monopolization of all decisions pertaining to that war, even to a greater extent than was the case in Kosovo. What is striking in the early phases of the US military intervention was the degree to which US war demands were totally accepted by the European Union, Russia, China and some Middle Eastern Arab regimes without any explicit quid pro quo. Needless to say, the Afghan intervention and the powerful role of the imperial state in defining the issues, alliances and political circumstances for market transactions hammers another nail in the coffin of "stateless empires" and strengthens the argument for a theory of a new mercantilist style of imperialism. The war in Afghanistan has led to vast increases in military expenditures, greater protectionism and military threats on all sides. Imperialism and empire are indeed doing well. Only the "multitudes" (i.e., peasants and workers) are suffering, a situation which raises two additional questions: Do peasants and workers react against empire and, if so, how?

Empire of the Subaltern?

When defining the configurations of power, Hardt and Negri operate at such a rarified level of abstraction that they obscure the most significant variations in regimes, states and class. As a result, their conceptualization of socio-economic change hovers uneasily in an epistemological penumbra, being either non-existent or wholly unconvincing. It comes as no surprise therefore that, given their postmodern predilection, change stems from the agency not of class but rather of the now fashionable and ubiquitous "subaltern."

It is tempting to search for and find in Negri's earlier writings theoretical elements that prefigure his present position on imperialism. In the light of the celebration of "marginality" by postmodernists such as Foucault and varieties of post-colonial/subalternist thinkers, therefore, it is perhaps significant that from the early 1970s onwards "Autonomia" embarked on a search for a new political class able to operate outside and against the existing party system.[4] In the absence of mass support from the northern industrial working class, which continued steadfastly to support the PCI (Italian Communist Party), those allocated this role by Autonomia were instead déclassé "marginals," composed of unemployed youth (migrants from rural areas in southern Italy), women and self-employed in the urban informal sector ("off-the-books" workers), or precisely those categories subsequently lionized by much postmodern theory as potentially or actually the rural and/or urban "empowered."

This earlier Autonomia perception does indeed permeate *Empire*, in which we are informed that "the new proletariat [which] appears as a constituent power... is a new proletariat and not a new industrial working class," the latter consisting of "all those whose labour is exploited by capital, the entire cooperating multitude" (p. 402). The same point is made earlier in the book where Hardt and Negri state that "our point... is that all of these diverse forms of labour are in some way subject to capitalist discipline and capitalist relations of production. This fact of being within capital and sustaining capital is what defines the proletariat as a class" (p. 53). The presence of the words "capitalist relations of production" notwithstanding, it is clear that for the authors of *Empire* the proletariat is not defined in terms of property relations. Rather, it is defined by the fact of being part of the same economic circuit as capital in which role it yields a portion of surplus to the latter. Not only is this definition not Marxist, but, conceptualized in this manner, a feudal landowning class yielding a portion of surplus labour to an emergent bourgeoisie could also be said to form part of the proletariat!

From the Autonomia days, therefore, *Empire* inherits the dubious proposition that a "refusal" of capitalist work (and work discipline) necessarily translates into a progressive politics, which, it is inferred, prefigures socialism or something like it. It is clear from an earlier text that Negri was prepared to accept the "subjective side" of grassroots agency without enquiring too closely as to how this was constructed, by whom, or in what political direction it was going. In short, for Negri it was earlier already the case that existing ideologies were wrongly identified as liberating simply because they were what a subject engaged in struggle happened to believe. Moreover, such views were regarded by him as evidence that the subject concerned was "virtually independent" of capitalist relations. The difficulty with this "refusal of capitalist work" argument is that — like postmodernists such as Scott and those associated with the Subaltern Studies project — it assumes any discourse-against is politically progressive by virtue of being discourse-against. No allowance is made either for the presence of capitalist agency or ideology or for the existence of a regressive or reactionary ideology among the working class elements within the broad ranks of the subaltern.

Like the catch-all category of "subaltern," therefore, the term "new proletariat" as deployed by Hardt and Negri embraces subjects whose class position is not just different but antagonistic and whose agency is accordingly designed to achieve what are mutually irreconcilable political ends. Thus, for example, in support of the view that peasants are generally "uprooted from their fields and villages and thrown into the burning forge of world production" (p. 247), the authors invoke the work of James Scott (1990) on peasant resistance against capitalism (p. 455, note 16), forgetting (or perhaps not knowing) that the latter's analytical approach has been heavily criticized for conflating not only rich, middle and poor peasants but also rural agency that is aimed at capitalism (e.g., by poor peasants opposed to low wages) with that targeted at socialism (e.g., by rich peasants opposed to land reform). In keeping with their enthusiasm for subalternism, Hardt and Negri categorize what they term "subaltern nationalism" as "progressive" (pp. 105ff.). The inference is that the struggles waged by the "multitudes" at the periphery of "Empire" are ipso facto progressive.

Just how flimsy the latter claim is emerges from the following statement: "The nation appears progressive... insofar as it poses the commonality of a potential community. Part of the 'modernizing' effects of the nation in subordinated countries has been the unification of diverse populations, breaking down religious, ethnic, cultural, and linguistic barriers" (p. 112). One is left wondering what planet Hardt and Negri were living on during the previous decade: the global situation after the fall of the Berlin Wall in 1989 has been exactly the opposite of that which they describe, namely, one in which the "other" of modernization has been the unleashing of rival nationalisms, culturalisms, religions and ethnicities, all of which have gone to war in order to sustain their specific kind of "difference." Hardt and Negri try to get around this problem by claiming that contemporary fundamentalisms are not backward-looking, an extremely dubious view justified in the following manner: "The anti-modern thrust that defines fundamentalisms might be better understood... not as a premodern but as a postmodern project" (p. 149). The antinomic and unsustainable character of this claim is something they recognize almost immediately but are nevertheless unable to explain, let alone escape from ("This marriage between postmodernism and fundamentalism is certainly an odd coupling considering that postmodernist and fundamentalist discourses stand in most respects in polar opposition: hybridity versus purity, difference versus identity, mobility versus stasis" [pp. 146ff.]). Because they equate postmodernism with a chronological transcendence of modernity, Hardt and Negri find it difficult to reconcile what is clearly a traditional discourse with a temporal "going-beyond." Unsurprisingly, the solution — that the very identities invoked by postmodernism are no different from those defended by a backward-looking fundamentalism (hybridity equals different purities, identity equals plurality of difference) — escapes them.

Conclusion

The concept of "empire" informing the analysis of Hardt and Negri resembles nothing so much as Immanuel Wallerstein's misconceived world system approach. Instead of core, semi-periphery and periphery, however, they write of "empire" and "multitudes," in the process subsuming peasants and workers under the catch-all category of "subaltern." This kind of simplistic abstract stratification of the world economy and power subordinates the dynamic of class relations to a static distribution of market shares. The abstract categories obscure fundamental differences in class interests among nations in each category — differences that determine how market shares are distributed, the ownership of property and living standards — as well as differences between dynamic and stagnant countries. In short, it erases class distinctions as reproduced by capital in more developed industrial countries and less developed agrarian contexts in erstwhile colonies. More fundamentally, by looking at market positions, Hardt and Negri overlook the ubiquity of the state in preserving and challenging the relationship between states and economies and reconfiguring the world economy.

After reading *Empire* it is no surprise that reviewers for *Time* and the *New York Times* welcomed the book and praised it so highly. In line with general "globaloney" theory, *Empire* argues that globalization is a progressive movement in history — a position that requires the abolition of imperialism by intellectual fiat — and that systemic alternatives are located within an amorphous multitude lacking both the structural cohesion and political organization necessary for contemporary revolutionary struggle. The book's citation of potted quotes from a sweeping array of thinkers provides the formal trappings for a celebration of US constitutionalism — at a time when its leaders were bombing Afghanistan (and its peasants and workers) into the stone age, after sending Iraq and Yugoslavia (plus their peasants and workers) into the iron age. *Empire* is a sweeping synthesis of intellectual froth about globalization, postmodernism, post-Marxism and post-history, all held together by a series of unsubstantiated arguments and assumptions that seriously contradict economic and historical realities. The "empire thesis" of post-imperialism is not novel. It is neither a great theory nor does it explain much about the real world. Rather, it provides for a wordy exercise devoid of critical intelligence. Readers who have encountered farmyard dunghills in the course of fieldwork in rural areas need no reminding as to the true fragrance of imperialism. It is a pity that Hardt and Negri appear to have lost their sense of smell.

2. THE ECONOMIC BASIS OF IMPERIAL POWER

IMPERIALISM HAS TAKEN DIVERSE FORMS OVER TIME: "PREMODERN," "modern" or "postmodern" — to use the language of Robert Cooper (2000b), advisor to Tony Blair — or, in more analytically useful terms, precapitalist or capitalist. Lenin, one of the major twentieth century theorists of capitalist development and socialism, defined imperialism as the most advanced stage of capitalism, in which financial and industrial forms of capital are merged into large corporate monopolies that, through the dynamics of state power (military force, principally), engage in a process of carving up the world into markets for their capital and surplus production, converting subordinate countries into colonies and local ruling classes into satraps and clients. However, whatever the form taken by imperialism, it entails the projection of state power in its various forms (economic, political and military) — whatever it takes for some nations to dominate others — to advance their class or "national" interests and subordinate other countries to these interests.

The dominant actor involved in this projection of power and creating the resulting relations of domination-subordination within the current arena of global politics is the capitalist nation-state. It has evolved diverse forms: democratic or authoritarian, and (with reference to its dominant policy agenda) liberal or neo-liberal. Other agents of imperialism include the largest capitalist corporations, which, in popular imagery or the dominant political "imaginary" of academia, roam the world in search of returns on their investments or capital. However, these corporations are not footloose or free from consideration of national interests. Indeed, the economic interests represented by these capitalist corporations converge with the national interests advanced and protected by the nation-states that make up what can be termed the "imperial state system," a system currently dominated by the US state. Furthermore, it is these states, in their projections of military and political power, that create the conditions needed for the home-based multinational corporations to take advantage of and operate profitably in the world's "emerging markets." The US imperial state, both directly (via the departments of state and defence) and indirectly (via control over financial institutions such as the World Bank and the International Monetary Fund), constitutes a directorate to manage the global system. Just like the government of the country, the decision-making power concentrated in this directorate of the new world order (the world capitalist or imperialist system) is backed up by a repressive apparatus; the armed forces of the US state, whose maintenance and global operations cost US taxpayers and US capital around $300 billion a year in 2003, at least $480 billion in 2004 and over $500 billion in 205, including Iraq and Afghanistan supplementary budgets.

The economic costs of building and maintaining this empire are enormous, raising serious questions about the foundations of the empire and the imperialist agenda. In fact, all earlier empires have in the end collapsed because of a combination of economic and political factors. The economic costs of empire ultimately tend to exceed the system's carrying capacity. And all forms of imperialism generate forces of resistance and opposition that are ultimately mobilized against the system. Sooner or later these forces are able to bring the system down as it collapses under the weight of its internal contradictions and the political forces generated by these contradictions. The capacity of the system to bear economic and political costs depends in part on the economic basis of the imperialist system, a topic to which we now turn.

The Economics of Empire

Discussions of economic power in the world economy centre on several critical issues. One of these issues is the role and agency of the multinational corporations of the competing states. MNCs are key units through which international economic power is wielded. Thus, to analyze the strengths of the different states, it is useful to compare the proportion of the biggest multinationals linked to each state.

The "general power" configuration measured by the number and percentage of MNCs linked to different states needs to be refined by looking at the particular subsector in which those corporations are concentrated. Our hypothesis is that different countries' MNCs concentrate power in different sectors. That is, power is not homogeneous across sectors; it is increasingly dispersed among the major competing power blocs. While a degree of dispersion by specialization reveals competing and complementary relations among the imperial powers, it is further hypothesized that one power center — the US — has greater domination over more sectors than the other power blocs.

In determining the five hundred largest MNCs, we rely on the criteria and calculations for March 2004 published in the *Financial Times* (*"Global 500: Special Report,"* May 27, 2004). The companies were ranked on the basis of their market capitalization, i.e., the stock market value of each company, as determined by multiplying the share price by the number of stocks issued. Companies with large state or family holdings were excluded.

Dominant Economic Power: The 500 Biggest MNCs—
the UN's Multi-billion Dollar Club

The US remains the dominant power by far in terms of the number and percentage of multinationals among the top 500, with 227 (45 percent) followed by Western Europe with 141 (28 percent) and Asia with 92 (18 percent). These three regional power blocs control 91 percent of the largest MNCs in the world. "Globalization" can overwhelmingly be seen as a derivative of the power of the MNCs based in these power blocs to move capital and control trade, credit, financing and entertainment. Almost three quarters (73 percent) of big corporate institutions are located in the Euro-US sphere of power. While Asian MNCs have become increasingly present and a possible challenge in the coming decades, in the short to medium term the US-European economic axis predominates. The current boom in China and India, and the belated economic recovery of Japan, reflect both the growth of endogenous capitalism and the expansion and conquest by Euro-American MNCs of these "emerging markets." Latin America, the Middle East and Africa have only eleven among the top five hundred MNCs. In Latin America only Brazil and Mexico have world-class MNCs, while Africa has none and Saudi Arabia controls four of the Middle East's six. Russia, following the catastrophic collapse of its economy with the transition to pillage capitalism, has only seven MNCs. The continents and countries which have the lowest number of economically powerful multinationals are precisely those that have been dominated by Euro-US MNCs and their imperial states. The incapacity to accumulate endogenous capital under client rulers servicing US-European MNCs is a leading cause of the continuing pillage of resources, transfers of earnings to banks among "the 500" and a general disaccumulation process. The few big multinational corporations of Russia and Latin America are by and large privatized state firms developed by the public savings and investment of previous statist regimes able to limit the presence of Euro-US MNCs.

A closer examination of the top multinationals illustrates the greater concentration of power in the US. Of the top ten MNCs, 80 percent are American and 20 percent are European. Among the top 20 percent, 75 percent are American, 20 percent are European and 5 percent are Japanese. Of the top fifty MNCs, 60 percent are US, 32 percent are European, 6 percent are Japanese and 5 percent are other. The greatest concentration of US power is among the biggest multinationals, while competition sets in as one moves to the lower tiers of the economic power hierarchy.

The US has the largest multinational corporations in industry (General Electric), oil and gas (Exxon-Mobil), software and computer services (Microsoft), pharmaceuticals (Pfizer), banking (Citicorp), retail sales (Wal-Mart), insurance (American International Group) and information technology hardware (Intel). Total capitalization of these giant MNCs is $1,979 billion. Those who write of the "decline" of the US empire have certainly ignored the consolidated power of America's top eight MNCs. What is called "globalization" is in reality the extreme concentration and extension of a US empire, or at least a Euro-US empire, which is complemented by the gradual emergence of Asian MNCs.

Russian multinationals, almost exclusively located in natural resources, are a special case: they result from the pillage and theft of huge state enterprises that were largely integrated in the domestic economy. Today the Russian MNCs largely "service" and supply Euro-US MNCs, are poorly integrated with the Russian state and have been operated by expatriate oligarchs in England, Israel and elsewhere.

Giant Canadian multinationals are largely active in banking, natural resources and information technology. They are linked in part to US MNCs and operate with little direct state involvement, except to follow US direction.

Beyond the top one hundred firms, however, the preponderance of US MNCs has narrowed and Euro-Asian MNCs have become a serious challenge. Here, European and Asian multinationals have become important operational units of the imperial system, moving beyond traditional regional boundaries and selectively entering into the US domestic economy.

Concentrated and Shared Dominance

Competition and complementarity in empire-building among the US, European and Asian multinational corporations is evident when we turn to specific economic sectors. Examining the top ten firms in several key economic sectors, we find monopolization, competition and displacement by US-based MNCs.

Retail Trade

US retail multinational corporations are the dominant group in the top ten — 80 percent of the biggest firms. This is not surprising given the fact that the US economy is heavily based on consumer spending, speculative bubbles and high levels of indebtedness. All leading US retail-sales MNCs began by dominating the domestic market, accumulating capital on the basis of exploitation of low-paid, non-unionized labour, and then moving overseas to reproduce these practices. In contrast, up until recently Europe and Asia's retail trade was based on family-owned small and medium-sized firms.

Information Technology

The US dominates IT with 80 percent of the top ten, followed by Europe, in part as a result of early state subsidies via military spending, the Y-2000 scam (the "end of the world scenario," which pumped tens of billions into the emerging IT enterprises) and the IT speculative bubble of the 1990s.

Mass Media and Entertainment
US multinationals dominate the world mass media and entertainment sector. Almost 80 percent of the top MNCs (eleven of fourteen) are control-led by US capital. With the dismantling of public media in the early part of the twentieth century and the monopolization of radio, television and film, the US giants "conglomerized," buying out or bankrupting local newspapers, music and cultural firms before repeating the pattern world-wide. The growth of concentrated US media and entertainment conglom-erates was achieved via favourable state intervention, "deregulation" and promotion, as media and entertainment served as an unofficial overt and covert propaganda arm of US imperial conquest, war, occupation and penetration.

The Military-Industrial Complex
US-based multinationals are leaders in the war-related, empire-building military industries. Of the top eleven giant military-industrial firms among the top five hundred, nine are US and two are European. Militarism has fueled US industrial expansion for over sixty-five years, lifting the US out of the Great Depression of the 1930s into a period of dramatic industrial expansion (World War II) and the "golden age of capitalism" (1948–73), but absorbing and wasting trillions of state-financed dollars and thus severely weakening the presence of the US within the non-military sector of industrial activity.

Software and Computer Services
US multinational corporations dominate the software and computer serv-ice sector, with six of the ten biggest firms. However, the supremacy of the US is being challenged by Japan and Europe, each of which has two of the top ten firms. The anti-monopoly challenge launched from Europe, the bursting of the IT bubble and the greater state funding of research and development has led to intense inter-imperial competition as well as fusions, buyouts and "unfair competitor practices."

Banking
US finance and banking capital has grown to become a leading force in the world economy. US multinational banks make up 60 percent of the top ten banks in the world, followed by Europe with 30 percent and Japan with 10 percent. US banking has grown through its debt holdings in Latin America, Asia and Africa, converting debt holdings into equities via neo-liberal policies of privatization and the deregulation of financial markets. US bonds have benefited disproportionately by facilitating the transfer of hundreds of billions of illicit funds by corrupt rulers, international crimi-nals and tax-evading business leaders, especially from Latin America. Big US overseas banks play a major role in shaping US imperial state policy via the international financial institutions promoting neo-liberalism, fi-

nancial deregulation, class-based austerity programs and foreign debt collection. On a lesser scale, but in the same direction, European banking giants influence the policies of the EU. However, more often than not, European multinational banks act in unison with US banks in the context of the "Paris Club" and in pursuit of the same goals of debt collection via common policies.

The European Challenge: Telecommunications, Oil and Gas, Insurance, Pharmaceuticals and Manufacturing

Europe is the leader in the telecommunications sector with 40 percent of the top ten multinationals. This hierarchy of economic power and world market share is followed by the US and then Asia, which accounts for 30 percent of the top ten. Similar patterns are found in insurance, where Europe has 50 percent of the largest MNCs, followed by 40 percent for the US and 10 percent for Japan. In the gas and oil sectors the US and Europe each have four of the top ten MNCs, followed by one each for Russia and Brazil. The same pattern is found in the pharmaceuticals sector, where the US and Europe dominate the top ten MNCs. In electronics and electrical equipment, the Japanese MNCs in particular, and Asian in general, control 70 percent of the largest producers, Europe 20 percent and the US only one MNC in the top ten.

The clearest expression of inter-imperialist competition is found in both light and heavy manufacturing, including metals, transport, chemicals, forestry and electronics. Among the largest light manufacturing firms, US MNCs represent 44 percent, European 48 percent and Japanese 8 percent. In heavy manufacturing, among the hundred largest firms, 32 percent are US, 30 percent are European, 22 percent are Japanese, 7 percent are other Asian and the rest are spread among five other countries. Similar proportions of corporate capital are found in the booming personal care and cosmetics sector, where the US and Europe each have 33 percent of the largest MNCs followed by Japan with 11 percent.

Relationships among the Imperial Centres

It is a mistake to refer to the US as "*the* global power," for it has strong competitors that have surpassed or compete favourably with it in key energy and productive sectors. While the US dominates the highly visible mass media and retail stores sectors, and is strongest in IT and finance, it is relatively weaker in manufacturing, telecommunications, electronics and insurance. It remains "competitive" in pharmaceuticals and oil and gas. US power is built on services, not on the production of tangible civilian goods. Without the heavily subsidized military-industrial MNCs, the US would have even less of a presence in industry. Moreover, the US-based manufacturing economy has been severely weakened by the expansion of American MNCs overseas, particularly into China. With their economic activities abroad engaged in empire-building, the MNCs maintain their home base in the US, thus maintaining powerful control over the direction, policies and personnel of the state and government.

The notion that Europe can be confined to being a "regional" power, as argued in the Wolfowitz-Perle doctrine, is out of touch with the overwhelming reality of Europe as a global imperial competitor of the US, with a solid manufacturing, financial and telecommunications power base. Moreover, the most recent data suggest that the US is gradually losing dominance. The data for 2004 showed that thirty US MNCs fell out of the top five hundred and there were only sixteen new entrants, a 5 percent decline. Europe stayed more or less the same, but Japan and the rest of Asia had a net increase of fourteen between 2003 and 2004, an increase of nearly 20 percent.

Two important caveats should be made. First, the decline in the percentage of US-based MNCs relative to Europe and Asia is in part balanced by the dispersal of European MNCs among several countries, and by the fact that, despite their common bond in the EU, they do not act as a unified body. And the same is true for Asia. Second, the US state, through the costly use of its military and secret police, can gain economic advantages even as its MNCs decline and face stiff competition.

The competition and disagreements between European politicians and Washington over trade policy and the Iraq War are subordinate to their long-term collaboration. Moreover, part of the political conflict revolves around Zionist ideologues in the Pentagon who have imposed a new Middle Eastern policy and global warfare.

Despite these ideologically induced conflicts, European and US capital have become increasingly interconnected. The Euro-US economy generates $2.5 trillion in total commercial sales and employs twelve million workers (*Financial Times*, June 9, 2004). In 2003, US MNCs invested $87 billion in Europe, an increase of 31 percent over 2002; and in the same year, European MNCs invested $37 billion in the US, an increase of 42 percent over the previous year. The high levels of trade and investment between the two biggest imperialist centres demonstrate that conflicts and rivalries are still less important than common economic interests. Nevertheless, despite structural affinities, the unilateralist, Israel-first crowd has and will continue to cause severe strains in the relationship.

The Israel-Palestine conflict, the Iraq War and Pentagon plans for possible, new Middle East conflicts (Iran, Syria and Kurdish areas of northern Iraq) will certainly create new tensions between the two imperial centres. The European empire, with its predominantly "trade-invest-ment-market" diplomatic strategy, faces a highly militaristic and imperial US. Europe proposes a multilateral, consultative and joint-sharing style of imperialism, while Washington looks to unilateral action, monopolization of rule and imperial plunder. Europeans look toward joint partnership in the Middle East with Arabs and Israeli elites; Washington, influenced by Zionists, values a strong relationship with Israel to the exclusion of Europe and Arab rulers, except as submissive clients. In this context we can expect deepening structural links between the imperial MNCs and imperial regimes, continued competition over market share and political conflict provoked by the Zionist extremists in Washington and their mentors in Tel Aviv.

Conclusion

The imperial policies adopted by Washington are a direct response to the power and centrality of the biggest MNCs in the US economy. Free trade agreements, IMF and World Bank policies, privatizations, the lowering of tariff barriers and the establishment of over 180 military bases in more than 130 countries are responses to the structural imperatives of the US economy and more particularly to the biggest US MNCs, which operate throughout the world. Imperialism is not a policy, a conspiracy or a product of any single administration, but a structural reality with political determinants and an economic basis. However, policies based on the economic imperatives of this structure are formulated by decision-makers in Washington and implemented via the state apparatus.

Most of the key policies that support US imperial economic interests are not made in the context of broad public debate. Nor are imperial interests stated as such. A small circle of mostly non-elected officials make decisions "behind closed doors" and plan imperial policies, aided by the "advice" constructed by a host of Washington-based policy forums such as the US Centre for Foreign Relations (the choice of east coast "liberal" trilateralists), the Heritage Foundation (preferred by George Bush the elder) and the Project for the New American Century (PNAC) (run by Dick Cheney's wife, and one of several forums used by the latest generation of neo-conservative neo-imperialists). The public is then fed the ritual rhetoric of "freedom," "democracy" and so on, presenting the imperialist project in its various forms (the Iraq War, for example) as an advance of the "forces of freedom, democracy and free enterprise" (to quote from George W. Bush's 2002 *National Security Report*).

The structural determination of strategic interests is compatible with, if not necessitated by, these "closed doors." Thus the argument that proposes "conspiracies" to be more significant than structural determinations is misplaced and based on false distinctions. Structural and "conspiratorial" determinants operate on different if not incompatible levels. Structural economic factors, such as MNCs, establish the general framework of US policy, while policymakers elaborate policies to advance these companies' interests. This process takes place out of public sight, and hence is conceivable as a "conspiracy," but not without the active participation of the CEOs of the major multinationals. Moreover, there are moments when particular policymakers can carve out a degree of independence from particular MNCs in specific regions and pursue their own ideological agendas even at the cost of the MNCs. The most striking example of this exceptional circumstance is the behaviour of sectors of the US state apparatus with relation to the Middle East during the George W. Bush presidency. An influential group of US Zionists, closely allied with and having strong loyalty to the Israeli state, formulated a strategy of permanent war in the Middle East based on the unilateral use of US military power to enhance the survival of Israel.

Zionist policymakers targeted several oil-producing countries that have provided exorbitant profits for American MNCs, purchased US Treasury notes to balance the current US account deficit and had major ties with US financial institutions. Moreover, these Zionist policymakers exacerbated the political and diplomatic isolation of the US in the world and created oil price volatility and huge budget deficits. In theory, and in their own eyes, these Zionists are not opposed to American MNCs, nor are they against forcefully building US imperial power. However, by harnessing US imperial power to Israeli interests, they effectively overrode the structural imperatives of some American MNCs.

This was clearly the case in the launching of the Iraq War. To destroy Iraq's economy, the infrastructure was destroyed and pillaged; to destroy Iraq's national unity, religious and ethnic groups were politicized and polarized. The result: Israeli power in the Middle East was enhanced and the US moved toward new targets. Syria was boycotted by the US; Iran became a target for attack; and Saudi Arabia has been the focus of fierce ideological critiques to the advantage of Israeli interests. As an unintended result, the US empire has become bogged down in a prolonged, losing colonial war, its budget and trade deficits have grown geometrically, the entire Middle East has been destabilized and the pro-Israel animus toward Muslims has awakened and transformed hundreds of millions into enemies of the US economic and military presence. Strategically, it has been argued, the US military has been stretched to and beyond its capacity to defend or expand the empire (Isenberg 1999). Conscription would polarize the country and weaken support for imperial politics. By any objective measure, the Zionist attempt to fuse US empire-building and enhanced Israeli power by inventing a joint US-Israeli power bloc in the Middle East has been a dramatic failure. In fact, it has eroded imperial power.

This is a clear example of how policymakers have acted not only behind the backs of the public, but behind the backs of the MNCs and against the structural imperatives of empire. Clearly there is not always a direct relationship between the structural imperatives of empire and the effective realization of corporate global interests. Ideological factors can lead policymakers to deviate from prioritizing MNC interests in favour of other loyalties, as we have seen today in the case of US Middle East policy. No doubt at some point in the not too distant future, Zionist policies may provoke a "correction" in US imperial policymaking. Already the state is divided between pro- and anti-Zionists, between Israel-firsters and empire-builders. To the degree that Israeli Middle Eastern ambitions jeopardize the greater interests of the biggest US MNCs, there is likely to be a major political showdown, with the Israeli power bloc in the US mobilizing all its resources to pressure Congress, the political parties and the President to back Israeli ambitions against the MNCs, and with the MNCs' spokespeople calling on the same to focus on the "bigger picture" of inter-imperialist competition, an overextended military and a hostile Middle East investment climate.

Ultimately the test is whether powerful economic structural imperatives based on the massive presence of US MNCs in the world economy will be a match for a politically powerful faction of Jewish capital located in leading economic sectors such as the mass media and finance. Ultimately the structural imperatives of empire-building will predominate over the parochial interests of the Israel-first crowd, but there may be profound domestic and international crises before the issue is resolved.

In conclusion, delineating the economic strengths and relative weaknesses of the US MNCs helps us to partially understand imperial politics. But it is also necessary to analyze the political and institutional sphere in which imperial policies are elaborated and pursued. While the imperial state represents the MNCs, it does so in its own manner, and occasionally policies pursued may sacrifice one set of imperial interests for another.

3. THE IMPERIAL STATE

ONE OF THE MOST PERVASIVE AND INSIDIOUS MYTHS OF OUR TIMES, perpetuated by academic works such as Hardt and Negri's *Empire*, is the idea that we live in a world with weak nation-states. Nothing could be further from the truth. In all regions of the world, the state — whether imperial, capitalist or neo-colonial — has been strengthened, its activities have expanded, and its intervention in the economy and civil society have become ubiquitous. The state in the imperialist nations — what we term "the imperial state" — is particularly active in concentrating power within the nation, projecting it overseas in a great variety of institutional, economic and political circumstances and establishing vast spheres of influence and domination. The US imperial state leads the way, followed by the EU, led by Germany and France, and Japan. The power of the imperial state is extended to international financial institutions such as the International Monetary Fund, the World Bank, the Asian Bank, the Inter-American Development Bank and the World Trade Organization. The imperial states provide most of the funds, appoint the leaders of the IFIs and hold them accountable for implementing policies that favour the multinational corporations of their respective countries. The advocates of a world without nation-states, or "globalists," fail to understand that the IFIs are not a higher or new form of government beyond the nation-state, but institutions that derive their power from the imperial states.

This chapter will discuss and criticize the unsubstantiated arguments of the globalists and proceed to establish the significance of the state in the contemporary world of global empire *with* imperialism. Prominent theorists of this view include Ignacio Ramonet and Bernard Cassen of *Le Monde Diplomatique* and their associates in the French NGO ATTAC.[1] The chapter will then turn to a brief explanation for the growth of statism in the new world order.

The Mythical World without Nation-States

The advocates of the thesis of a world without nation-states, dubbed by us as "globalist theorists" or "globalists," depart from very dubious assumptions. There are variations and nuances in the arguments presented by the globalists, some arguing that the nation-state is an anachronism, others arguing that it is in decline, and yet others that it no longer describes reality. While these differences continue to provoke debate, more significant is what unites them — a set of highly questionable and misplaced assumptions, which will now be addressed.

Assumption 1

Globalists assume that multinational corporations are global corporations that have no specific location in any particular nation-state. Instead, they form a new world economy divorced from national control, the institutional expression of a new world ruling class — what some sociologists (Sklair 1997, for example) term "the international capitalist class."

This assumption is based on the fact that the biggest capitalist corporations are "multinational," operating in a number of countries; they are highly mobile and have the power to evade taxes and in many national jurisdictions escape the regulatory controls of the state.

There are several conceptual and empirical problems with this assumption. First, that MNCs operate in many countries does not detract from the fact that the headquarters where most of the strategic decisions, directors and profits are concentrated are predominantly located in the US, the EU and Japan (see Chapter 2 above, and also Doremus, Kelly, Pauly and Reich 1999). Second, mobility is based on strategic decisions taken by directors in these headquarters in the imperial centres, and these decisions depend on the political and economic conditions created by the imperial state and its representatives in the IFIs. That is, the mobility of the capital of the MNCs is contingent upon the structure of inter-state relations. Third, evasion of taxes and regulations is only possible because of deliberate policies pursued by the imperial states and their multinational banks (US Senate 1999 and 2001). Non-enforcement of laws against transfers of illicit earnings from the neo-colonial countries to the imperial states favours a concentration of wealth and strengthens the imperialist state's external accounts. The flouting of state regulations by the MNCs is part of a broader set of imperial, neo-colonial state power relations.

Assumption 2

Globalists also assume that the governments of the old nation-state have been superseded by a new "world government," the institutionality of "global governance" made up of the CEOs of the IFIs, the WTO and the MNCs. While they carry seeds of truth, arguments advanced on the basis of this assumption tend to be very superficial and lack understanding of the structure of global power. While it is true that the IFIs make many important decisions in a great many geographical locations affecting significant economic and social sectors, these decisions and their makers are closely linked to the imperial states and the MNCs that influence them. Top IFI officials are appointed by their national/imperial governments, and all the crucial policy guidelines that dictate lending conditions and requirements are set by the finance, treasury and economy ministers of the imperial states. The vast majority of funds for the IFIs come from the imperial states and representation on the executive boards of the IFIs is based on the proportion of funding by the imperial states. The head of the IMF and the World Bank have to be European in the case of the former, and American in the latter.[2]

The globalist vision of IFI power is based on a discussion of derived power rather than its source, which is the imperial state. In this sense, global or international power derives from the imperial state, not from supranational entities. Those that argue otherwise overestimate the autonomy of the IFIs and underestimate their subordination to the imperial state.[3] The real significance of the IFIs is how they magnify, extend and deepen the power of the imperial states and how they become a terrain for competition between rival imperial states. Far from superseding the old states, IFIs have strengthened the strategic role of these states as quarterbacks for the international plays of global capital.

Assumption 3

A common argument of globalization theory is that an information revolution that has eliminated state borders and created a new global economy has taken place (on this see Castells 2000). Globalists argue that a new technological revolution has provided a new impetus to the development of productive forces, a new dynamism that has transformed capitalism as a system. However, the claim that information technologies have revolutionized the nature of capitalism and created a new global economy in which nation-states and national economies have become superfluous is extremely dubious.

First of all, a comparison of productivity growth in the US over the past half century fails to support this globalist argument. From 1953 to 1973, in the heyday of capitalism's global age, but before the so-called "information revolution," productivity grew at an annual average rate of 2.6 percent per year. With the onset of a system-wide crisis and the introduction of computers — one of several measures adopted in search of a solution to this crisis — productivity growth continued to lag, and from 1972 to 1995 the annual rate was actually less than half of the pre-crisis rate (Wolf 1999: 10). Even in the so-called boom period of 1995–99, productivity growth was 2.2 percent below the pre-computer period. Japan, which of all countries makes the most extensive use of computers and robots, witnessed a decade of stagnation and crisis (the 1990s), two decades into the so-called "third technological revolution."

In 2000 the information sector went into a deep crisis; tens of thousands of workers were fired, hundreds of firms went bankrupt and the value of computer-related stocks dropped by 80 percent. The speculative bubble that had defined the so-called "information economy" burst. In addition, the major source of productivity growth in the US claimed by globalists was restricted to computer manufacturing or derived from an increase in the rate of absolute exploitation — from an increase in the annual number of hours worked (from 120 to 360 hours more than European workers). Studies have also shown that computer use in offices is directed more toward personal use than toward exchanging ideas. It is estimated that up to 60 percent of computer time is spent in activity unrelated to the enterprise. Computer manufacturers account for only 1.2 percent of the US economy and less than 5 percent of capital stock (Wolf 1999). In addition, the US population census provides another explanation for the higher productivity figures: five million uncounted workers, mostly illegal immigrants, flooded the US labour market in the 1990s. Since productivity is measured by output per worker, these five million uncounted workers inflate the productivity data. If these five million were included, the productivity figures would be below 2 percent.

With the decline of the information economy and its stock valuations, it is clear that the information revolution is not the transformative force that it is made out to be, one that defines the economies of the major imperial states. Even less is it the basis of a new world order. The facts that most people have computers and browse the internet and some firms have better control over their inventories, etc. do not mean that power has shifted beyond the nation-state. As investors in world stock markets shift funds away from the fictitious high-tech firms that show no profits and only losses, publicist claims about an information revolution ring hollow.

Assumption 4

Related to the prior assumption, globalists argue that we are living in a "New Economy" that has superseded the "Old Economy" of manufacturers, mining, agriculture and social services. A number of globalists argue that the market creates a more effective and real democracy in which ordinary people are able to make choices about their futures, and that new efficiencies produced by the new technologies ensure high growth. But the recession of late 2000 and 2001 certainly refutes this argument. The so-called "normal" boom-bust business cycle continues to operate, as does an underlying propensity towards crisis, which, as it happens, is accentuated by the highly speculative nature of so much investment in the New Economy. The New Economy demonstrates all the features of a volatile speculative economy, driven by exorbitant claims of high returns. In the absence of profits or even revenues, it turns out that much of what was touted as a New Economy was a colossal financial swindle, where the high returns to early investors led to financial ruin for later investors.

The new efficiencies promised by the New Economy publicists could not resist the logic of the capitalist business cycle. "Just-in-time production" is premised on a stable and continuous growth of demand, but the sudden decline in demand associated with the 2001 recession led to an accumulation of inventories among producers and sellers, and to the layoffs, cash-flow problems, increased indebtedness and bankruptcies that had characterized the Old Economy.

It is clear that the so-called "New Economy" does not transcend the propensity of capitalism towards crisis. In fact, it is more vulnerable and has fewer resources to fall back on, since most of its cash flow depends on speculative expectations of continuous high returns. The sharp decline in commercial advertising earnings on the websites and the saturation of the computer market has led to a structural crisis for producers of hardware and software, leading to a giant shakedown in the industry; the exorbitant paper value of most stocks has tumbled and the major internet companies are struggling to survive, let alone define the nature of a new economy.

Assumption 5

Globalist theorists like Hardt and Negri (2000) write of an imperial system as opposed to imperialist states as if the one could exist without the other. The system has no centre since all states have lost their special significance before the all-powerful MNCs that dominate markets. This approach fails to recognize the class and institutional power of nationally owned and -directed banks and industries. Even more problematic, these systems theorists fail to link the structures, operations, legal codes and linkages between imperial states, the MNCs and their offspring in the IFIs. The vast reach of their power concentrates profits, interest, rents and royalties in the imperialist countries. The system not only derives from the combined force of the imperial state and its MNCs but is sustained by it. To abstract from the specificities of ownership and state power in order to describe an imperial system is to lose sight of the basic contradictions and conflicts, the inter-state imperial rivalries and the popular struggles for state power that define its working at the political level. The chimera of a stateless empire contains the same problems as the notion of a world without nation-states: it exaggerates the autonomy of capital from the state and parrots the false propositions of the free market ideologues who argue that the market (or, in the words of Negri, "the collectivist capital-ist") dominates the imperialist system.

Assumption 6

Globalists operate at such a level of abstraction in defining the configura-tions of power that they obscure and gloss over the most significant variations in regimes, states and class configurations. As a result, they have a very unconvincing conception of socio-economic change. The most egregious example of such a misconception can be found in the world system approach of Immanuel Wallerstein (1976) and its categories of "core" (centre), "semi-periphery" and "periphery." This type of sim-plistic abstract stratification of the world economy and power subordi-nates the dynamic of class relations (property in the means of global production) to a much less dynamic analysis of competition for increased world market shares. The abstract categories of world system theory obscure fundamental differences in class relations and interests within each nation-state, differences that determine how resources are allocated and income is distributed, property relations in the means of production, living standards and associated political dynamics. More importantly, by focusing on market relations rather than production relations world system theorists and globalists underestimate and misunderstand the crucial role of the state in determining how the global economy is structured and reconfigured. To all appearances the global economy, together with its institutionality, is determined by forces beyond any political control. In reality it is the outcome of actions taken by agencies of the internationalist capitalist class on the basis of strategies designed by self-appointed guardians of the new world order who constitute a sort of "imperial brain trust" for the system (Salbuchi 2000). In other words, the issue is not structural but political.

The Centrality of the State

In the contemporary world the nation-state in both its imperial and neocolonial forms has multiplied and expanded its activity. Far from being an anachronism, the state has become a central element of the world economy. There is some appearance of fragmentation, "disaggregation" and even disintegration in the system of nationstates, and thus, according to Hobsbawm (1987), a presumed weakening of state power vis-à-vis the power of the giant corporations that dominate the world economy, which has generated an as yet unsettled debate on the relative power of MNCs and governments (Wolf 2002). Thus in Eastern Europe the number of nationstates has multiplied from ten a decade ago to twenty-eight. And in Western Europe the various nationstates that originally formed the EU have also embarked on a process of amalgamation and political union, to some extent diminishing the powers of the individual nationstates within the union. However, in these and other cases of "disaggregation" it is clear that the issue is not at all economic versus political power — the relative power of the MNCs versus that of the nation-state. Nor is the issue the "great question" identified by Hobsbawm as facing the twenty-first century: "the interaction between the world with states and the world without states" (1999).

Contrary to the arguments advanced by globalists, the great question facing us today, a question not for the left but for the right, is *how to strengthen the state power of the MNCs in support of their domestic and global operations.* Furthermore, the activities of the state, be it imperial or neocolonial, modern or postmodern, are shaped by the relationship of the state to the social structure — to the social forces behind the exercise of state power. In every case, all over the world — in each world, in every world — the state, where not directly captured by the economically dominant capitalist class, has been restructured to better serve the inter-ests of global capital, the MNCs, etc. Thus, in Hobsbawm's world of small or weak states, on the south of a global divide between the imperialist "centre" (strong states) and the colonized "periphery" (weak states), the state must be open at the border and at customs, indulgent towards taxes and tariffs for foreign investors, obedient to the IMF's privatization poli-cies and liquidation of state economic sectors, punctual in payment of debts accumulated with international banks and institutions, and ruthless in keeping workers' wages low (Vasapollo 2003). Finally, the neo-colonial state, be it democratic or authoritarian in form, must, by any means possible, ensure domestic stability to provide security for foreign inves-tors and the profitability of MNC operations. In addition, the creation of supranational political institutions, as in the EU, serves the same purpose — to fulfil the state's strategic function to support and advance the process of capital accumulation. The *Financial Times* reports that the meetings of the EU more and more resemble the meetings of corporate CEOs, both in form and content, focusing on how to advance the interests of European MNCs in concert with the interests of the EU.

Imperial State Crisis Management

The centrality of the imperial state has been evidenced in fundamental areas of political, cultural and economic activity that buttress imperial power. In recent times several major financial and economic crises have occurred in various regions of the world. In each instance, the imperial states, particularly the US, have intervened to bail out capital, to protect and reimburse capitalists for investments gone sour and to avoid the collapse of the fragile architecture of global financial transactions and cross-country flows. For example, in December 1994, when the Mexican financial system was on the verge of collapse, then President Clinton intervened by dispatching $40 billion to bail out US investors, who domi-nated the trade in government bonds on the stock market, and to stabilize the peso. Another such example is provided by the Asian crisis of mid-1997, which spread like a virus (the "Asian flu") to Russia in 1998 and then to Brazil. During the Asian crisis the US and EU governments approved an IMF–World Bank multi-billion-dollar bailout package in exchange for an opening of economies, particularly that of South Korea, to foreign takeovers of hitherto protected domestic markets and basic industries. In fact, some analysts (for example, Patel 1998), as well as the prime minister of Thailand, seriously suggested that the sinister motives of global compe-tition (and a strategy orchestrated by the US), rather than the unantici-pated effects of large volumes of volatile capital, were behind the crisis. In the Brazilian crisis of 1999 and the Argentine crisis of 2001, Washington pressured the IFIs and the governments of the day to protect foreign investors and the banks, most of which had been privatized and were under US or EU ownership. Within the US the threatened bankruptcy of a major international investment bank led to intervention by the Federal Reserve, which again pressured for a private bank bailout of another $40 billion. In short, the imperial state, with increasing frequency and with enormous resources, has played a dominant role in crisis management, saving major investors from bankruptcy, propping up insolvent MNCs and preventing the collapse of currencies, and of the entire system. More than ever the MNCs and the so-called "global economy" depend on the continuous and massive intervention of the imperial states to secure benefits (buyouts of local enterprises, etc.) and manage crises.

Inter-imperialist Competition

Competition between rival imperial powers and MNCs is spearheaded by rival imperial states (see Chapter 8 for more analysis). For example, the US imperial state is leading the fight to open European markets to US beef and US exports of bananas from South and Central America, while state officials in Japan and the EU negotiate with US officials to increase export quotas and other conditions of regulated access to the US market. Trade and markets in this context are largely defined by state-to-state agreements. Globalization is thus not just a by-product of the growth and activities of the MNCs but also an artifice of state-to-state agreement. Competition between capitalist enterprises is mediated or influenced, when not directed and shaped by the state, which functions as a quarterback for the MNCs, calling the plays. Markets do not transcend the state but operate within it.

Conquest of Markets

The state plays a profound and pervasive role in the conquest of overseas markets and the protection of local markets. First the state provides indirect and direct subsidies to export sectors. For example, in the year 2000 the US financed more than $15 billion in export sales. Currently, the US ranks seventh among countries in subsidization of exports — behind Japan, France, Germany, the Netherlands, Canada and South Korea (*Financial Times*, March 6, 2001, p. 4). US agricultural exports receive subsidized water and electrical power and export subsidies in the form of tax relief. Second, the imperial state, via the IFIs, pressures loan-recipient states in the Third World to lower or eliminate trade barriers, and to privatize and denationalize enterprises through conditionality agreements. This allows American, European and Japanese MNCs to penetrate markets and buy local enterprises. Most exports are financed by agencies of the state. So-called "globalization" would not exist were it not for state intervention, nor would the markets remain open were it not for the interventions of the imperial state in the form of political threats, economic pressure, recruitment of local clients, offers of aid and military force. Imperialism takes many forms, from aid and local development to war and military aggression (see Chapters 10 and 11), but in all of its diverse forms, whether it entails the projection of economic, political or military power, the fundamental aim is essentially the same: to dominate the world through conquest of "emerging markets," penetration of competing economies and protection of the home market.

The US, Europe and Japan have elaborate sets of trade barriers in a wide range of product areas of strategic importance: auto imports are limited by quotas, as are sugar, textiles, steel, etc. The US and the EU manipulate anti-dumping regulations to protect uncompetitive industries from more efficient producers (*Financial Times*, March 6, 2001, p. 8). A multiplicity of non-traditional constraints and informal agreements limit access of foreign imports to the US market and regulate access to it via a system of state-to-state negotiations. And the US plays hardball in these negotiations, using WTO rules when it suits, and bending or ignoring these rules when US interests are at stake. In many cases, in its dealings with neo-colonial regimes such as Brazil under Cardoso, the US state rejects reciprocity, demanding (and securing) the liberalization of the information industry while restricting Brazilian steel exports, on the bogus pretext of anti-dumping charges. Relations with Mexico and Canada, countries that are heavily dependent on the US market (which consumes up to 80 percent of their exports), are fraught with such power plays by the US state.

Trade Agreements

All the major economic agreements, liberalizing trade and establishing new investment regulations, are negotiated by states, enforced by states and subject to state modification. The GATT, WTO, Lomé, etc., which established the framework and rules for global trading networks, were formulated by states. In addition, bilateral and regional multilateral trade pacts such as NAFTA, LAFTA, etc. were initiated by the imperial state to open new markets for their MNCs. The imperial state operates in synergy with its MNCs. The expansion in markets has nothing to do with multinational corporations superseding anachronistic states. On the contrary, most movements of capital to new markets depend on state intervention to knock down barriers and, in some cases, to destabilize nationalist regimes.

Investments Agreements

New bilateral and multilateral investment agreements are formulated at the state level with the agreement and active participation of the MNCs. The reason is clear: the MNCs want state participation to guarantee that their capital will not be expropriated, subject to discriminatory taxes or restricted in remitting profits. The state is the enforcer of investment guarantees, a crucial element in corporate investment expansion. In many cases, the imperial states use their representation and power in the IFIs to impose new investment codes as conditions for stabilization or development loans.

Protection, Subsidies and Adjudication

The imperial states of the EU, the US and Japan regularly and systematically restrict imports, setting up diverse barriers to protect local producers and domestic industries, imposing the rules of free trade (liberalization, etc.) on competitors while pursuing protectionism at home. US and European states heavily subsidize agriculture with low rates for electricity and water use. Research and development of new technology is heavily financed by the state and then turned over to MNCs. At each stage prior to, during and after the expansion of MNCs in the world market, the state is deeply implicated. Where national enterprises are non-competitive, the imperial states invent pretexts to protect them from more efficient producers. Japan protects its rice producers, even though the final price is ten times more costly to consumers. The US provides huge subsidies to California agribusiness exporters in the form of research, cheap water rates and loans tied to the purchase of US grain exports. The EU subsidizes the formation of its high-tech industries, agriculture, etc.

Statism or neo-statism is the leitmotif of global economic expansion. The rhetoric of free markets promoted by conservative ideologues has been consumed and parroted by the globalist left. While the left has talked about the declining role of the state, the right has been active in promoting state activity to further the interests of the MNCs. While the left talks of globalization of markets, the MNCs from the imperial countries and their states carve up emerging and available markets, enlarging their spheres of domination and control, and, as in the nineteenth century, in the era of industrial capitalism, battering down closed doors to potential foreign markets. The imperial state, in other words, is not simply an economic institution; the overseas expansion of the MNCs is heavily dependent on the military and political role of the imperial state.

Expansion of the Political and Military Power of the Imperial State

The overseas expansion of the MNCs has been made possible by the military and political expansion of Euro-American imperialism via NATO and surrogate armies in southern Africa, Latin America and Asia. In Russia, other states of the former USSR and Eastern Europe, client regimes have been sponsored and supported by the imperial states, laying the groundwork for the takeover of a vast array of strategic industries, energy sources, etc. The triumph of the US imperial states over the USSR provided the impetus for dismantling the welfare states in Europe and what passed as a welfare state in the US. The Euro-American wars in the Gulf and Balkans have consolidated the imperial states' dominance and extended their influence over dissident states. The destabilization of the former Communist regimes and the destructive wars against nationalist regimes in southern Africa, Latin America and elsewhere opened these regions to neo-liberal policy prescriptions. Imperial military expansion directly related to state military apparatuses accompanied and promoted MNC overseas expansion. "Globalization" grew out of the barrel of a gun held by the imperial state.

To further protect overseas capital, the US and the EU, at a NATO meeting on April 23–24, 1999, created a new doctrine ("the Strategic Concept of the Atlantic Alliance") that legitimates offensive war inside and outside of Europe against any country that threatens vital economic interests (their MNCs). NATO was expanded to incorporate new client states in Eastern Europe and new peace associates among the Baltic states and the former republics of the USSR (Georgia, Kazahkstan, etc.). In other words, imperial-state military alliances have incorporated more states and involved more armed state apparatuses than before, all to ensure the safe passage of MNCs into these countries and the easy flow of profits back to their headquarters in the US and Western Europe.

The State and the Mass Media

While the mass media crosses more borders than ever, and more quickly and frequently, ownership and control is highly concentrated in the hands of US and European MNCs. The message is increasingly homogenous, and the source and inspiration is closely coordinated with policymakers in Washington, Berlin, London, etc. Global flows, imperial controls: this is the essence of the mass media today. The mass media multinationals look to the imperial states and their officials to set the political line and define the parameters for discussion, while they reap the profits.

On this point we conclude that the imperial states, far from being superseded by the overseas expansion of capital, have grown and become essential components of the world political economy. Globalist theorists mystify the role of the imperial state, an essential adversary, in the front lines of defence of the privileges and power of the MNCs.

While a few globalist writers might concede the importance of the imperial state, they would still argue that the recolonized states are withering away under the weight of global corporations that undermine their capacity to make decisions and regulate national economies.

The Recolonized State as a Terrain for Struggle

The starting point for any discussion of Third World states (TWSs) is historical. Most TWSs developed socio-economic policies contrary to IMF and World Bank prescriptions between 1945 and 1975. The basic reason had little to do with the USSR. The main reasons were the social classes, political alliances and ideologies that directed TWS policy, and pressure from mass movements. Throughout this thirty-year period, the imperial states, specifically the US, pressured the TWSs to liberalize their econo-

ratize public enterprises, etc. Most TWSs resisted these imperial (which are now dubbed "globalization").

basic changes took place that altered this scenario: imperialist powers led by the US launched a military offensive, utilizing mercenary and client military-political forces in southern Africa, Central and South America, and Asia to destroy economies and topple nationalist and socialist regimes that rejected the liberal program. The second change was the formation and ascendancy in the Third World of what Sklair (1997) and others term the "transnational capitalist class," which includes top political functionaries as well as capitalists linked to international financial circuits, with overseas bank accounts and investments and largely engaged in export markets. Devotees of the neo-liberal program of the imperial powers, this class became the ruling and economically dominant class in much of the Third World and proceeded to implement policies that privileged the interests of their imperial overlords and class allies. The dynamic interplay between the transnational capitalist class and imperial power produced what is mistakenly described as globalization. What in fact took place is the recolonization of the Third World.

The Third World state (TWS) is described by globalization theorists as powerless, lacking the attributes of a state and incapable of resisting the forces of globalization. There are several problems with this theory (see Weiss 1998). First, it amalgamates all TWSs under the same rubric, thus failing to distinguish between diverse forms of the post-colonial state. Second, it fails to take account of the fact that the TWSs have been active agents in advancing and implementing policies that have facilitated the "globalization," "liberalization" and "privatization" of their economies. Third, globalization theorists cannot account for variations in TWS policy with regard to the neo-liberal agenda of the imperial powers. Fourth, they overlook the importance of the new configuration of the capitalist class, whose members and political representatives in so many cases have achieved state power, using the state apparatus to advance the neo-liberal agenda. Fifth, globalists generally understate the scope and depth of state intervention in the economy and society, equating a weak state with the absence of social welfare. In fact, the neo-colonial state is as active, and as regulatory and interventionist, as the populist or welfare state, but the form of its intervention is different, often oriented as it is towards the interests of global capital and its local representatives.

While the recolonized state is beholden to global capital and serves the interests of the international capitalist class — and this class's states — it requires (and disposes of) substantial resources and power, both economic and non-economic, that enable it to fulfil its mission. Indeed, without a strong (that is, recolonized) state, imperialism would be imperilled. "Strength" in this context is defined and measured by the capacity of state actors and institutions to carry out fundamental structural "reforms" and secure the political conditions needed to sustain them — "political order" in the face of a popular movement against the new world order of globalization, neo-liberalism and capitalist development. While the colonized state might have an appearance of weakness, of being unable to withstand the forces of globalization and forced to respond to the agenda and policies of corporate capital, often it is quite "strong" in its capacity to translate this agenda into national policy. Since the recolonized TWSs are coterminous with the policies of the imperial state and its MNC associates, the notion of a weak minimalist state hollowed out and powerless in the face of global capitalism is of dubious analytical value.

The centrality of the recolonized states in advancing the neo-liberal counter-revolution is evident in several interrelated policy areas, outlined below.

Privatization

The recolonized state, in consultation with the IFIs, implements its liberal agenda through the privatization of strategic and lucrative public enterprises. Privatization requires intensive state intervention, including the formation of political alliances, repression of trade unions and/or firing of militant workers, socialization of the debts of enterprises, securing the advice of overseas investment banks in organizing the sale, intervening to ensure that favoured buyers have purchasing advantages and eliminating any rate or price controls if the public enterprise operated with fixed fees.

Imposition of Structural Adjustment

A structural adjustment program (SAP) means far more than mere economic adjustment, and "structural" in this context refers to class power, wealth and control (Veltmeyer, Petras and Vieux 1997). The role of the recolonized state in this connection is vital since a SAP involves a change of ownership in the means of production (from public to private, from national to private); the imposition of regressive taxes (replacing progressive income taxes with value-added taxes and reducing taxes on the rich and foreign capital); a reconcentration of income and property (regressive wage policies, freezing minimum wages, promoting agro-business at the expense of peasant agriculture, etc.); lower tariff barriers (bankrupting national producers in the process, providing MNCs "improved access" to local markets, etc.); reducing social programs (expenditures for health, education and social welfare); and increasing subsidies for exporters, etc. A SAP is a strategy of the dominant ruling class (transnational capitalism) directed against the great majority of local producers, workers and peasants. Implementation of a SAP requires a strong state willing to "stay the course," with enough "political will" to persist against the resistance of the majority — an ideologically committed state willing to shed its historical role as an independent entity, rejecting the idea of popular sovereignty in order to implement unpopular policies (by executive decree if possible, or by other means if necessary).

Those who speak and write of a neo-liberal regime speak or write of a powerful state that imposes and implements its policies.

Labour Flexibility

This is a euphemism for concentrating power in the hands of employers and the recolonized state. The new so-called "labour and pension re-forms" are policies that increase the powers of employers to hire workers on precarious contracts and fire them with little or no severance pay. It represents the total subjection of labour to capital. Workers are excluded from any voice in hours or days worked, or safety or health conditions. Workers possess no job security as employment is based on short-term contracts without vacations, pensions, etc. The privatization of pension funds put billions of dollars in the hands of private investment houses that receive exorbitant management fees and access to funds for speculation and fraud, enriching the few and threatening the retirement income of millions. Implementing regressive labour and pension legislation requires a strong state that can intervene against the popular sectors of civil society and repress and resist strong trade-union protests. Enforcement requires consolidating support among the capitalist class and securing backing from the IFIs, which is readily available. A weak state would not be able to resist the pressures of the popular classes. Instead, it would make conces-sions. A strong state can ignore protests and proceed to implement regres-sive labour and pension legislation.

In examining the most important policies pursued by the recolonized state, it is clear that the scope and depth of state intervention is as strong as ever. The main difference is in the socio-economic direction of state activism and intervention: liberal neo-statism involves intervention to transfer wealth and property to the private rich, especially to foreign capital. The recolonized state has not deregulated the economy; it has established new rules governing income policy, pensions, labour relations, import-export policies, flow of capital, etc. The new rules favouring for-eign capital require a new regulatory regime in which labour-capital populist-nationalists are replaced by representatives of the new liberal ruling class.

In the dismantling of the previous regulatory regime and social economy, and the construction of a new liberal economy and society, the recolonized state plays an essential activist and interventionist role, albeit one operating under the dominance of the imperial state(s).

Why the State Plays a Central Role

The imperial powers of the Third World have a much more realistic and pragmatic understanding of the centrality of the state, whether imperial or recolonized, than the theorists of globalization purporting to be on the left. While the publicists of the ruling class mouth the globalist rhetoric, in practice they strengthen and extend the power of the state. They do so because it is essential for the expansion and survival of their interests. There are several reasons why the state continues to play an essential role in the contemporary world.

Volatility of Markets

The contemporary world economy is profoundly influenced by financial sectors and by speculative activity that is highly volatile and constantly requires state intervention to prevent periodic financial crises in particular regions from spreading. Stock market speculators in the imperial countries are highly dependent on interest rates fixed by central banks. Collapsing financial and banking systems depend on state intervention to restructure bad loans (and pay depositors with taxpayers' money) as in the case of Japan, South Korea and Russia. Stagnating economies, such as Japan, depend on state intervention to stimulate growth. The number of examples could be expanded, but the main point is that movements of speculative capital have multiplied and increased the role of the state in trying to stabilize the anarchy of the market, with whatever resources can be mobilized from whatever sources are available, but mainly via added burdens to lower income taxpayers.

Financial Deregulation

The lessening of state control over financial transactions has increased the role of state intervention in bailing out crisis-ridden financial systems and enterprises, as was the case in the savings and loan crisis in the US. Lack of capital controls and free convertibility have allowed speculation on currencies and massive outflows of capital in times of panic. The state has intervened by supporting currencies, or letting them float, and/or tightening lending by raising interest rates. The frequency and increasing intensity of crises have changed the role of the state from one of police officer to firefighter — putting out financial conflagrations.

Inter-imperial Competition

The imperial states have increasingly taken part in the struggles for market share, each defending their own MNCs. And the recolonized states are active in promoting joint ventures between their capitalist enterprises and the MNCs. The imperial states have negotiated quotas on imports, taken competitors to the WTO, organized boycotts, etc. to strengthen their own MNCs at the expense of rivals. The US imperial state has fought for its cattle exporters against the EU, threatening boycotts and retaliatory measures, and it has limited imports of agricultural products from sugar-producing tropical countries. In short, competition between national MNCs has become conflicts between states, in which states become the final arbiters. Given shrinking markets and recession, we can expect greater state intervention and protection, not less.

The Scope and Depth of Transformation
No single multinational corporation or collectivity has the power to transform the economic and social structures that have allowed capital to flow en masse to overseas markets. The state created the institutional and systemic framework for the flow of capital and established the rules of the game that have guided overseas expansion. However, given the fragility of this "financial architecture," the state must continuously involve itself in bailing out capital and propping up recolonized regimes, keeping their allies and neo-colonial satraps in line.

Buttressing the IFIs
Since international financial institutions depend directly on the imperial states for their direction, programming and priorities, the support of the imperial state is essential to allow IFIs to continue to intervene in the new colonies. IFI funding depends on the imperial states, without which the IFIs would not have either the authority or leverage to enforce their macroeconomic policy prescriptions. IFIs serve as a link between the imperial and colonized states, and their power derives from the imperial centre. For these reasons, the state continues to be essential in the world political economy. Far from being a residual power derived from the past, the continuing relevance of the state is a structural feature of imperialism in its current form.

Conclusion

The theories constructed within the globalization paradigm fail to explain the central role that the state continues to play in the political economies of the contemporary world. In fact, the notion of an imperial system has no meaning unless we understand the activities of the imperial state and the multiplicity of roles it plays in opening markets for the expansion of its MNCs.

The current configuration of power in the world economy is not based on stateless or global corporations, but on MNCs working closely with their imperial states. It is absurd to speak of "globalization" when the largest MNCs are American (48 percent), European (35 percent) or Japanese (11 percent). IFIs like the World Bank and IMF do not form a new global state but derive their power and funding from the imperial states. Imperialism and not globalization is the key concept for understanding inter-state conflicts and inter-corporate competition. The imperial states and the MNC are not polarities; there is a synergy between neo-statism and neo-liberalism. In today's world, contrary to neo-liberal free market ideology, policymakers in both the imperial and recolonized states pick winners and losers through incentives, subsidies and tariffs, resulting in the expansion of specific big capitalist groupings and the decline of small, medium-sized and large firms without close ties to the regime.

The debate among bourgeois economists is over whether the large-scale, long-term intervention and bailout of MNCs is a moral hazard, about whether the knowledge of corporate directors that the state will subsidize losses encourages reckless speculative behaviour or not. "New Economy" economists have set aside their free market ideology when faced with a crisis and looked to the state for financial resources to stave off bankruptcy. On the other hand, fundamentalist neo-liberals argue that profits are earned on the basis of investment risks and, therefore, if the state eliminates risk it undermines the market's efficient allocation of resources and promotes destructive speculation.

The basic problem with globalization theory is that it focuses on the overseas expansion of national corporations but fails to take account of the headquarters of these corporations. MNCs buy and sell globally, but their strategic decisions on technology and investment are controlled by their national headquarters. The dynamics that flow from this fact are analyzed in subsequent chapters.

4. SPOILS OF EMPIRE
The US in Latin America

NOWHERE IN THE CONTEMPORARY WORLD HAVE ECONOMIC RELATIONS between inperial states and Third World regimes been so one-sided, so beneficial to the former and so detrimental to the latter, as in Latin America. To discuss these imperial state–client state relationships it is first of all necessary to establish a chronology that distinguishes degrees of domination and control, specifics of class collaboration and different forms of empire-building in recent decades.

To speak of imperialism as "five hundred years of exploitation and domination" is both *generally true* and *specifically misleading*. While European and US empire-builders have exploited many of the countries in Latin America for most of the past half millennium, it is also true that Latin American popular movements and nationalist and socialist regimes have managed to significantly modify or transform their relations with the imperial states at different conjunctures. Imperialism is based on class and state relations that by nature imply a process of conflict, confrontation, conquest, revolution, counter-revolution and transformation. The history of the region is replete with such "developments."

National-populist regimes from the 1930s to the 1960s were successful in partially transforming Latin America from a raw-material-based export economy into a relatively diversified urban industrial economy oriented towards the domestic market. A feature of this populist and nationalist development was the gradual incorporation of the middle class and elements of the working class into the political and economic process. Also, landless, near-landless and proletarianized peasants were offered "development" and land reform as means of staving off growing pressures for more radical change and revolution. However, in the mid-1970s the capitalist class both in Europe (Davis 1984; Crouch and Pizzorno 1978) and in Latin America launched a counter-revolution that in Latin America was aided and abetted, when not led, by the agents of American imperialism.

In alliance with Latin American transnational capitalists (linked to international financial, trade and marketing networks) and the armed forces, this counter-revolution was designed to arrest and reverse reformist change and development. To this purpose a "new economic model" of neo-liberal capitalist development was introduced by military force in

Chile and Argentina. In the 1980s, in an entirely new context of a region-wide debt crisis, these early "neo-liberal experiments" were reproduced and imposed on client regimes across the region by the economic agents of the imperialist states, working in concert to bring about policy reforms that would pave the way for a new wave of "investments" and the subjugation of the national economies in the region to the dictates of capital and the requirements of empire (for details see Veltmeyer and Petras 1997 and 2000).

Having taken control of the strategic and dynamic sectors of the economy and consolidated its hold on a client political class, "the empire" in the 1990s was well on the way towards a denationalization and recolonization that would facilitate a pillage of resources that would undermine and cripple the biggest economies in the region. This process generated in some countries conditions of a severe economic and political crisis, and new forces of resistance and opposition in the form of anti-systemic social movements. By the end of the decade this recolonization process — facilitated by several rounds of neo-liberal policy reforms and based on traditional right-wing leaders and the recruitment of new client rulers from the ranks of Latin America's renegade leftists and populists — was well advanced.

Imperial State–Client State Relations in the Latin American "Periphery"

In brief we can identify four recent periods of imperial state–client state relations. The 1930–70s period of relatively limited imperial domination was based on the *eclipse* rather than the displacement of the liberal agro-mineral collaborator classes, and on the emergence and expansion of national state and private industrial enterprises, foreign trade and exchange control regimes, and national banks. The 1970s (from 1965 to 1982 to be precise) marked a transition from a period of liberal reform and national development under the aegis of the "old economic model" of nationalization, regulation and state protection (as well as some import-substitution industrialization) towards a period of neo-liberal capitalist development and incorporation of Latin America into the "global economy" and the "new world economic order" (that is, the Euro-American empire). The 1983–99 period included massive privatization of public enterprises and the denationalization of banks, industries, telecommunications, strategic energy services, etc. The current period involves the transformation of strategic economic conquests into a new political-legal regime — the Free Trade Area for the Americas (ALCA) Commission — that vests US empire-builders with formal rulership of the region.

Empire Building: Phase I

The transition from national-populism to neo-liberalism was consummated through a process of violent conflicts, military coups, massacres, forced exiles, establishment of a state (military and police) apparatus loyal to the imperial states and a political class of willing accomplices. The empire-builders and their client rulers, both military and civilian, immediately opened the region to a massive invasion by US and European "investors" and multinational corporations.

Economic empire-building was made possible by the military empire builders who directly and indirectly intervened to repress, disarticulate and fragment the popular opposition. Military coups in Brazil (1964), Bolivia (1971), Chile (1973) and Argentina (1976), and civilian military coups in Uruguay (1972) and Peru (1993), created the political framework and international agreements with international financial institutions that halted and reversed the national industrializing project of the region's national (and nationalist) bourgeoisie, opening up Latin America to eventual conquest by US and European interests. This process was initiated in the 1970s in the Southern Cone of Chile, Argentina, Bolivia and Uruguay under the aegis of US-trained and supported "armed forces," which facilitated the process with an initial round of neo-liberal policies.

The imperial project was further advanced in the 1980s by a second round of neo-liberal policies under the aegis of constitutional-civilian regimes that had materialized in the process of "democratic renewal" — return to the rule of law and a reincorporation of the "private sector" (domestic and foreign capitalist enterprises) into the economic development project.

Under pressure from the popular movement, the US in the 1980s brokered a "negotiated transition" from military to elite electoral authoritarian political rule, safeguarding the "neo-liberal" policy and institutional framework needed to further the expansion of economic empire. In the next decade, facilitated by a massive inflow of capital in the form of foreign direct investment (FDI), the economic empire — both European (mostly Spanish) and US — underwent dramatic expansion as trade barriers fell and American, European Union and Asian commodities flooded Latin American markets, displacing millions of small farmers, local producers, manufacturers and retailers. It was for good reason as well as for symbolic value that the Zapatistas struck on January 1, 1994, the day set for the implementation of the North American Free Trade Agreement. As Subcomandante Marcos announced at the time, this agreement was the "death knell" for both Chiapas and the economies of the region.

The year 1989 saw the last of the one remaining military regime (in Chile) in the region, ending a ten-year process of "redemocratization" or "democratic renewal." The new "democratized" client regimes pillaged their economies, privatizing and selling off thousands of public enterprises, while MNCs bought local banks, manufacturers, land and real estate. According to a study in Brazil, in 1989 foreign banks owned 9.6 percent of bank stocks, but by 2000 they controlled 33 percent. By 2001, foreign finance capital controlled twelve of the twenty biggest banks in Brazil. In Mexico this process was even more advanced, with all of the country's banks falling prey to various consortia controlled by foreign-owned banks. Regionwide over 50 percent of all bank assets were privatized and denationalized.

The growth of foreign capital is almost exclusively the result of the acquisition of national public and private banks, not the creation of new firms. In Latin America a study of 212 directors of nineteen financial associations representing banks in fourteen Latin American countries revealed that 55 percent were representatives of foreign banks. A majority of the leaders of financial networks in Latin America today are North American or European bankers. These financial networks in turn directly or indirectly control industrial, commercial and real estate properties. Equally important, they establish the conditions for external financing in collaboration with the IFIs. US client ideologues in Latin America are mostly trained at elite academic (propaganda) universities such as Chicago, Harvard and Stanford. Through state terror, coercion and subservience to imperial demands communicated through imperially controlled IFIs, they imposed an imperially centred and designed neo-liberal model. The IFIs imposed this "model" through their structural adjustment policies and associated "reforms" that benefited local financial elites linked to US multinational banks.

The Spoils of Empire: The Sharks Feed

The imperially designed neo-liberal model led to a long-term and large-scale systematic pillage of every country in Latin America with resources to pillage. Calculations from data provided by the Economic Commission for Latin America and the Caribbean (ECLAC) (2002a and 2000b) on remittances for payments of profit and interest (see Table 4.1) show that returns on the operations of US capital in Latin America averaged close to $60 billion a year in the 1990s. Over the decade, $585 billion in interest payments and profits were remitted to the centre of the empire, the vast bulk of it to US home offices.

This volume of returns on capital for investments and loans in Latin America is perhaps sufficient to explain the "sluggish growth" in the region and the failure of Latin America to meet the expectations of economic recovery and economic growth by the World Bank, the IMF and many analysts throughout the 1990s. However, the data in Table 4.1 provide only a part of this sad and sordid story. Neither UNCTAD nor the data in Table 4.1 collected by ECLAC include the significant revenues drawn from royalty payments, shipping, insurance and other service fees;

Table 4.1. Export Earnings and Remittances for Payment of Profit and Interest, Latin America, 1980–2001 (billion US$)

	1980	'85	'90	'93	'94	'95	'96	'97	'98	'99	2000	'01
Export earnings	109	116	165	183	221	271	300	333	333	347	413	392
Profit remittances	32	47	43	45	48	54	60	66	72	71	82	78

Source: ECLAC *2002a and 2002b.*

nor do they include the scores of billions of dollars illegally transferred by Latin American elites via US and European banks to overseas accounts. According to the *World Investment Report* (UNCTAD 2002) royalty payments of developing countries to the MNCs from 1986 to 1990 — crucial years in the "decade lost to development," in which Latin America experienced a huge capital drain in the form of interest payments on external debts — increased by 22 percent a year to a total of $73 billion. As for Latin America it turns out that data on royalty and related payments are difficult to come by, but Table 4.1 summarizes the available data for the 1990s.

Saxe-Fernández (2002) estimates that with just the "legal" transfers of financial resources the total pillage of Latin America for 2000 is closer to $100 billion than $70 billion. If we multiply this sum by the ten years of the past decade we can estimate that Latin America made a net contribution to the imperial states of over a trillion dollars. Table 4.2 provides a snapshot of some of the mechanisms and capital flows involved in this "resource transfer" from Latin America to the major centres of the European-US empire. In five of the years in the 1990s outflows exceeded inflows.

What these data show is that the outflow of capital to the imperial centres — "international resource transfers" in official lingo — is an enormous drain, drawing out huge pools of accumulated and potential capital. In the late 1970s, Latin America was the primary recipient of both foreign direct investment and international commercial bank loans placed in developing countries. The newly industrializing countries in East Asia were generally financing their own development. Governments in Latin America, many under a military regime, however, were eager to attract FDI, notwithstanding the regulations in place, and to borrow heavily at the very low rates of interest offered by banks anxious to hook foreign clients. As a result, these countries acquired a huge debt load, pushing them into crisis when the US Federal Reserve hiked interest rates to an all-time high. In the late 1970s the income received by the MNCs on their accumulated and new investments exceeded new outflows by a considerable margin — $30 billion (on an accumulated stock of $188 billion) from 1977 to 1979. Reported income on direct corporate investments represents an

Table 4.2. Net Capital Inflows and Outflows, Latin America, 1980–2002 (billion US$)

	1985–90	'91-2	'93	'94	'95	'96	'97	'98	'99	2000	'01	'02
Capital inflows	105.1	123.7	125.6	66.7	98.8	103.7	109.2	96.5	96.5	83.1	49.6	
ODA	37.5	10.0	5.4	5.6	5.7	5.5	-8.6	10.9	1.6	11.1	20.2	12.6
Private flows	-	95.1	118.3	120.0	61.0	93.3	112.3	98.3	94.9	85.4	62.9	37.0
FDI	42.5	29.4	17.2	28.7	31.9	43.8	66.1	73.4	87.8	75.8	69.3	42.0
Portfolio[b]	-	44.7	74.4	63.1	4.8	12.2	13.3	-2.1	-3.6	-0.4	2.3	1.0
Loans	63.8	21.0	26.5	28.2	24.3	37.9	32.9	27.0	10.7	10.0	-8.7	-6.0
Returns on capital		142.0	74.1	73.2	78.5	79.2	82.9	99.4	107.8	90.9	100.0	96.8
Profit on assets	62.0	34.7	36.6	40.9	42.8	48.2	51.2	52.2	53.4	54.7	52.5	
Interest payments[c]	211.2	76.0	38.0	35.0	36.0	35.0	33.0	46.3	53.6	35.3	43.1	41.9
Royalty payments[a]	5.4	2.2	1.4	1.6	1.6	1.4	1.7	1.9	2.0	2.2	2.2	2.4
Net Resource transfers (on assets)	-150.4	30.7	31.5	10.1	19.4	22.7	32.3	27.2	-3.1	-0.2	-4.6	-38.8
Accumulated capital stock												
Debt	420.0	480.2	520.6	564.4	619.3	641.4	666.6	747.6	763.7	740.5	727.8	725.1
FDI	-	-	167.8	186.2	225.8	320.6	375.4	396.8	190.6	207.1	216.4	269.9

(a) as of 1995 — World Bank, *World Development Indicators*, 2002
(b) World Bank, *Global Development Finance*, Statistical Appendix, Table 20, 2002
(c) World Bank 2000 and 2002

Sources: ECLAC 1998; UNCTAD 1998: 256, 267–68, 362; 2002; US Dept. of Commerce 1994; World Bank 1997. FDI stock 1999–2001 for US only (US Census Bureau 2002).

average profit rate of 12 percent on FDI as calculated by the US Department of Commerce, but from 22–33 percent as calculated by ECLAC (1998).

In just three years at the turn into the 1980s American MNCs made over $15 billion in profits from their Latin American operations. Although this level of returns on invested capital might pale in comparison to the profits made by the commercial banks in the 1980s (some $211.2 billion from 1985 to 1989, and $300 billion over the decade), it was enough to stimulate another surge of new FDI in the 1990s, as one government after another in the region was forced to liberalize its capital markets and remove the remaining barriers. The statistics on this are both revealing and startling (see Table 4.1).

Over the course of the decade the MNCs turned towards Latin America in a big way, stepping up new investments from $8.7 billion in 1990 to $61 billion in 1998 — a seven-fold increase in FDI inflows, twice the rate of growth experienced anywhere else (the worldwide average was 223 percent). Notwithstanding the enormous and rapidly growing capital and commodity markets emerging in China and elsewhere in the East, and frenzied merger and acquisition activity elsewhere (especially in Europe and the US), Latin America experienced the highest rate of growth in directly invested capital. However, the bulk of this capital — some $400 billion over the decade (and another $160 billion from 2000 to 2002) — involved mergers and acquisitions of privatized firms rather than productive investments.[1] Even so, the MNCs and IFIs managed to generate from this direct investment $368 billion in profits and another $18 billion in royalty charges.

The financial resources sucked out of the region in the 1990s were more than sufficient to explain the sluggish growth of the economies in the region over the decade — less than 3 percent per annum and down to 0.3 in 2001 and -0.9 in 2002 (on a per capita basis, virtually zero growth over the decade) (World Bank 2003: Table 8). ECLAC (2002) has, in this context, identified retrospectively the beginnings of another "decade lost to development." If we take into account less obvious mechanisms of surplus transfer to the various imperial centres, then the pillage of the region's wealth reaches truly gigantic proportions, a veritable hemorrhage of resources sucked out of the region's economy by, in the poetic language of Subcomandante Marcos (1994), "the bloody jaws" of the "wild beast" (imperialism), whose teeth, he notes, have "sunk deeply into the throat of southeastern Mexico, drawing out large pools of blood" [tribute in the form of "petroleum, electrical energy, cattle, money, coffee, banana, honey, corn"] through "many veins" — oil and gas pipes, electrical lines, traincars, bank accounts, trucks and vans, clandestine paths, gaps and forest trails. The financial mechanisms of resource transfers and capital flow reflected in Table 4.1 are primary means of surplus value or unpaid labour extraction and transfer — "exploitation," to be more precise. But, as Marcos has suggested, the imperialist system can count on diverse agents and a number of different of mechanisms to pillage the resources of dominated economies, some of them well hidden or disguised.

These other largely hidden mechanisms of surplus transfer ("net international resource outflows") can be placed into two categories: (1) the structure of international trade, regarded by neo-liberals as the "engine of economic growth" (with capitalist corporations as the drivers of this engine), and (2) the structure of capital-labour relations, and the organization of labour within this structure.

As for trade, an empire-building process is evident in the systematic takeover of production facilities within the region, the penetration of local markets and the push to dominate both inter- and intra-regional trade via policies designed to open up Latin America's economies and liberalize access to US-produced goods and services while limiting and controlling the access of Latin American competitors to the US market.[2] According to Bilbao Vizcaya Argentaria Bankus (BBVA), headquartered in Spain, over one-third (56) of the 150 biggest enterprises in Latin America are now foreign-owned, half are nationally/privately owned and almost 13 percent (19) are national state firms.[3] However, the 75 nationally privately owned firms only generate 30 percent of the total sales of this group of enterprises and 22 percent of their exports. The foreign-owned firms, however, account for 63 percent of the group's export earnings. Other studies indicate that American and European MNCs control a substantial share of Argentina's domestic market, while the remaining national public firms are the major foreign-exchange earners. In Brazil the pattern is all too similar (Petras and Veltmeyer 2003b).

American and European MNCs not only dominate inter- and intra-regional trade but also dominate domestic markets in the region, largely displacing local producers in the process. The imperial formula for Latin America is to export capital so as to capture the domestic markets and to import raw materials from the publicly owned enterprises. In 2002, MNCs repatriated $22 billion in profits on direct investments of $76 billion — an almost 35 percent rate of return.[4] Some data for the 1990s are presented in Table 4.2. Most of the net outflow of resources in the 1980s was in the form of interest payments on the external debt. In the 1990s, however, FDI or equity financing (mostly to purchase the assets of already existing or privatized enterprises) replaced debt as the principal source of capital,[5] becoming, in IMF language, "the backbone of private sector external financial flows" to the less developed countries (LDC) (IMF 2002: 2).

Although public or state enterprises accounted for $245 billion in sales, of which 35 percent represented exports, it is clear that the strategic goal of US empire-building is to seize control of the assets and enterprises in this sector. In the 1980s this process was most advanced in Mexico, which, from 1982 to 1993 devolved almost all of its state enterprises, some 1,152, to the "private sector." The crowning event in this process, which netted the government $31.5 billion in revenues, was the sale from 1992 and 1993 of the country's eighteen state banks, the largest of which have subsequently fallen into the hands (i.e., banks) of the Euro-American transnational capitalist class — Banamex went to Citibank and Bancomer to Bilbao Vizcaya. That the anticipated revenues from the sale of these state enterprises were not the primary object of the privatization agenda is evidenced by recent reports of Banco de Mexico and the Secretaría de Hacienda (*La Jornada*, July 25, 2003) that the total revenues derived from these privatizations in all economic sectors was only $31.5 billion, barely 28.8 percent of the debt ($89.4 billion) subsequently assumed by the government in the process of bailing out the banks in the wake of the 1995 financial crisis. Amador (2003) estimates that the bailout of private capital in recent years has cost Mexico $109.2 billion.

In the 1990s the privatization agenda was widely implemented as part of a second round of sweeping reforms mandated by the "new economic model" of free market capitalism (Bulmer-Thomas 1996; Veltmeyer, Petras and Vieux 2000). The privatization policy, although pioneered in Chile by Augusto Pinochet in the 1970s and advanced in a spectacular fashion by Carlos Salinas de Gortari in the late 1980s and early 1990s, achieved its paradigmatic form under the Carlos Menem regime in Argentina in the 1990s. The World Bank has viewed the Argentina experience as a "model" for other countries across the world as well as the region to follow, and Brazil, under Fernando Henrique Cardoso, did just that (Petras and Veltmeyer 2003b). Just as Argentina, Brazil and Mexico in 1983 accounted for 50 percent of all Third World debt, in the next decade they represented some of the most important privatizations in the world.

The strategic focus of the privatization agenda has shifted over the years. Currently, the strategic focus of the empire-builders in the region is on the state petroleum and gas companies of Mexico, Venezuela, Brazil, Ecuador, Colombia and Bolivia, as well as the Chilean Copper Corporation (*La Jornada*, June 15, 2003). A study by Saxe-Fernández and Núñez (2001) analyzes in detail the machinations of the World Bank in this regard. They detail the systematic efforts of the World Bank to bring about the de facto privatization of Pemex, Mexico's state oil company, and to facilitate thereby a massive expropriation of Mexico's denationalized natural and productive resources and to transfer to the US empire enough surplus value and capital to seriously undermine the Mexican economy and substantially contribute to the US economy. The devil, it is said, is in the details, and this study by Saxe-Fernández and Núñez is certainly detailed. They calculate (2001: 150–51) that, with Mexico's turn towards the neo-liberal model under IMF and World Bank conditions between 1983 and 1997 an economic surplus of \$457 billion was sucked out of Mexico by various means into the US and EU imperial centres. This calculation with regard to Mexico includes two forms of surplus transfer: (1) debt service and (2) trade losses via the payment of rents, an unequal exchange in trade relations and payment for franchises, concessions and patent rights.

At another level, the system of trade between the US and Mexico — and, for that matter, Latin America generally and other developing countries — is based on a structure that is highly skewed in its distribution of economic benefits. However, at the level of world trade the US economy is not the behemoth it would like to be — that it was, for example, in the immediate post-World War II period when it commanded a lion's share of the world's productive and financial resources (up to 50 percent in some estimates) and had a commanding position in world industrial production and trade in both goods and services, accounting for 59 percent of the world's developed oil reserves, 46 percent of total energy production, over 80 percent of total motor vehicles and 50 percent of the world's monetary gold and currency reserves (Maizels 1970).

However, as shown in part in Table 4.3, over the years the US has

Table 4.3. US Trade Balance, 1990–2003 (billion US$)

	1990	'91	'92	'93	'94	'95	'96	'97	'98	'99	2000	'01	'02	'03
World	-101	-66	-85	-116	-151	-160	-170	-181	-230	-329	-436	-412	-469	-354
Mexico	-1.9	2.2	5.4	1.7	1.4	-15.8	-17.5	-14.6	-15.9	-22.8	-24.6	-30.0	-37.1	-27.7
LA Other	-9.7	-2.6	1.7	2.4	3.3	7.5	3.1	9.3	13.1	-3.3	-14.1	-9.2	-18.0	-17.7
EU	6.3	17.0	9.0	-1.0	-8.1	-8.2	-15.2	-16.8	-27.4	-43.4	-55.0	-61.3	-82.0	-59.9

Source: US Census Bureau, "US Trade Balance" <http://www.census.gov.foreign-trade/balance>.

steadily lost its market share in world trade, although this apparent trend reflects in part the growing share of this trade that is accounted for by affiliates of US MNCs whose output and sales are not included in the US trade account. These affiliates, according to UNCTAD (2002), by now account for at least 13 percent of world trade today. Another 50 percent of this trade in goods and services takes the form of intra-firm transfers, which is to say, they do not enter the market at all. In any case, what can be said with certainty is that the US national trade account has been in deficit since the late 1960s. At the time — in 1971 to be precise — the US administration began to institute a series of strategic measures, beginning with a unilateral abandonment of the Bretton Woods fixed-rate regime for the US dollar, designed to improve its position in the world market vis-à-vis its major competitors (Aglietta 1982).

However, as shown by Aglietti's study of strategic responses by the US administration to the crisis in global capitalism, these responses did not arrest a long-term trend towards ever-larger deficits on the US national trade account. The US continues to be in a substantial trade deficit situation, the deficit growing from $63.3 billion in 1991 ($101 billion in 1990) to $468.3 billion in 2002 and $354.1 billion in 2003. The US continues to post a trade deficit with economies in every major region in the world even in Latin America. For most of the 1990s, Latin America helped the US government reduce the deficit in its trade account (see Table 4.3). However, as of 1999 (and as of 1995 in Mexico) this was no longer the case and the US had to rely even more on finance capital to cover its growing trade deficits. This situation in the US trade balance is represented in statistical terms for 2002 in Table 4.4.

The US generally sustains these deficits by attracting from all over the world financial and investment capital seeking higher rates of stable returns secured by the strength of the US dollar as the dominant world currency. Nevertheless, the capacity of the US economy to ride out its propensity towards crisis, and to finance the enormous deficit on its trade account, to some extent depends on its capacity to capture new markets for its exports and to dominate existing markets. Hence, the ongoing efforts of the US administration to establish a Free Trade Area for the Americas

Table 4.4 US Exports, Imports and Trade Balance, by Region, 2002 (billion US$)

	Exports	Imports	Trade Balance
Latin America	-56.9	142.3	199.1
APEC	-316.8	448.9	765.7
OECD	-88	156.2	245.1
Total	-482.9	681.9	1,164.7

Source: US Census Bureau, "US Trade Balance" <http://www.cednsus.gov.foreign-trade balance>.

(FTAA, or ALCA in Spanish). It is clear to the US that Latin America has to make a greater contribution to the ailing US economy, notwithstanding its enormous contribution over the years, particularly in the 1990s. However, the precise nature and total of this "necessary" contribution is not so easy to calculate. To do so would require a closer look at the diverse mechanisms of productive resource flow built into the structure of trade between the US and Latin America, and in this regard no country is as important as Mexico, the US's major trading partner in the region, with the US absorbing up to 80 percent of Mexico's exports.

Recent studies by UNCTAD (2002 and 2003) and ECLAC (2000b) expose one of the hidden elements of this structure — deteriorating terms of trade between economies at the centre of the system and on its periphery. In this regard, UNCTAD (2002: 42) estimates that Latin America (together with other areas of the developing world) since the early 1980s has lost at least 10 percent of the marketed value of the labour embodied in the production of its exported commodities — a 13 percent loss just in 1998 and another 14 percent in 1999.[6] The magnitude of this loss, via a "downward pressure on export prices" is enormous. In the long run it might very well exceed the total value of the economic surplus sucked out by other means, such as FDI. And this by no means is the end of the story of resource pillage. A series of built-in barriers erected against Latin American exports and the corresponding liberalization[7] of Latin America's capital and product markets vis-à-vis the US — dubbed by UNCTAD as a "lack of balance in the liberalization process" (liberalization for the LDCs, protection and subsidies for the Organization for Economic Co-operation and Development [OECD] countries)[8] — has resulted in an outflow of "productive resources" (potential capital) that compares with the total value of Latin America's "capital flight" (investment capital deposited or marketed in the US), which in itself approaches, if not exceeds, the total value of external debt payments over the years.[9] And these payments have been, and continue to be, a significant factor in the expropriation of productive resources generated in the region. Joao Pedro Stedile (2003), leader of the Landless Rural Workers Movement (MST) in Brazil, estimates that up to $480 billion in debt payments have been made by the

Brazilian government since its turn toward neo-liberalism in 1991, but over the course of these payments the accumulated debt has increased from $6 billion to a staggering $250 billion. These "reforms" have not only facilitated a process of globalization and asset appropriation, but have also been a means of transferring to the centre of the empire a significant supply of productive and financial resources.

Notwithstanding the disguised nature and the difficulty of accurate measurement of these transfers, the magnitude of surplus value transferred probably exceeds the more visible outflow of financial resources. What is clear is that through the structure of its trade with the US in particular, Latin America not only loses a large mass of surplus value extracted from its direct producers and workers but makes a significant contribution to the US economy. Indeed, trade with Latin America is one of the economic pillars of US imperialism.

US–Latin American trade represents a major contribution of different classes of producers and workers to the US economy. It is well established that labour is a major factor in the production process, the principal source of added value and the major contributor to "total factor productivity." What is not so well known is how the organization and export of labour can be used — and is used — as yet another means of pillaging a country's resources and transferring them to the imperial centre. A recent study of transnational (Mexico-US) labour migration by Delgado Wise (2004: 7) is revealing. He estimates that the direct and indirect contribution of Mexican labour to the US economy in balance of payments — and the corresponding loss to the Mexican economy — is in the order of $29 billion a year. This "contribution" does not include the massive export of natural resources (oil) and assets (when MNCs acquire assets of privatized public companies at knockdown prices).[10] What it does take into account is the hemorrhage of potential capital which enters the US economy through diverse conduits, including: (1) the remuneration of labour in the *maquilladores* that account for the bulk (70 percent) of Mexico's manufacturing exports at a level that is well below the value of the labour-power employed and generates an enormous reservoir of surplus value in the form of repatriated profits, at a rate of 35 percent return on invested capital;[11] (2) the direct export of agricultural and farm labour in the form of seasonal, controlled or "illegal" migration of both documented and undocumented workers, accounting for up to 80 percent of the agricultural labour in the US, with a clearly depressive impact on the wages of employed wage-labourers in the sector; and (3) direct immigration into the US of educated and highly qualified forms of Mexican labour, estimated to constitute 40 percent of all Mexican migrants, without the US having had to bear any of the reproduction costs of this labour.[12] Although there are no studies into the magnitude of this transfer of labour-added value, the contribution to the US and the cost to Mexico are undoubtedly considerable. Delgado Wise (2004: 7) estimates the contribution of Mexican labour to the balance of trade with the US in 2002 to be in excess of $28 billion.[13] Although the remittances of Mexican migrants are in the order of $9.8 billion — the country's third-largest source of foreign exchange earnings (behind revenue from exports of oil and manufacturing, but ahead of tourism and agricultural exports, and comparable in volume to FDI) — these remittances are derived from economic activities by Mexican repatriates who, working *within* the US, contribute substantially more to the US economy than to Mexico's.[14] Like trade (the export of natural resources and commodities), migration (the export of labour) constitutes a substantial net loss to Mexico and an equally substantial net benefit and boost to the US economy.[15]

If one were to add up both overt and hidden mechanisms of surplus transfer, the contribution to the US of the Mexican "economy" (the labour of the 80 million or so who participate directly and indirectly) and the corresponding capital drain from Mexico is nothing less than staggering. If we consider similar forms of capital drain from the other countries in the region, particularly Brazil, Latin America can be seen as a major economic pillar of the US empire, explaining the lengths that the US state will go — and periodically has gone — to ensure by political or military means the subservience of its many client states in the region.

Building the Empire in Stages

To summarize, it is possible to identify four stages of empire-building:

1. ideological-military-political intervention to impose the "new economic model" within the parameters of a "realistic" approach towards international relations and to overcome inevitable "obstacles" — popular resistance, the timing and sequencing of implementation, incompetent rulers, etc.;
2. implementation of the policies of empire — privatization, deregulation, liberalization and decentralization — leading to increased integration into the "new world order" and, at the national level, processes of expropriation, denationalization and dominance of local elites linked to the IFIs and MNCs;
3. conversion from national privatization to foreign control via debt payments, loans and buyouts, leading to the takeover of large market shares in sales and banking; and
4. the drive for direct imperial political-military *control* to repress mass resistance resulting from the pillage in phases 1–3, and to extend and deepen privatization to include lucrative public energy, raw material, and light and power enterprises. Stage four is a preparation for the imposition of the FTAA (ALCA) — the final stage of empire-building — *the recolonization of Latin America.*

The Mechanics of Imperial Rule

The key to empire-building — the dynamic of imperialism — is the role of the imperial state and its "quasi-private/public" auxiliaries in the private sector. The MNCs and financial expansion in Latin America are crucial for accumulation and to counter the tendency for the rate of profit to decline, but it is also important to recognize the role of the imperial state in resolving the fundamental question of the geographic and economic locations where these processes play themselves out, the timing of the resolution or attempted resolution of economic crises, and the necessary social relations and political framework that enable economic contradictions to be resolved. Overproduction may drive the capitalist to turn to the conquest of overseas markets, but these "markets" will not open if local regimes are not forced to lower barriers via military invasions, coups and the placement of imperial-centred economist-ideologues in decision-making positions. The leverage of the IFIs linked to the imperial state is also a basic component of market openness. The falling rate of profit of key economic sectors (and their leading MNCs) cannot be reversed if labour legislation in the client states is not "reformed" through the IFIs, and mass organized resistance is not repressed by the police and military apparatus of clients.

Thirty-five percent rates of return are not secured in democratic, participatory societies with full employment and labour rights. Exorbitant rates of return, pillage of public resources, saturation of markets and prompt full payment of debt in the midst of mass poverty requires bloody repression by client rulers, which is far beyond the capability of "market forces" alone.

Strategic openings for the MNCs clearly require the massive systematic involvement of the imperial state. Economic empire-building is intimately related to *client regime–building* (what liberals and imperialists term "nation-building"). The imperial state in Latin America not only creates the initial foundations of empire-centred development but is deeply involved in controlling, disciplining, recruiting, corrupting, co-opting and threatening electoral politicians to serve as local collaborators.

The empire rules via the IFIs, which enforce economic discipline via loans, conditionality and threats — the purpose being to use debt obligations to deepen privatization and enforce compliance with "open markets" policy.

The rule of the open market applies to Latin American but not to the US or the EU, where selective protectionism reigns. The imperial states have established over 120 military bases throughout the world, including more than two dozen bases and operational locations throughout Latin America, to recruit officials and to train them to identify ideologically with the empire, oppose anti-imperial adversaries and intervene in time of regime crisis. Most important, the imperial state intervenes to influence political elites, financing candidates and parties, and buying, co-opting, threatening or seducing ascending political figures. Imperial policymakers encourage greater links with the MNCs and greater distance from popular constituencies. The latter activity involves long-term cultivation of opposition figures from what the US State Department calls the "responsible left" or the "democratic left," who provide the "right signals" — supporting electoral as opposed to mass struggle, compromises favouring concessions to MNCs, and an affinity for individual over collective mobility. The empire favours personalistic rule that provides an authoritarian setting for implementing harsh austerity rules for the many and large-scale concessions to the rich, particularly the foreign rich.

The most recent successes of the imperial state's strategy of client regime-building are found in Brazil and Ecuador. In both cases, political leaders, Luis Inacio (Lula) da Silva and Lucio Gutiérrez, were backed by radical popular movements before they "turned" or converted to empire-centred policies via ideological persuasion in line with a rightward shift in the leadership of their party apparatus.

The imperial state, through its formal and informal links to US-based private and public cultural institutions, recruits media "stars," upwardly mobile intellectuals, students and journalists to design and promote empire-centred cultural practices and institutes that train activists and influence public opinion. The head of USAID recently demanded that US-funded non-governmental organizations (NGOs) drop their "non-governmental" facade and openly declare that they are "an arm of the US government" (*Financial Times*, June 13, 2003). There are many "arms of the US government," admitted or not, that combine cultural entertainment and ideological indoctrination, world news and imperial propaganda, and scholarship and foundation grants with empire-centred thinking and acting. The imperial state has created and defended this "public-private" cultural universe for economic empire-building in Latin America. In summary, Washington spends US tax dollars to finance the expansion of the US economic empire, depleting the resources of the republic. Nowhere are the direct ties between political-military empire-building and rulership more clearly related to economic empire-building than in Latin America. And the process marches towards imperial colonial rule.

New Directions for the Empire

Empire-building has taken a new and more aggressive direction in the new millennium — a series of imperialist wars and conquests driven by the imperial state and directed by militarist ideologues. Since 2001, the US has engaged in two wars of conquest, innumerable assassinations and interventions throughout the world through clandestine "special forces operations," and the recruitment and co-optation of client rulers throughout Asia, Africa, Latin America and the Balkans. The empire-builders have consolidated control over their Eastern European and Baltic clients and moved on to cement ties with the far right regimes of Spain and Italy. Under pressure, the initial resistance of the European Union has given way to its members becoming *subordinated associates* of the US, protecting US puppet regimes in Afghanistan, providing assistance to the US colonial regime in Iraq, backing US threats and demands against Iran and joining the attack on Cuba by supporting US-funded Cuban agents.

The US empire-builders have accelerated the process of colonization of Latin America via ALCA. There are several reasons why the US is pressing the colonization process:

• clients and collaborators in Latin America are still in place, but their power is tenuous at best;
• mass resistance is building up throughout the region;
• the mercantilist, liberal-protectionist model of empire is provoking opposition among sectors of Latin American export elites;
• the US seeks to monopolize the takeover of the remaining major public enterprises as they are privatized, avoiding losses to Europe as occurred, especially to Spain, during the previous wave in the 1990s;
• military clients are still in place but they are not present everywhere or to the same degree, particularly in Venezuela, Brazil, Ecuador and Bolivia;
• the US can use the momentum of its military-political conquests in Asia to pressure and blackmail conformity among Latin America political elites; and
• the surprise conversion of two regimes — Lula's in Brazil and Lucio Gutiérrez's in Ecuador — to ALCA, and their vulnerability to mass opposition, caused the empire-builders to move with haste.

US empire-builders have moved toward colonial domination with naked power and imperial-centred demands, ignoring concessions to their client regimes and thus severely weakening their bases for compliance. Mexico provides the clearest case: the US has refused President Vicente Fox's request to legalize the status of four million Mexican migrant workers and to abide by reciprocity in trade agreements on transport, textiles and a number of other commodities. Instead Washington demands the complete privatization of Mexico's public petroleum industry (Pemex), the biggest revenue and foreign-exchange-earning firm in the country.

The historical precedent for the current process of US empire-building in Latin America is the mercantilist system of the European colonial empires. Some common features include:

• overt imperial controls via a political authority (ALCA) that establishes the economic regulations and legal framework for US monopolization of a privileged economic position in Latin America;

- imperial military command structures, bases and direct involvement in field operations to repress popular insurgencies;
- non-reciprocal trade involving total liberalization of Latin American trade regimes and selective protective measures to prevent competitive Latin producers from competing successfully in the US market; and
- the effective exclusion of European, Japanese and other economic powers from competing in Latin American markets.

The neo-mercantilist imperial system is explicitly being implemented via ALCA on the economic front and via Plan Colombia, the Andean Initiative and the continental coordination of military "assistance" on the military front.

Empire-building, recolonization and consolidation rest on three political pillars: (1) co-opting "popular" leaders such as Lula in Brazil, Gutiérrez in Ecuador and Néstor Kirchner in Argentina; (2) acceleration of ALCA military accords in the face of decaying clients (Alejandro Toledo in Peru, Gonzalo Sánchez de Lozada in Bolivia and Alvaro Uribe in Colombia); and (3) isolation and/or overthrow of the Venezuelan and Cuban regimes and defeat of the growing popular opposition in Latin America. ALCA will provide US empire-builders with control over an institution, the ALCA Commission, which will make policy on every aspect of trade, investment, public-private relations and services, including education, health and pensions. Just as the debt refinancing of Latin American regimes facilitated liberalization, the current neo-liberal regimes facilitate recolonization via ALCA. Under US colonial rule, the Latin American administrative structures will stay in place, reduced and reconfigured, to implement US colonial policies expressed through the ALCA Commission. Latin American legislative, executive and judicial powers will be reduced to debating the methods, pace and application of ALCA/US-dictated policies. As in former colonial systems, vertical authoritarian structures will be superimposed over electoral institutions.

The growing military power of the US and its projections in Latin America have emboldened the empire-builders to act more aggressively. In Venezuela a military-civilian coup and employers' lockout were orchestrated by US intelligence agencies. In Colombia, US military involvement has intensified the carnage and displaced hundreds of thousands of peasants to deprive the popular insurgents of recruits, food and logistical support. Washington has openly organized nuclei of counter-revolutionary cadres against Cuba (dubbed "dissidents") to engage in propaganda and recruitment, while explicitly listing the revolutionary regime as its proximate military target. Throughout Latin America, US military bases have been established for future intervention where client regimes might be overthrown by popular majorities.

Equally important are the *political conquests* of the empire-builders. In Brazil, the Lula regime has been converted into a satellite of the imperial states, indiscriminately embracing the financial and agro-export elites who play an integral role in promoting ALCA and recolonization. In Ecuador, Gutiérrez and his partners, the Pachakutik party, have moved swiftly to privatize the state petroleum and electrical companies, embracing dollarization, US military bases, Plan Colombia and ALCA, breaking strikes and militarizing petrol refineries.

The "new perspectives" for colonization in Latin America existed before the events of 9/11 and the so-called US "war against terrorism." The new militarism after 9/11 accelerated the process of colonization and gave greater impetus to militarization and direct intervention. The most significant change since 9/11 has been the total exclusion of any consultation and concessions to client regimes, making for even more lopsided relations.

5. THE US REPUBLIC AND THE WEIGHT OF EMPIRE

Until its recent revival, the notion of "imperialism" had disappeared from academic and political discourse. However, except for the odd intellectual dinosaur, many writers, journalists and academics have reintroduced the concept of imperialism into their analysis of world power. Forms of analysis that employed the Gramscian notion of "hegemony" have generally proven inadequate for explaining the dynamics of empire-building today, particularly in relation to the new emphasis of the US empire on the projection of military power and rule by force — "the new imperialism," as opposed to the machinations of economic empire in the post-World War II period.

Close to fifty years ago the Economic Commission on Latin America (CEPAL) described the world economy in terms of a "center" and "periphery," and twenty years later the world system theorist Immanuel Wallerstein added to academic discourse on the structure of international relations the rather peculiar notion of a "semi-periphery." But these and other such terms, devoid of any historical, class or state specificity, have now been discarded by most critical writers in the contemporary world as meaningless and thus useless. In addition, as we have argued in a different context (Petras and Veltmeyer 2001), the recent and by now rather widespread intellectual turn towards the notion of "globalization" as a means of describing what is going on in the world today is even less useful.

Not that long ago, Hardt and Negri (2000) could write of an "Empire" where "imperialism is over." Today, however, the notion of imperialism, particularly as regards the aggressive unilateral projection of state power by the US, has been put back on the intellectual map and on political agendas. All the major questions we face today regarding the nature of international power relations and the reality of multiplying conflicts, patterns of conquests and resistance revolve around the nature and dynamics of imperialism, particularly as regards the most powerful and aggressive imperial power: the United States of America.

However, no sooner has the spectre of US imperialism raised its ahead and reasserted itself in our minds and global politics than it has faced serious questions regarding its sustainability in the current circumstances

— which begs the question as to whether US imperialism in its most recent incarnation is all that "new." The ideologues and advocates of US empire in the current context speak and write at length about the need for a "new imperialism" — an imperialism that does not hesitate to resort to "an organized... coercive force" (Cooper 2000b: 13) or "revert to the rougher methods of an earlier era — force, pre-emptive attack, deception, whatever [might be] necessary" (Cooper 2000b: 7).

In its simplest form, the question is whether the US empire is ascendant or in decline. But while this appears to be the "central issue," it actually obscures more fundamental questions that must be addressed, questions that involve relations between domestic politics and the economy to the empire, the dynamics of the forces of resistance and opposition to empire, and the political capacity of the imperial state to sustain its outward expansion and deal with domestic decay. To argue as some academics do that the empire is declining because it has "overreached itself," that it is "overextended" (Kennedy, Hobsbawm, Wallerstein), overlooks the capacity of the imperial ruling class to reallocate resources from the domestic economy in defence of the empire, the efficacy of state and private institutions (the media, etc.) that gird the empire-building project and, most importantly, the ability of state officials to recruit clients in the service of empire.

The continuing dynamic of imperial expansion, including the military conquest of the Balkans, Afghanistan and Iraq, takes place with the active support and approval of the vast majority of US citizens, who are suffering the worst social and economic cuts in governmental programs and the most regressive tax legislation in recent history. Clearly those impressionable commentators who saw in the occasional mass demonstrations against globalization and the Iraq war in Seattle, Washington, Cancun and other cities as a challenge and weakening of the empire were wrong.

Once the war began, the large demonstrations ended and today there is no mass movement in opposition to continuing bloody colonial occupation or in support of the growing anti-colonial resistance. Equally serious, the critics of imperial power are unable to account for the *worldwide* nature of the imperial doctrine — of fighting imperial wars "everywhere and for the foreseeable future" as George W. Bush enunciated clearly in his 2002 national security doctrine. Latching onto the most visible and obvious objective — oil, in the case of Iraq — the activist critics fail to consider the multiple sites of continuing imperialist military intervention in Latin America, Africa and Asia (Colombia, Djibouti, the Philippines, etc.). Oil is an important issue in the empire-building project, but so is state power in its various forms (particularly economic and military) and the domination of clients, rivals and independent states.

To fully understand the worldwide political and military aggression of the US empire-builders, we must focus on the scope and extent of the empire. To appreciate whether the US empire is on the decline or expanding, first of all we must distinguish between the domestic economy (what we term "the republic") and the international economy (what we term "empire").

The Economic Structure of the American Empire

Most economic analysts agree that the driving force of the world economy, the institutions that are central to the international flow of investments, financial transactions and world trade, are the MNCs, which, according to UNCTAD (2004), number some 65,000, with an estimated 860,000 affiliates. Equally important, no state can aspire to global dominance if its principal economic agent, the multinational corporation, does not in the aggregate exercise a paramount role in the world economy. Any serious discussion of the present and future of US imperial supremacy must include an analysis of the distribution of US power among the competing MNCs, particularly the top 500 — UNCTAD's "multi-billion dollar club."[1]

US-based MNCs dominate the listings of the top five hundred corporations in the world (see discussion in Chapter 2). To reiterate, almost half of the biggest MNCs are US-owned and operated, almost double the share of its next regional competitor — Europe. Japanese-owned MNCs comprise only 9 percent of the total and the rest of Asia (South Korea, Hong Kong, India, Taiwan, Singapore, etc.) account for fewer than 4 percent of the five hundred biggest firms and banks. The concentration of US economic power is even greater if we look at the fifty largest MNCs, over 60 percent of which are US-owned; and the power of the US economic giants is even more evident when we examine the top twenty MNCs, over 70 percent of which are US-owned. Among the top ten MNCs the United States controls 80 percent.

Many analysts — with a rather impressionistic and superficial view and citing the decline in stock market values of US MNCs as an indicator of a general decline in the US global position — fail to recognize that the stock value of the MNCs of Europe, Japan and the rest of the world also fell to an equal or greater degree. Their analysis also fails to take into account the financialization of world capital and the dominance of this capital by the US. The frenzied "merger and acquisition" activity of the MNCs in recent years,[2] can be explained in terms of the dominance of US-based finance capital and its inextricable links to "globalizing" forms of corporate capital.

We can examine several other measures of the continued economic power of the US empire. If we compare net capitalization, we find that the value of US MNCs (among the "top 500") exceeds the combined value of MNCs of all other regions. The valuation of US MNCs is from $5.141 billion to $7.445 billion. Thus US MNCs have a market value more than *double* that of its closest competitor — Europe.

The argument for a consolidated and growing US world economic "hegemony" is further strengthened if we examine the eight leading economic sectors of the world economy, namely banking, pharmaceuticals, telecommunications, information technology hardware, oil and gas, software and computer services, insurance and retail sales. American MNCs are a majority of the top-ranked in five of these sectors, are half in oil and gas and are a minority in insurance. The same pattern is true if we examine the so-called "old economy." US-owned MNCs in the old economy, including mining, oil, automobiles, chemicals and consumer goods, number forty-five of the top hundred. Among the top forty-five MNCs connected with manufacturing, US MNCs number twenty-one, Europe seventeen, Japan five and the rest of the world two. The US has the top-ranked company in twenty-three out of thirty-four industry groups. US MNCs control nearly 59 percent of the leading manufacturing and mining firms, almost equal to the combined European and Japanese MNCs. The major area of US weakness is in the electronics sector, where the US has only two of the top twenty-three firms.

Insofar as MNCs are the driving force for economic empire-building — the primary agent of "economic imperialism" — it is clear that the US is still dominant, showing few to no signs of "weakening" or being "in decline" compared to Japan or Europe.[3] The thesis of an overextended empire or declining economy has no apparent basis in fact. The speculative bubble of recent years only affected the IT (information technology) sector, but this was also true for the US's competitors. Moreover, while the IT sector declined, sectors of the "old economy" revived or expanded; and within the IT sector there has been a concentration and centralization of capital, with Microsoft, IBM and a few other US giants advancing in rank while many others declined.

While fraud and corruption have affected investor confidence in US MNCs, this has also been the case in Europe and Japan. The result has been a *general* decline in the market valuation of all MNCs in the three competing imperial centres (the US, the EU and Japan). The worldwide decline in stock valuation is evident if we compare the total from one year to the next: in 2002 the net value was $16,250 billion compared to $12,580 billion in 2003 — a decline of 22.6 percent. However, approximately half of this decline took place in the IT hardware sector.

The indisputable fact is that the US economic empire is dominant and in an ascendant phase, its depth and scope surpassing its European and Japanese rivals by a multiple of two in most instances. The advocates of a "declining empire" thesis either fail to grasp the economic structural elements of the US empire or resort to long-term forecasts based on historical comparisons to conclude that sometime in the future the US empire will, like all empires, decline (Hobsbawm 1987). Long-term historical forecasting of an inevitable decline has the virtue of consoling both the billions of people facing exploitation and destructive wars and the rulers of nations threatened with military invasion and the takeover of their natural resources. However, it is irrelevant for diagnosing the structure and dynamics of economic power today, or grasping the forces ranged against it. The thesis of decline is based on abstract theorizing, at worst on wishful thinking and at best on invalid extrapolations from the *domestic* economy to the empire.

What needs to be emphasized is that the "contradictions" that threaten the US empire are not simple economic deductions from an assumed "overextended empire" that presumably will energize "the people" to topple or force the imperial policymakers to rethink their imperialist project. The US empire is built and supported by both major political parties and all branches of government, and has followed an upward trajectory via imperial wars, colonial conquests and corporate expansion, particularly since its defeat in Indochina. Imperial defeats and moments of decline are a direct result of political, social and military struggles, most of which have taken place in Latin America and Asia, and to a lesser extent in Europe and North America.

Militarism and Economic Empire

There is little doubt that the US global economic empire has had a long and significant connection to the US military. They are two parts of the same project. The US has military bases in 120 countries around the world, which form the core of its military empire. US militarism, involving wars, proxy interventions via mercenaries, contracted combatants, special forces and covert intelligence operations over a prolonged period of time, has created, in many regions of the world, favourable conditions for the expansion of the US economic empire. Regimes that impose restrictions on US-based direct investments, refuse to pay debts owed to US banks, nationalize US overseas holdings or support nationalist movements have been threatened into submission, subverted or invaded, resulting in the imposition of client regimes favourable to US empire-building. There is no precise sequence for economic expansion and military action, although there is a vast network of ties. In some cases, economic interests dictate military bases or Central Intelligence Agency (CIA) intervention (as in Chile in 1973); in other instances military action, including wars, have been used to force countries to submit to the project of economic empire-building (Iraq in 2003).

Nor is there a perfect symmetry between imperial military spending and engagement and economic empire-building. At times military engagement lags behind corporate multinational expansion, as occurred during the mid-1950s to the early 1960s and later between the end of the Indochina wars and the early 1980s. At other times the reverse has taken place, with military involvement dominating the political economic agenda.

Instances include the Korean War (1950–53), the Indochina ("Vietnam") War (1964–75), the Reagan era (1981–89) and, it would seem, Iraq. The construction of empire does not follow a line of perfect symmetry between economic and military components. Nor does a periodic, disproportionate emphasis on one or the other lead to the demise of the empire. A review of the past half-century of US empire testifies to this.

The notion of an "overextended" empire is based on the speculative and ahistorical assumption that empire-building follows some ideal or stylized pattern where military costs and economic benefits go hand in hand. This is false for several reasons: most of the benefits of empire go to the overseas and domestic corporate elite, whereas the costs are borne by US taxpayers and the low-income families that provide the combat and occupation soldiers. In addition, what appears to be a military-economic disproportion in one period appears "balanced" in the following. For example, US Cold War military expenditures and interventions contributed to the downfall of Communist regimes, which led to windfall profits and the lucrative exploitation of mineral resources in ex-Communist countries as well as to a reduction in social welfare programs in the West. To argue that "excessive" militarism and military expenditures (the "new imperialism") are harmful to economic empire-building, it would be necessary to show that US corporate control over the world economy has declined; that the access of the US to strategic resources has diminished and that the US citizenry refuses to suffer the social cuts, regressive tax burdens and budgetary allocations that sustain the empire-building project. However, to date there is no evidence for any such developments.

The thesis of the "overextension" of the US military empire overlooks the capacity of US empire-builders to recruit subordinate allies and client states to accept police, administrative and financial duties in the service of the empire. In the Balkans, the Europeans have over 40,000 troops serving under US-dominated NATO command. In Afghanistan, Canadian and European military forces, UN administrative personnel and a number of Third World client states supply the personnel to safeguard the Karzai puppet regime. In Iraq, subordinate allies like Britain and vassal states like South Korea, Poland and other Eastern European clients supply military and civilian auxiliaries to enforce US colonial rule. Washington's client building in Eastern Europe, dating back to at least the 1980s with Solidarity in Poland, has provided a large reservoir of political and diplomatic support and mercenary armies in the current drive for empire. Huge airbases and troop deployment platforms are currently being constructed in Romania and Bulgaria to match those in Kosova and Macedonia.

US empire-builders have shoved the Russians out of Central and Southern Asia, building airbases in Kazakhstan, Uzbekistan, Georgia and Afghanistan. The recruitment of client regimes from the Baltic to the Middle East, Central Asia and Southern Asia demonstrates the rapid growth of the US military empire and furthers new opportunities for US MNCs to expand the economic empire. This extended empire has led to the formation of regional, imperially dominated alliances that provide new military recruits to bolster and consolidate the expansion. Rather than viewing US empire-building as a process of "overextension," we should see it as a process of *widening the pool* for new recruits to strengthen the US military command. US power has learned to discard multilateral power-sharing with its European imperial allies and competitors in favour of subcontracting military occupation and police functions to new clients from Eastern Europe and Central and Southern Asia.

Throughout the growth and expansion of the US empire, the European Union has followed in the wake of its conquests, financing and providing military and civil administrators. The brief interlude of German, French and Belgian dissent prior to the US invasion of Iraq was followed by almost total subservience to the US's bellicose and intrusive demands and attacks on Iran, North Korea and Cuba; commitments to follow the US lead in promoting a rapid deployment force; backing for the US occupation of Iraq (Security Council Resolution no. 1483); and a general recognition that, in the words of compliant EU foreign secretary Javier Solano, "We don't want to compete with the United States — it would be absolutely ridiculous — but see the problem jointly." The EU generally accepts its role (as defined by Rumsfeld and Wolfowitz) as a subordinated ally in the US drive for worldwide domination, seeking to secure a place at the economic trough and to be delegated power and minority shares in contracts and privatized companies.

Imperialists who argue that heightened European independence and competition would weaken the US empire should read Romano Prodi, President of the European Commission, who in a press statement in Washington on June 2003 said, "When Europe and the US are together, no problem or enemy can face us; if we are not together any problem can be a crisis." Prodi and Solano represent the new thinking in Europe: better to collaborate with a winning imperialism and secure minority benefits rather than be chastised, bullied and left out in the cold, excluded from the new colonies. Given the promise of being helped to foot the initial costs of occupation and colonial state-building without a challenge to US supremacy, the empire-builders tend to welcome and encourage this new thinking.

There are no signs that global militarism is eroding US economic empire-building, and this includes the current phase of US wars of imperial conquest. US MNCs continue to dominate banking, manufacturing, IT, pharmaceuticals, oil and gas and other strategic industries. The Iraqi invasion has strengthened US control over the second-greatest reserves of oil and gas in the world. In addition, there is no imminent popular revolt or rejection of empire-building within the US "homeland." In the midst of colonial conquest, over three-quarters of US citizens — the highest proportion in the world — report they are "very proud of their country"; more than eight out of ten supported the invasion of Iraq and continue to support the US occupation even when President Bush's justification for the war — to destroy weapons of mass destruction (WMD) — was demonstrated to be a pure fabrication.

Despite the most regressive tax reduction in recent history, large-scale slashing of social spending and huge budget deficits, growing evidence that US occupation forces have nothing to do with "liberating" the Iraqis, and even the regular body count of young American soldiers, the citizens of the US show little to no signs of mass protest. The anti-war movement of January–February 2003 almost completely disappeared with the successful military conquest and occupation of Iraq. In short, the extension of military activity from the Balkans through the Middle East to South Asia has not adversely affected the international economic position of America's MNCs, nor has it undermined domestic political support for the empire-building project and its architects.

Decline of the Republic

Notwithstanding the continued growth and consolidation of the American empire, there is another side — an underside, if you will. While the empire prospers and US military bases proliferate, the "republic" — the economy within the boundaries of the territorial United States — declines, its class society more and more polarized, its politics more repressive and divisive.

There are two distinct but interrelated "economies" and state activities in the United States: (1) the empire that encapsulates the world of the MNCs, the global military apparatus and the international financial institutions linked to the imperial state, and (2) the republic — the economy, state institutions and social classes that provide the soldiers, executives, tax dollars and markets that sustain the empire. The growth of the empire has visibly impoverished the domestic economy in a variety of ways while enriching CEOs (and their extended entourages) who benefit from and direct the overseas activities of the MNCs. In 2002, US empire-builders added over $100 billion to military spending to finance the Iraq and Afghanistan wars, in the process cutting health, education and welfare programs. And on the 2003 anniversary of 9/11 the administration requested another $86 billion for reconstruction efforts (in addition to a $800 million package for the preparation of a final report on the whereabouts of Iraq's "weapons of mass destruction"). The social costs of empire are staggering. Today, according to the Institute for Policy Studies, there are more than 40 million Americans without any health coverage at all; another 50 million have only partial and clearly inadequate coverage; and millions more have to spend up to one-third of their net income for adequate medical coverage. As for the government's social welfare system, the pension and social security funds needed to ensure and protect the welfare of American citizens have been depleted to cover current expenses and to keep the budget deficit from ballooning out of control. At the same time, through the machinations of corporations like Enron, a large number of employee pensions, funded up to $40 billion, were wiped out virtually overnight. Corpfocus, a citizens' corporate watchdog, has shown that Enron is not an isolated case but only the most visible manifestation of an entire system of corporate greed and malfeasance, costing "society" (through appropriations for personal enrichment) millions if not billions of dollars a year.

The financing of imperialism led to an estimated $400 billion budget deficit in 2003, which was likely to increase as the military occupation of Iraq was to cost at least another $86 billion, according to the administration's appeal to Congress, to assure the victory of the forces of "freedom." Domestic industrial production, particularly in the automobile sector, has experienced sharp declines in profit margins. Ford has taken several billion dollar losses, while the majority of US manufacturers have invested abroad or subcontracted to local producers in Latin America and Asia. The result is that the subsidiaries of American MNCs have captured an important share of China's exports to the US market but have also increased the US external deficit — a deficit that has passed beyond $500 billion. The super-profits earned by the MNCs relocated throughout the new colonial and semi-colonial economies of Asia and Latin America strengthen imperial institutions while weakening the domestic economy, the government's budget financing and external accounts.

But the "unbearable costs of global domination" (financier Felix Rohatyn) are in fact quite "bearable" — at least to America's ultra-rich and the eroding but still extensive middle class. There is no mass revolt despite widening inequalities in the distribution of income, declining living standards, depleted or non-existent social services, extended working days, higher individual payments to health and pension funds, and massive corruption and fraud that rob millions of US investors and pensioners of their savings and pension funds. Unemployment is growing. Including those who no longer bother to register, the unemployment rate in mid-2003 exceeded 10 percent. Of course, in certain populations and sectors of society — in residential areas and communities populated disproportionately by Blacks, for example — the unemployment rate is much higher — as high as 80 percent in some areas. And the statistics on this phenomenon do not include the larger problem of underemployment, whereby up to 40 percent of the labour force works in what in the popular vernacular are referred to as "shitty jobs" with poverty-level wages, poor working conditions, and/or in irregular forms of nonstandard (part-time, temporary, etc.) employment. The combined statistics on this dimension of the US empire — its underside, behind the domestic ramparts of empire — point toward a stagnant economy and a decaying society in serious pain where not falling apart.

In this context of domestic decay the empire-builders spend massive sums to conquer the world based on fabricated claims. They terrorize the domestic population with paranoiac visions of imminent attacks, in pursuit of endless foreign wars, world conquest and horrific carnage of defenceless people. They sponsor or protect domestic anthrax terrorists who terrorized American citizens and served to justify US state terror. By and large the great majority of Americans have just "sat back and watched" (Harold Pinter) or taken pride and vicarious pleasure in being identified with the victorious rampaging armies. While major US cities are bankrupt or heavily indebted, the federal government spends billions subsidizing agro-export elites to the tune of $180 billion dollars over ten years, handing giant MNC building contractors (e.g., Halliburton) with close ties to the empire-builders lucrative billion-dollar contracts, and spending billions to subsidize mercenary armies in Afghanistan, Iraq and Colombia. In the midst of domestic stagnation the empire-builders give massive tax cuts to the corporate elite — those most likely to invest in the MNCs and their overseas "operations."

To attract overseas investment, as a means of financing a huge deficit on the country's trade account, the imperial state allows US multinational banks to launder tens of billions of dollars in illicit funds from multimillionaire tax evaders, corrupt bankers and elite political officials from Latin America, China, Africa and elsewhere (the US Congress, for example). The funds to sustain the empire are in part based on a massive corruption of overseas clients who "invest" in the US economy while pillaging their own countries or opening up their economies to imperial pillage. Nevertheless, as the dollar weakens and profitable opportunities shrink, the declining economy of the republic no longer attracts the hitherto high levels of foreign investment. FDI inflows, for example, declined from $300 billion in 2000 (over 20 percent of total world FDI inflows) to just $124 billion in 2002 and $50 billion in 2003 (UNCTAD 2002). The problem is that the republic needs $2.7 billion a day in capital inflows to finance the external deficit on the trade account, which climbed to an historic high of $354 billion in 2002 (US Census Bureau 2003).

The result of a strengthened empire and a weakening republic is greater social sacrifices at home, more protectionism, greater transfers of profits and interest payments from Latin America and other neo-colonial regions, more moralizing crusades, more forceful mass media blitzes, even more blatant official lies and new wars to charge up the chauvinist juices. In this context, the corporate swindle of millions of US investors and pensioners personally enriched CEOs, financed the expansion of MNCs abroad and impoverished many. Corruption is not an aberration of a few deviant CEOs; it is a structural feature of US empire-building, both abroad and at home.

Imperial War and the Republic

Despite occasional criticism by European leaders and inconsequential dissent from within the republic's legislature, the Bush regime has vastly expanded the empire-building project using the political and military networks of his predecessors. Under Clinton the military empire was extended from the Baltic to the Balkans and beyond, including a partial occupation of Iraq. The Bush militarists, however, have managed to expand the US military empire via the conquest of Iraq, the Caucasus, Central Asia, Afghanistan and Southeast Asia, and the construction of a vast archipelago of airbases, military supply zones and fortresses from which to attack and conquer the entire southern tier of Asia, up to and including North Korea. In the Middle East, Bush has announced a "free trade zone" — from North Africa to Saudi Arabia (including Israel) — controlled by the US.

As Wolf (*Financial Times*, February 5, 2002) points out, the current adventures of the Bush administration in this strategically crucial region relate to two concerns behind all forms of empire: control over coveted resources (oil in this case) and a "security vacuum" — that is, opposition to the empire. Never has the US military empire grown so widely, so quickly and with such ease, making talk and writing about the "decline of the empire" idle chatter or a self-indulgent exercise in "faith healing."

As with the regime's irrational foreign policy on Cuba, certain economic sectors in the US have undoubtedly suffered from the empire's hysterical "anti-terrorist" propaganda designed to secure public support for imperial wars and conquests. Adversely affected sectors include the civil aeronautic industries, tourism and related service activities. However, large state subsidies and interest-free loans have cushioned some of the corporate sector from adverse effects.

Empire-building in our time is driven by systemic and political forces, and reinforced by ideological extremism. Simplistic attempts to explain the wars by reference to the influence of the military-industrial complex fail to take account of the relative decline in the weight of the major aerospace and defence sector among the top 500 firms in recent years. Imperial conquests today are based on the drives to dominate the world — a project the United Nations was set up to prevent — and to open *future* opportunities for MNCs. The military empire is designed to secure future access to wealth, not to generate it in the process of conquest. War and the network of military satellites are an adjunct to a system set up to facilitate the making of monopoly profits with the compliance of client rulers disposed to offer exploitation rights to MNCs.

"Empire-building is no tea party," a retired colonel from the US

Marines once told us, referring to the systematic human rights violations which accompany imperial wars and conquests. Nothing captures the deliberate and planned violence embedded in US empire-building than the US *opposition* to the international criminal court, and the vicious arm-twisting of the US that has forced more than fifty countries to sign bilateral pacts giving impunity to US military personnel. But it is not the inhumanity of imperial wars, nor the gross violations of international law, nor the fabrication of provocations to justify colonial conquest that bring fissures in the ruling power bloc of state officials and corporate elites. It is the debate between the governing military empire-builders and the economic empire-builders on the best way to build the empire and consolidate the structure of rule and domination *without undermining the republic's capacity to finance the imperial state.*

Intra-imperial Conflict

The inter-elite struggle over how best to build the empire takes place at several levels. The first and most general issue has to do with the relationship between the militarists and the corporate empire-builders. While they share a common vision of the US empire, some disagree over the degree of "autonomy" with which the militarists are able to act, at times elaborating military strategies that concentrate on conquest rather than economic costs and benefits. Successful military conquests have increased the power and enhanced the independence of the militarists in shaping strategic global strategy over and against some of the concerns of the economic empire-builders in the private sector.

The second issue has to with the distortions in US empire-building policy generated by key empire strategists with ties to Zionism. Zionists such as Paul Wolfowitz and Richard Perle and a host of other architects of the strategy of global conquest, in support of Israeli state policy, are almost fanatically concerned to direct US policy toward destroying Israel's Arab adversaries throughout the Middle East, even when a "negotiated" approach to the expansion of the US empire — and peace — are feasible. This is clearly the case with Iran and Syria, despite the emergence of liberal pro-US political movements and personalities who are pursuing non-violent methods.

Equally damaging, in the eyes of conventional military and intelligence strategists, the Zionist empire-builders have projected a paranoid Israeli point of view of politics — perceiving a world full of enemies, including the Europeans, who cannot be trusted, and people all over the Third World as potential terrorists. Influential Zionists like Richard Perle follow the precepts of an infamous Israeli military-politician (Moshe Dayan): "the Arabs only understand force." While the Israeli-Zionist "philosophy" is deadly enough in the Middle East, its exponents in Washington have global power and the capacity to implement it on a world scale. The Israeli strategy of preventive wars, colonization, occupation, collective punishment and the unilateral use of force in defiance of international law has been adapted by US militarists, who have long-standing ties to Israel and have made Israeli practices the doctrinal guide for their empire-building project.

The result of this "Zionist bias" in US strategic empire-building has generated several points of conflict within the imperial elite: for example, among economic empire-builders who look toward alliances with Arab oil rulers to expand their domain and among professional elites in the US military and intelligence agencies who have been castigated and marginalized by the Zionists for not providing the "right" intelligence to justify the wars that destroy Israel's enemies. Such thinking led Under-Secretary of Defense Paul Wolfowitz to form a parallel intelligence structure compatible with the Zionist policy of "destroying Israel's enemies." This bogus intelligence group, calling itself a "cabal," is less an intelligence agency for collecting reliable information than a propaganda agency to fabricate "reports," justifying predetermined war policies based on the pro-Israeli worldview.

A third example of intra-regime conflict is that between Secretary of Defense Donald Rumsfeld and military-intelligence professionals. Rumsfeld, as the key figure involved in the military empire-building process, has been vigorously involved in concentrating power in his hands and that of his personal coterie led by Wolfowitz, Perle, Bolton and other extreme militarists. Rumsfeld has overruled Pentagon professionals on the reorganization of the armed forces, weapon procurement, war strategy and intelligence operations. He has promoted loyalist military officers over those with greater seniority and military experience, and humiliated those who express the slightest dissent. His tyrannical behaviour toward high military officials is his method of stifling elite discussions. His most loyal subordinates and influential advisers are those who adhere to his extremist military empire-building strategy: sequential wars that overlap and combine with worldwide, terrorizing covert assassination programs.

No doubt, Rumsfeld has been the controlling figure in the formulation and execution of the strategy of world military conquest — an imperial strategy that closely resembles, if not parallels, that of Nazi Germany. Rumsfeld's concentration of power within the imperial elite and hostility toward professionals was dramatically expressed in his nomination of retired General Peter Jan Schoomaker, former commander of Special Forces Delta, described to one of the authors (Petras) by senior military officers at the Delta headquarters at Fort Bragg as a collection of "psychopaths trained to murder." Clearly the ex-Delta general was selected precisely because his ideological and behavioural profile harmonizes with Rumsfeld's own.

The first major conflicts between Rumsfeld and the military-intelligence hierarchies surfaced in the aftermath of the Iraq War over the issue of the non-existence of weapons of mass destruction in Iraq. As WMD were the Bush administration's major justification for the war, this issue provoked debate in the mass media and among some congresspeople. The conflict surfaced when "professionals" in the military and the intelligence agencies leaked reports and made statements that questioned Rumsfeld's allegations in the run up to the war. Clearly the "professionals" were hoping to point to Rumsfeld and Wolfowitz's personal "intelligence" coterie as responsible for cooking the data to justify their war plans. In short, the intensity of the inter- and intra-elite struggle for bureaucratic power had reached a point at which pro-empire professionals were willing to question a successful imperialist war to rid themselves of a bureaucratic tyrant who was jeopardizing their empire-building project to advance his own personal power. However, with the aid of Congress and the mass media, the militarists were able to bury the issue and even succeeded in securing public compliance with the war.

A fourth conflict within the governing imperial elite is that over relations between military and economic empire-builders. The latter clearly see military action as a *means* to an end — a dominant and hegemonic American empire. For military imperialists, military world conquest has become the strategic goal, which, they assume, will redound eventually to the benefit of the economic empire-builders. This has led some critics and ideologues among the economic empire-builders to question the militarists' knowledge of the short- and long-term economic costs of an indiscriminate policy of military intervention and permanent war. This may become an important debate over the *methods* of empire-building but not about the empire itself, which is supported by both sides. Adding fuel in this debate is the dispute over the "economic cronyism" that afflicts the militarists, who have handed over lucrative post-war contracts to favoured MNCs linked to the Rumsfeld-Cheney-Bush clique while ignoring the claims of other corporate elites.

These disputes between capitalists and military empire-builders, however, are clearly secondary to the powerful interests and policies that unite them. Despite the occasional and passing concerns expressed by some capitalists about imperialist war policies, the capitalist class, particularly the MNCs, are powerful backers of the Bush administration's empire-building.

There are at least eight reasons why the MNCs back the Bush administration, despite certain misgivings among individual capitalists concerning the neo-Nazi doctrine of permanent warfare. While a few editorial writers in the financial press and individual capitalists have criticized the Bush administration's budget deficits, weak dollar and growing external accounts deficits, the majority of the capitalist class continue to provide solid support for Bush's empire-building regime for concrete reasons.

First, the regime has rejected all international treaties, including the Kyoto agreement that imposes environmental controls on industry, thus lowering the costs of production for American firms. Second, the Bush administration provides billions in export subsidies, particularly to big agribusiness export firms, thus increasing their market share, "competitiveness" and profits. Third, the Bush administration provides protective measures for over two hundred products, involving tens of thousands of non-competitive producers who sell in the republic's domestic market, thus limiting the entrance of more efficient competitors. Fourth, the Bush regime has decreased taxes for the entire capitalist class, benefiting CEOs of the MNCs and the capitalists operating in the republic, thus increasing gains from dividends, capital gains and salaries. Fifth, the administration has largely tolerated (or participated in) the cover-up of corruption, fraud and auditing felonies in most of the major MNCs and banks. Sixth, the regime continues to tolerate loose banking regulations, in effect promoting the laundering of billions of dollars by American multinational banks. And seventh, the Bush administration has refused to increase the minimum wage and has pursued an anti-labour agenda, lowering labour costs for big and small business groups engaged in sweatshops and the service sector.

These and similar policies provide the economic bases for strong structural linkages between the Bush administration and the capitalist class as a whole. This explains the close collaboration between military empire-builders and the business class of the republic. The "trade-off" involves state economic payoffs to the domestic business elite in exchange for the capitalist class's political and financial support of military empire.

What allows US military empire-builders to proceed in their quest for world conquest, despite inconsequential criticism from European allies, is the knowledge that they have the solid backing of Wall Street and "Main Street" (capitalists producing for the domestic market of the republic). Moreover, the overseas power and corporate links of US MNCs and banks with their European counterparts has weakened European resolve to challenge US supremacy and strengthened the hands of the right-wing regimes in Italy and Spain.

Circuses, but No Bread

Empire-building does not provide any payoffs for workers, employees, small farmers and most businesspeople within the republic. Their support of the empire is based on the consumption of state propaganda via the mass media. They experience the symbolic gratification of being citizens of "the most powerful country in the world" and take a servile attitude toward established state authority. The lack of a credible left-wing political party or movement further undermines or prevents the formation of popular opposition. Even worse, what pass for left or progressive journals and intellectuals were in large part supportive of the US wars against Yugoslavia, Afghanistan and, to a lesser degree, Iraq.

Even more telling, the great majority of the American intellectual left joined the Bush administration in attacking Cuba over the execution of Cuban terrorists and the jailing of US-financed propagandists and subversives. "Progressive" movements and journals in the US, with few notable exceptions, have not demonstrated solidarity with current or past anti-colonial resistance movements, national liberation struggles or revolutionary regimes, neither the National Liberation Front in Vietnam, the Iraqi resistance nor the Cuban Revolution. Most of the US opposition tends to be legalist (citing constitutional law) or moralistic (citing universal precepts) and divorced from any form of struggle for social change — divorced from revolutionary practice certainly, but even from reformism.

The state, mass media and corporate world all encourage a mindless, passive engagement in mass spectator sports and entertainment that creates an apolitical ethos (providing athletic and celebrity heroes and heroines) that reinforces the imperial worldview of "good" and "evil," where the "good guys" defeat the doers of "evil" in the end through violence and destruction. What is most surprising, perhaps, is how few sociologists address this issue or even conceptualize it as a problem, even though it is one that goes to the very foundation of US "society" and "culture."

As the empire grows, corporate-funded pensions disappear, medical and pharmaceutical costs skyrocket, and unemployment and poverty grow beyond the numbers recorded by the flawed official statistics. As of July 2003 the official unemployment rate was 6.5 percent but the unofficial rate was close to double that. Empire-building does not create a "labour aristocracy" concerned to share the crumbs of empire — at least if we consider the several thousand trade union officials who draw hundreds of thousands of dollars in annual salaries, pensions and payoffs while the dues-paying union members in the private sector, only 9 percent of the labour force, are both demobilized and demoralized. Social inequalities within the republic are widening and deepening: the ratio of CEO income to that of workers has gone up from 80:1 twenty-five years ago to 450:1 today and is growing. From 1990 to 2000, executive pay at the top US corporations increased by 571 percent, and more recent announcements point towards a continuation of this trend. Wages are compressed — the share of labour in national income has significantly declined, by 12 percent over the same decade alone — while the salaries, stock options and other benefits of the top CEOs has grown apace, and the share of "capital" in national income (money available for investment) has steadily increased.

One of the mechanisms used by the government to reduce the share of workers and households in national income and to increase the share of capital (in the belief that workers will only spend their wages, while the rich have a higher propensity to invest their savings and thus promote "economic growth") is increasingly regressive taxes and tax cuts. According to Citizens for Tax Justice, corporate taxes were to plummet to only 1.3 percent of GDP in 2003. Over half of the tax cuts enacted in 2002 favoured the richest one percent of US taxpayers, continuing a trend initiated under the Reagan presidency.

On the other side of the ledger, workers in general are subject to increasing pressures on their wages, reduction of social benefits, deterioration of their conditions of work and the possibility of losing their jobs and not finding new ones. Relative to their counterparts in Europe, US workers have on average considerably less vacation time, fewer and reduced benefits, a longer work tenure with longer working hours per week and, since both of the two dominant political parties are controlled by empire-builders, no political representation. As a result, American workers are further left out in the cold with each assault on their conditions of life and work, and on their capacity to negotiate these conditions. The working class has lost battle after battle in the long struggle waged by capitalists against it.

The period from 1968 to 1973 was the highpoint for workers in this struggle, both in Europe and the US, but, from the perspective of the working class, the following thirty years brought a steady decline in organizational capacity, share of national income, quality of life and political clout. While US corporate capital launched a series of relatively successful global campaigns in a battle for its share of the "emerging markets" in Asia and Latin America, and advanced its project for economic empire within the institutionality of the new world order, the American working class was squeezed, cast aside or trampled underfoot.

Never has capital had it so good than since the 1980s. Conditions have been even better than during the "golden ages of capitalism" in the 1950s and 1970s. And labour has never had it so bad, at least since the 1930s. Average wages today in the US are at or below the wage rates of 1973 and, according to the Economic Policy Institute (EPI), a fourth of the working population today in the US is earning poverty-level wages. In a situation of skyrocketing executive compensation and wealth accumulation, the American working class has borne the brunt of the adjustment of the US economy to the requirements of the economic and military empire. The social costs of this empire, borne disproportionately by the working class in its many forms and multiracial divisions, are absolutely staggering, and no more so than under the George W. Bush regime.

What is surprising, or at least not well explained by anyone, is that the *objectively* defined and well-documented losses of the working classes have not led to significant opposition to empire-building except, it seems, among Blacks, who opposed the Iraq War by a substantial margin. Of course, in many areas up to 40 percent of Blacks, particularly the youth and those of "productive age," are either unemployed or caught up in the machinery of the justice system, or both. The erosion of the welfare state, heightened levels of exploitation and oppression of workers (and recent immigrants) of colour, together with the upward transfer and concentration of wealth, serve to finance the regime's empire-building project. This is clear enough. Equally clear are the negative social and political side effects of this process. Large-scale corporate corruption, a stagnant speculative economy and rising unemployment have accompanied a dramatic rightward shift in imperial politics.

There has also been an increase in corporate crime, national chauvinism and the spread of social Darwinism, which pits the self-seeking individual against others in a struggle for survival and advantage. In this context, unemployed and undereducated minorities choose in large numbers to join the imperial army, while many poor white workers express their socially constructed hostility towards Muslims, Arabs and other Middle Eastern peoples. The affluent leaders of the major Jewish organizations give unconditional support to the butcher Ariel Sharon and their own ideological counterparts in the Bush regime as they plan new imperial wars, the next one perhaps aimed at Iran. Meanwhile, "progressives" once again begin their perennially futile effort to transform the Democratic Party from an imperial to a truly democratic party of the republic.

A major challenge to the empire does not exist in the US, at least in the foreseeable future. Neither dissident capitalists (viz. the growing gap between the empire and the republic) nor the working class in its many divisions can form the social base of an effective opposition. The main threat to the empire comes from the outside, from the ongoing mass and class struggles in Latin America, the Middle East and Asia.

6. DYNAMICS OF EMPIRE-BUILDING AND IMPERIAL RULE

IT IS FUTILE AT BEST AND MISLEADING AT WORST TO SPECULATE AND take consolation from the fact that in some distant future time "all empires decline." Before that unspecified time takes place, millions of lives are at stake, national sovereignties are at risk and popular struggles are taking place. To place "final judgments" at the centre of analysis is to distance oneself from the actors for change and from the real power of empire today, and its logic and direction. Tendentious truisms such as "empires decline" provide us with no analytical framework for understanding the driving forces of imperialism and the rising forces of opposition. Abstract and non-specific historical analysis and superficial discussion of the empire-builders ("their decisions are frivolous") are themselves frivolous and superficial. A "long view of history" divorced from concrete analysis of the dominant power of the US empire today and its drive for worldwide conquest, and of class-based anti-imperialist struggles, is a mirror of the style of the ideologues of the empire. There is no end of imperial pundits who write of "the American Century," "Pax Americana," "Global Power" and other vacuous "long views" of history.

To understand the current contradictions of empire, we have to analyze concrete classes, ethnic classes, the specific natures of regimes with their class configurations, and the organizational capacities of the popular movements to mount challenges to imperial clients and the empire. To pontificate using abstract historical analogies and the truism that empires eventually decline has neither intellectual nor practical political relevance.

Class and State in the American Empire

US empire-building and decay are built on class and state relationships. Collaborator classes are formed through a complex process of internal class and political formation and external integration into subordinate but beneficial elite relations. Hegemony and domination by transnational Latin American ruling classes, for example, are essential to shaping and supporting imperial client states that implement the empire-centred "neo-liberal policies." The role of the imperial state is central to the formation of client states, providing financial and political backing as well as the threats and personal rewards that induce the privatization of lucrative public enterprises and the one-sided elimination of foreign trade and investment barriers.

What appears to overseas academic critics as "irrational" imperial aggression is in fact a highly rational calculus based on the historical ease with which imperial policymakers have secured a dominant position in the colonized economy, the compliance of client states and the eager support of financially speculative transnational elites. Easy success in imposing empire-centred "models," in overthrowing and/or invading recalcitrant or nationalist Latin American regimes (in Chile, Brazil, Panama, the Dominican Republic, etc.) has encouraged US empire-builders to act with greater violence, brazenly wielding force as the most reasonable weapon, given its efficiency in securing imperial goals. We should remember that the US interventionary success in Guatemala (1954) caused the US to repeat such actions in Cuba in 1961 — a policy that led to defeat. The US later successfully orchestrated military coups in Brazil (1964) and Indonesia (1965), and the invasion of the Dominican Republic in 1965 encouraged the US to deepen and extend its military invasion of Indochina, which led to a profound weakening of domestic political support and an historic but temporary defeat of US imperial policymakers.

The reconstruction of the empire-building project under President Carter focused on political-ideological warfare on the favourable terrain of Eastern Europe and the USSR, and the reconstruction of covert military surrogates in Central Asia (Afghanistan) in alliance with fundamentalist Islamists. In southern Africa (Angola and Mozambique) imperial policymakers financed and supplied tribalist surrogates backed by racist South Africa. In South and Central America (Argentina, Chile, Bolivia, El Salvador and Guatemala) the US acted via its client military regimes, and in Nicaragua via client drug-running mercenaries. From the late 1970s on, the empire-builders reconstructed the US military imperial apparatus and gradually regathered domestic political support for overseas conquests through military invasions of Panama and Grenada.

The ideological formulae for imperial conquest are very similar to those used by the Third Reich: opposition leaders are demonized, the invasion and imposition of client regimes are described as liberation and the restoration of democracy, and incorporation into the US sphere of influence is described as becoming part of the "free world." The Carter-Reagan military empire created the foundations for Bush the father's launch into a new US-centred "New World Order" with the Gulf War, a project which was premature and lacked a "colonial occupation" to insure uncontested control.

The Clinton era (1992–2000) witnessed the massive expansion of empire-building on a world scale — wars in the Balkans, the conquest of a third of Iraq via Kurdish clients in the North and "no-fly" zones in the south (combined with punishing bombardments and economic blockades to destroy the state and economy), military alliances with new clients and military bases from the Baltic states to Central Europe to the Balkans and the Southern Caucuses. Aggressive military conquest and colonization began under the banner of humanitarian imperialism under Clinton. Doctrinal radicalization came with Bush, Rumsfeld and Wolfowitz. It is a serious and egregious error to view "9/11" as the point of departure for military empire-building. What has occurred after 9/11 is the systematic, unilateral pursuit of empire-building through a more explicit doctrine of global warfare, as opposed to the piecemeal but equally violent practice of humanitarian imperialism propounded by Clinton.

Inter-imperialist and National and Class Conflicts

Imperial power is embedded in class and state relations: prior to the movement of capital and the imposition of imperial state power, a national and class struggle takes place, a struggle that varies in intensity but recurs throughout the period of imperial occupation and domination. As pointed out earlier, in Latin America the imposition of empire-centred neo-liberal regimes was established through a violent class-state struggle "from above." The victorious transnational classes reconfigured the state in order to "reconstruct" social relations (labour-capital relations, public-private and foreign-national property) to conform to the empire-centred model. The neo-liberal regimes and neo-mercantilist empires were products of class struggles, as are the continuing antagonistic relations that confront the empire-builders' recolonization project.

Antagonistic class relations are a constant of contemporary empire-building. However, the social relations and class, ethnic and gender forces that confront each other today are different from the recent past due to the transformation of the class structure wrought by a quarter of a century of neo-liberal rulership. It is important to summarize the changes in class formation in order to understand the contemporary social classes confronting the empire-builders and local client states. The new class forces have in turn developed new tactics, strategies and leadership that are central to their efforts to overthrow imperial domination.

Changes in Class Structure and Social Relations
Since the onset of neo-liberalism in the 1970s, several key political and socio-economic changes have emerged in class structure. The opening of the economy to cheap foreign manufactured imports has had two major impacts on class structure: it has reduced the size of the industrial working class, established a "captive labour force" in the free trade zones and *maquiladores*/assembly plants, reduced the number of skilled metal work-

ers and created smaller and more exploitative decentralized "contract labour" industries. As a consequence, the size of the employed stable industrial labour force has declined in most Latin American countries (such as Bolivia, Peru, Colombia, Brazil and Argentina), while those who remain employed fear their replacement because of the willingness of employers to deploy the reserve army of unemployed. The relative weight of industrial workers within the working class has declined, as has the percentage of unionized workers, the number of strikes and labour militancy in the industrial sector. On the other hand, the number of unemployed and underemployed workers has increased geometrically, running from 40 percent to 80 percent in countries such as Argentina, Peru, Bolivia, Colombia, Brazil, Venezuela and Mexico. The older *maquiladora* industrial regions — the northern Mexican border regions, the Caribbean — have experienced plant closings as US capitalists relocate to China or to the "rural areas" (southern Mexico) where salaries are lower and working conditions even more exploitative, with longer hours and fewer safety, health and environmental regulations. The growth of a "critical mass" of unemployed workers has led to the growth of autonomous movements of these workers who attack the capitalist class outside of the site of production (the factory), in the streets, blocking the circulation of machinery and raw materials (inputs) and finished products (outputs) transported to market, thus putting constraints on the realization of profit.

The promotion of an "export-growth strategy" along with the import of subsidized low-priced food, particularly grains, has led to the displacement of peasants and the bankruptcy of family farmers producing for local markets. Over 90 percent of state agricultural subsidies are channeled to large agro-exporters, denying small producers state credits and financing. Empire-centred agricultural policies have increased the percentage and number of landless rural workers, polarized the countryside and radicalized small family farmers facing extinction because of the client state's intervention in favour of food imports and agro-export elites. Growing land concentration, encroachment on indigenous people's land, the high cost of farm inputs and low prices paid for food products have radicalized the peasant and Indian-peasant communities, while depriving them of land, markets and profit margins. The growth of literacy and social interaction with progressive church and trade union nuclei and the recent experiences of struggle have turned the countryside into a centre of anti-imperialist movements.

Contemporary rural movements are not composed of "primitive rebels," backward-looking "traditionalists" resisting "modernization." The *campesino* movements are led by educated sons and daughters of downwardly mobile rural families, seeking to secure credits and market shares, recover land occupied by capital and state protection from subsidized cheap imports. Seeking modern means of production, market shares, inexpensive credits and "fair prices," and working and struggling collectively, are the hallmarks of the modern but impoverished rural classes. They are knowledgeable about the negative impacts of empire-centred policies (ALCA, neo-liberalism). In Brazil (the Landless Rural Workers Movement, or MST), in Bolivia (the *cocaleros*), in Colombia (the peasant and rural guerrilla movements), in Ecuador (sectors of the Indian-peasant movement) and to a lesser extent in Paraguay, Peru and Mexico, peasant-based movements have been the best-organized and cutting edges of anti-imperialist resistance.

The contradictions between the empire and the peasantry have become acute, not because of greater exploitation and extraction of surplus value, but because of the threat of *total displacement* (from land, home, family and community), *violent appropriation of the means of production* and denial of a location to "earn a living." The rural labour force is highly stratified and in many cases ethnically diverse, leading to socio-political divisions; however, where these "differences" have been overcome, the combative organized rural classes have been most successful in challenging the empire's expansion — in the countryside as well as the cities. The MST has occupied big landholdings and settled 350,000 families in less than twenty years and had 120,000 families organized to occupy uncultivated estates in July 2003. In Bolivia, over 40,000 families earn a living farming coca in vibrant communities with stable families thanks to the organization and struggles of the *cocalero* farmers' union. The major military challenge in Latin America to client regimes and US military empire-builders is in the Colombian countryside, where the two major guerrilla groups, the Revolutionary Armed Forces of Colombia (FARC) and the National Liberation Army (ELN), control over 40 percent of the countryside. Many of the major national organizations organizing urban demonstrations against the ALCA are located, more often than not, among the militant rural organizations.

Given the visible and dominant role of modern, rural-based agrarian movements in opposing the US empire, it is surprising that *no* systematic discussion occurs in the writing of Hobsbawm, Wallerstein or other prophets of eventual imperial decline. These writers emphasize inter-imperial rivalries and inter-elite conflicts (capitalists against empire), basing their arguments on specific trade disputes and differences concerning the modes of empire-building or general, tendentious and emotionally gratifying notions that "all empires decline," all "capitalist systems eventually go into crises," leaving it to the magic of the marketplace to bring about what they call "systemic changes" from "chaos." A visit to a meeting of peasants in an occupied estate would likely provide sufficient stimulus for these armchair, empire-centred prophets to rethink their theories of imperial decline.

The New Urban Proletariat: Public Sector Workers

From June to July of 2003, in Ecuador, Bolivia, Peru, Brazil, Argentina and Colombia, public employees — mostly public school teachers — were engaged in indefinite strikes involving millions, and in some cases inciting work stoppages by private-sector wage workers. In the cities, public employees have been at the cutting edge of the biggest and most militant urban struggles against client regimes and their empire-centred policies. This is necessarily the case because imperial expansion is premised on the privatization of public enterprises, resulting in massive firings and loss of pensions, other social benefits and job tenure. Further, imperial creditors demand budget surpluses to pay off debts to foreign creditors, meaning cutbacks in all social services and public development spending, which leads to further slashing of the number of public employees, reductions of salary, pension and social benefits, and greater intensification of workloads (for example, teacher-student and doctor-patient ratios). The loss of tenure and the hiring of contract workers (NGOs) have undermined the job security of public employees, making them subject to the same "market insecurities" as manufacturing workers. In short, the empire-building strategy of privatizing public firms, the priority of debt payments in budget allocations and the proletarianization of living standards and working conditions are the objective factors driving public employees into the streets and into prolonged nationwide strikes.

The principal coalition partners in all the major confrontations with client states and their imperial patrons are public employees, especially teachers, and peasants. The most militant trade-union actions in the provincial and capital cities are led by public employees and involve the occupation of municipal and federal buildings, the blocking of streets and the ousters of public officials. Frequently, public employees have been reduced to near indigence because of delays in payment and/or payment in devalued currency. In Brazil, public employees lost 20 percent of their real income as salaries were frozen from 1998 to 2003. In the Argentine provinces, municipal workers have been delayed payment for three to four months and then paid in local, provincial currency.

The new protagonists of anti-imperialist politics include the rural landless, farmer and peasant movements, the urban unemployed and self-employed (especially in Argentina, Venezuela, Bolivia and Peru) and public employees throughout the region, particularly workers in the petroleum and gas industries targeted for privatization. Their specific demands are frequently linked to the rejection of ALCA, US military bases and the empire-centred policies of client regimes.

Empire-building: Omnipotence in the Eyes of the Observer

In the US mass media and in the public utterances of the Washington elite, the advance of the US empire appears to be an inevitable, always successful, totally justified and irreversible process to be applauded or suffered. To critics, the "internal contradictions" or "overextension" of empire will lead the empire-builders to their own downfall.

The sense of imperial omnipotence permeates both the celebrants and the pessimists who take a long-term view of empire. What both "long term" historical speculators and short-term apologists lack is any in-depth understanding of the *concrete struggles* that shape the correlation of forces today and will determine whether the US empire is with us for a few years, a decade or a century.

US empire-builders have suffered several important defeats in a series of important confrontations. In Venezuela, the urban poor, unemployed and self-employed in the hundreds of thousands came down from the *ranchos* in Caracas and provided the impetus to military loyalists to overthrow the dictatorial Fernando Carmona regime, imposed by a military-civilian coup orchestrated by the US, and to restore the popularly elected Hugo Chavez to the presidency. A year later, US-backed economic, media and trade union clients attempted to overthrow the regime by paralyzing the petroleum industry. They were also defeated, by an alliance of loyalist military officials, sectors of the working class and the mass of urban poor, many organized in "Bolivarian circles," barrio-based mass organizations.

In Colombia, the US effort to establish dominance through paramilitary and state terror campaigns ordered by client President Uribe have been decisively contained by the Revolutionary Armed Forces of Colombia — People's Army (FARC–EP) and the National Liberation Army, despite thousands of US-financed mercenaries, contract workers and combat advisers working with a budget of over $2 billion and the most up-to-date military technology and helicopter gunships.

In Bolivia the *cocaleros* have successfully resisted the US-orchestrated campaign to destroy the coca farmers and their organizations. Despite US client President Gonzalo Sánchez de Lozada's violent repression and direct intervention by the US ambassador in Bolivian politics, the *cocaleros* have created, in association with miners, the urban poor, factory workers and the self-employed in Cochabamba, La Paz, Sucre and Oruco, a formidable coalition capable of blocking neo-liberal policies — such as the privatization of water — building a national political movement, which is the main opposition party in Congress, and building a national leadership with the capacity to prevent Bolivia's entry into ALCA.

In Cuba the urban and rural mass movements provided solid support to the revolutionary regime's successful effort to dismantle US-financed terrorist networks as well as embryonic propaganda cells promoted by US intelligence services.

The most successful challenges and defeats to US empire-building have come from autonomous organized class forces in the Third World. The least consequential opponents of empire-building are the former social democratic, centre-left and populist electoral regimes that have largely adopted the empire-centred economic and social strategies and have allied with Latin American transnational capitalists and US and EU multinationals. The most striking example is Lula's Workers' Party (PT) regime in Brazil. This regime has been converted into a servile client of the United States, appointing key economic ministers and a central banker who are totally integrated into the empire-centred "development" project. Lula's monetarist economic program of reducing public employees' pensions, sharp cuts in social spending, regressive taxation and pro-employer "labour reform" is only part of a pro-empire agenda. Similar processes have occurred with other pseudo-populist electoral politicians, Gutiérrez in Ecuador and Toledo in Peru. The most significant development is the speed with which the mass of the class-based movements — particularly public employees, peasants and the self-employed — mobilize to confront and attack these new clients of empire. In each instance, the masses that voted for the "centre-left" are the identical forces in the streets demanding their resignation as collaborators with imperialism.

Throughout Latin America, there is virtually no organized mass movement organized by the capitalist class, or for that matter by the small and medium-sized business people or farmers, though a minority occasionally support particular protests on issues of debt payment, interest rates and protectionism. What precludes inclusion of the bourgeoisie into the mass struggles is their support of neo-liberal anti-labour legislation, the low level of the minimum wage, the reduction in social security taxes and the regime's tolerance of widespread tax evasion and corrupt links with lower-level customs and trade officials regarding import duties and export licenses.

The socio-political movements that have close links with "centre-left" regimes that have converted into imperial clients have been severely disoriented and in some cases are in the process of internal debates and discussions. The Landless Rural Workers Movement (MST) and CUT (the United Trade Union Federation) in Brazil, the National Confederation of Indigenous Nationalities of Ecuador (CONAIE), the unemployed workers movement in Argentina and the trade unions in Uruguay all face the problem of choosing between anti-imperialist class struggle or collaboration with the new "centre-left" electoral client regimes of the empire.

In contrast to the class-based, politically oriented struggle for state power, which has dealt blows to imperial expansion, the amorphous "anti-globalization" movements and World Social Forums have not defeated any of the empire-building projects, nor have they been successful in preventing a single military conquest. Moreover, the "anti-globalization" leaders have not created any mass support for the popular anti-imperialist resistance to US military occupation and pillage in the Balkans, Afghanistan or Iraq. Mass "anti-globalization" demonstrations are merely ritual events limited in time and space. They lack tactics or strategies that will have a major impact on imperial expansion, war preparations, privatizations, structural adjustment policies or any other empire-centred measures. Only when US imperial rivals in Europe (particularly France, Germany, Italy and Spain) take measures to make their MNCs more competitive by lowering pensions, increasing the retirement age or slashing social expenditures do workers demonstrate. Only in France is there any effort by the workers' movement to go beyond limited "ritual" strikes — symbolic protests that may delay but certainly do not eliminate the imposition of domestic burdens in order to finance imperial expansion.

Orderly, time-bounded mass anti-war demonstrations symbolically confront state power — they marched through the city of London to Hyde Park to hear anti-imperialist speeches — but lack the capacity to paralyze the system or engage in serious political warfare. It is the nature of "crowds" to come and leave as they please, lacking any organized political structure. The leftist sects are confined to selling their newspapers or distributing leaflets for radical forums, while self-described anarchists (and police provocateurs) break a few shop windows to convince themselves that they are anti-capitalists.

The strength of the anti-imperialist movement is found among the guerrillas in the jungles of Colombia, the Bolivarian circles in the urban slums of Caracas, the street demonstrations of Cuba, the landless workers occupying the *fazendas* of Brazil, the coca farmers of Bolivia, the underemployed and unemployed urban poor of Peru and Argentina — in short, among the organized classes, displaced, exploited and impoverished by empire client regimes.

The Future of Empire?

It is difficult to speculate with any accuracy when the moment will come when the US empire begins to decline. It is even more difficult to determine if this decline will be structural or conjunctural. The best that can be done is to delineate the principle contradictions. The major contradictions are political and social as much as they are economic. The fundamental contradiction and challenge today is between Latin America's organized rural and urban masses and the US empire-builders and their client rulers, transnational capitalists and NGO/trade union auxiliaries. The second major contradiction is between the expanding empire and the declining republic, and the capacity of the imperial ruling class to commit wealth, revenues and personnel to empire-building. The third contradiction is between the conquest and occupation countries and mass national anti-colonial resistance movements, as in Iraq and Afghanistan.

A fourth contradiction is between the growing military empire and the inability to extract profits from the newly colonized regions, future oil revenues notwithstanding. The centrality of Third World struggles to weaken the US empire is best illustrated by the effects of the Iraqi resistance on the US occupation army. The US colonial occupation forces are taking casualties daily — deaths and injuries throughout the country at the hands of popularly backed Iraqi guerrillas. The most immediate effect is to lower the morale of the US occupying forces. The US military's rapid disenchantment and openly expressed hostility toward long-term occupation is one of the weakest links in the US empire — as it was in the aftermath of the Second World War, and the Korean and Indochinese wars. This key weakness of the US imperial armed forces means that the militarists will have a serious problem in sustaining colonial conquests unless there is a major infusion of foreign legionnaires from India, Pakistan, Turkey, Eastern Europe or other client regimes.

The vast technological superstructure of the US imperial war machine ultimately relies on ground troops to occupy and consolidate imperial rule. The problem, however, is that the nature of US ground troops is not compatible with long-term policing of colonies. First, much of the occupying army is made up of reservists and National Guard members — not lifetime enlisted soldiers — who joined the military to supplement their civilian pay and secure health and pension benefits not otherwise available. The reservists' idea of "military service" is one night a week training and short-term summer exercises, with calls to short-term active duty in times of national emergency. This outlook is incompatible with long-term colonial occupation. This sector of the military has little stomach for prolonged absence from job, family, school and community, especially in Iraq and Afghanistan, facing the harsh conditions of intense heat, lack of water and decent living facilities, widespread popular hostility and frequent attacks.

Second, many of the enlisted soldiers joined to escape unemployment or low-income, dead-end jobs with the hope of "learning a trade" and returning to civilian life. Few volunteers expected face-to-face combat on hostile terrain.

Third, the "professional soldiers" resent being assigned colonial police duties, particularly given the hostile day-to-day environment and the incompetence of the higher echelons of the military command in reconstructing a basic infrastructure.

Fourth, there is a profound gap in "soldiering" between the affluent, upwardly mobile, media-savvy and air-conditioned generals and colonels, who fly to the occupied countries for reports, reviews and press conferences and fly out to their secure, well-serviced headquarters in Qatar,

Florida or Washington for filet mignon dinners, and the occupation forces lodged in flea-bag tents, eating plastic-wrap rations, lacking water for showers and toilets, and facing the nearly universal hostility of the conquered Iraqi people.

Fifth, the occupation forces are increasingly resentful and frustrated by the lies and deceptions of the high command regarding their tenure of service. The gap between the ideals and promises and the reality is sending shock waves throughout the occupation forces. First, they were told they would be welcomed as a "liberating army"; instead they confront general hostility and are justifiably considered an army of oppressors. They were told they would work with "free Iraqis" to rebuild the country; instead they patrol broken streets in armoured carriers, engaging in housebreaking and massive military sweeps. Most significantly, they were told they would fight a war, conquer the country and return home as heroes; instead, they now realize they will have to spend years ducking grenades and bullets to sustain a puppet regime.

The US military, which was trained for high-tech war, faces urban warfare in the streets, universities and neighbourhoods where the Iraqi resistance has the advantages of knowing the terrain and having the support of local people. Rumsfeld's propaganda about the urban resistance being simply a "remnant" of the defeated Baathist forces rings false to soldiers who experience hostility from grammar school children and the millions of Muslims who were previously persecuted by Saddam Hussein.

The dilemma of the civilian militarists is that the 160,000 or so US troops in Iraq are inadequate to control 24 million Iraqis demanding self-determination. Given the fact that the US military requires at least five non-combat soldiers for every active combatant, and given the decline in recruitment of "volunteers" in the face of the harsh demands of an occupying army, civilian militarists have no choice but to limit the rotation of troops and to seek "multilateral" assistance from clients and allies. What the civilian militarists are not willing to do is to return to general conscription. As past draft dodgers themselves, the militarists in the Bush administration have no desire to call up their own children or grandchildren to risk their lives for the empire. Both upper-middle-class gentiles and Zionists have no desire to pull their progeny from elite universities or professional schools, or lucrative banking or financial careers, to fight "international terrorism."

Finally, the civilian-military rulers in charge of the colonial policy are themselves totally divorced not only from the swelling mass opposition in Iraq and from their own increasingly rebellious ground troops, but also from groups of their own military officials. The Rumsfeld-Wolfowitz ideologues have discredited and bypassed military and CIA intelligence sources and created their own "inner circles" in order to impose their own highly politicized "intelligence" to justify military conquest. Their obsession with imperial conquest and military dominance is fuelled by racist anti-Arab animus and driven by the idea of a greater US-Israel "co-prosperity sphere" in the Middle East. The organizational-ideological division at the top of imperial military intelligence could over time seriously erode the power of the civilian militarists.

As the republic gives way to the empire, it is likely that one of the principal sources of conflict and rebellion may occur within the military, and this may eventually have an impact on domestic politics. The war and the drive for colonial control have generalized strong anti-colonial popular resistance in the occupied countries and generated daily casualties among imperial ground forces. Resistance, casualties and military discontent are beginning to affect the popularity of the latest imperialist wars. At issue here are the negative images in the United States resulting from growing American casualties, the economic and political chaos in Iraq, the escalating costs of conquest and the apparent incompetence in managing the occupation. Even noted imperialist apologists are bemoaning the lack of "preparation" or "capacity" of strategists for colonial domination. Unilateral US military action benefited the militarists intent on short-term unrestricted warfare, but it undermines the bases for securing multilateral financial and military support for post-conquest colony building.

The highly charged and emotional diatribes of the civilian militarists with their neo-Nazi "will to world power" is crashing into the reality of reluctant vassal states, Iraqi opposition and the growing rebelliousness of US troops in the occupied lands. Those ideologues and politicians who take their cues from the Israeli strategy of massive unilateral force to secure colonies, forget that Sharon could not exist without the support of the US government and the Zionist diaspora, and that the US has neither a supporting power nor affluent benefactors.

Some observers, focusing on tactical and commercial disputes, argue that inter-imperialist rivalries are growing between the EU and the US. What is significant about these conflicts is how quickly they are defused, how small is their impact and how quickly the disputants are reconciled to jointly pursue empire-building. For example, the opposition of some European countries to the US-British invasion of Iraq was subsequently followed by an agreement within the European Union to build their own rapid deployment forces. France sent paratroopers into three African countries shortly after the Iraq War. Europe's decision to follow the United States is illustrated by its decision to reduce relations with Cuba, collaborate with the US in isolating Iraq, approve US resolutions against the spread of "weapons of mass destruction," etc. The imperial linkages between Europe and the US are far stronger than their competing interests. Equally important, the strength of the US military and economic empire and its aggressive approach has intimidated would-be critics in

France and Germany, who are surrounded by US satellites in Eastern Europe, the Baltic nations and the Balkans.

The economy of the US republic is built on speculation, fraud, credit, debt, cheap immigrant labour, huge direct and indirect state subsidies, foreign borrowings and large and growing trade and budget deficits. When the economy moves from stagnation into a major recession, it will weaken the empire *if* the state is unable to foist the burden of recovery on the backs of the waged, salaried and small business groups, and *if* the state is forced to reallocate resources and personnel from empire-building to the republic. Unfortunately the record of the last quarter century tells us that the US public has shown little active resistance to military spending in times of war and only minority opposition to imperial conquest.

The trade unions are politically impotent and linked to the empire through their ties to the Democratic Party. There is no national political and social movement in existence capable of challenging the empire-builders today or in the foreseeable future. With more than 90 percent of the private-sector workforce non-union, workers show little if any political influence and do not even possess a social organization that could potentially reallocate the budget toward greater social, instead of military, spending. One of the great advantages of the US empire-builders over Europe and even Japan is their capacity to exploit workers (with longer hours of work and no national health, pension or vacation plans), fire workers easily and cheaply, and relocate firms. The US empire-builders' key comparative advantage against its potential European and Japanese rivals is their control over the most backward working class in the industrialized world.

The highly exploitative social relations of production in the US provide the surplus necessary for overseas expansion and limit the possibilities of the downwardly mobile waged and salaried classes from challenging the decline of the republic.

The argument for the decline of empire cannot count on any automatic economic collapse, internal rebellion or consequential division between economic and military empire-builders. The empire will be defeated from without or it will not be defeated at all. Only with external defeats will internal dissent or opposition emerge, activating the exploited and the poor, and particularly the Black and Hispanic populations.

The particularity of the US empire in contrast to Europe, Asia and elsewhere is that it lacks a tradition of working-class or left-wing anti-imperialism. Opposition in the recent past has been directed at "global capital" and the policies and practices of the MNCs. Except among a small minority, there is no sense among "anti-globalization" activists that the central issue is the US imperial state. Not even at the height of the recent anti-war movement was there any understanding of the imperial-colonial nature of the Iraq War. This was evident in the virtual disappearance of the anti-war movement once the war began. During the US occupation, colonial rule and massacre of Iraqis protesting the US occupation and destruction of their economy, there was virtually no anti-colonial movement. The only long-standing internal opposition to US imperial policy occurred during the Vietnam War *because of the prolonged length and effectiveness of the Indochinese resistance movements, the defeat of the US and the large number of US military deaths and casualties.*

The current empire-builders have learned from their previous defeats and do not hesitate to launch massive aerial attacks, use uranium-tipped shells or mobilize mercenaries from their new client regimes in England, Poland, the Ukraine, etc. Thousands of private mercenaries have been subcontracted by the Pentagon in implementing Plan Colombia and the pacification of the Balkans. The problem of "overextension" is then not an irremediable problem, particularly since the EU has implemented a similar program of rapid deployment forces to invade and occupy countries where clients are in danger or independent states or movements emerge.

The dynamics of US empire-building are still in full force even as contradictions deepen and fissures appear. The imperialist state commands the allegiance of its domestic ruling class and substantial sectors of a fragmented, chauvinistic and downwardly mobile population despite growing unease among the public about the Iraqi resistance. The imperial economy continues to dominate key sectors of world investment, trade and finance through its multinationals. The military empire-builders have established more military bases in more regions than ever before, openly embracing a doctrine of permanent warfare and military intervention anywhere in the world, with the acquiescence of Europe and Japan.

Has the US empire "peaked"? Perhaps. But the current imperial projections are for further wars. New imperial colonial networks are being consolidated. In Latin America the conversion of the Da Silva regime to ALCA and the formation of a US-Brazil-Mexico nexus assures the US of new and bigger markets and privileged opportunities for US MNCs. The US-Israel nexus promotes a Middle East "Free Market Zone" dominated by the two powers.

The promoters of US imperial-colonial conquest draw no limits, experience no internal constraints and possess willing accomplices among the other great and lesser powers, most of which are eager to make amends for their meek dissent over US tactics in the run-up to the Iraqi conquest. The evidence is clear. The EU has taken up the US cudgels in attacking Cuba, Iran and North Korea with unprecedented vehemence and threats, gaining merit points from Washington. On the basis of the successful US conquest of Iraq, the empire-builders in the EU and Japan have decided that it is better to join the US war machine and share the spoils of conquest rather than be excluded in the future.

If our evidence and arguments hold, it is clear that imperial rivalries, internal opposition and economic contradictions will not play a decisive role in the "decline of the empire." Mass political-social struggles in the colonized nations and client states are the driving forces that will call into question the durability of the empire, its longevity and its successes and losses. Mass popular resistance in Iraq is delaying oil deliveries, undermining military morale and bringing out the ugly totalitarian features of a murderous occupation force. The large-scale guerrilla force in Colombia blocks the expansion of US MNCs and undermines US military strategy. The continuing Palestinian resistance blocks the consolidation of Greater Israel and US-Israeli plans for a wider free trade zone. The urban mass uprising in Venezuela defeated the US-backed bosses' lockout and undermined US efforts to monopolize petrol from Venezuela to Iraq. The Cuban revolutionary regime remains a model and hope of resistance to hundreds of millions in the Third World.

Only when these and other struggles detonate wider regional uprisings and radical struggles, increasing US casualties and costs, will opposition emerge in the US and the EU. Rival imperial powers may take advantage of the decline to assert their own imperial interests and dissociate themselves from a weakening empire.

US empire-building is not merely a product of US "accumulation on a world scale," nor have the military empire-builders "overreached" the boundaries of economic possibility. The buildup of empire has proceeded with ups and downs for over half a century and has accelerated in the recent period with the demise of the Sino-Soviet bloc and its nationalist allies in the Third World. Both Democrats and Republicans, both Clinton and Bush administrations, have eagerly seized opportunities to establish military bases, launch colonial conquests and impose client regimes, even as their ideological justifications varied. Rulers from both major US parties have subordinated the economy of the republic to the empire. Both parties pursue ALCA — the first promoted it and the second implemented it. The US political party system, Congress, the court system and the mass media are totally embedded in the imperial system. The imperial values and interests of Christian fundamentalists, Zionist ideologues, civilian militarists, bankers and CEOs of MNCs support US empire-building.

Most US citizens who defend the empire may participate in financing it but do not receive its spoils. Nevertheless, they appear to have consumed a racial-nationalist ideology that arrogates all good to themselves and only evil to the critics and overseas adversaries of the state. Change will only come when the reality of Third World resistance and revolt undermines the US military will to conquer.

7. THE CLASS DYNAMICS OF ANTI-IMPERIALIST POLITICS

TO UNDERSTAND ANTI-IMPERIALIST POLITICS IT IS IMPORTANT TO ASK several key questions such as: What constitutes an anti-imperialist movement (AIM)? Do the anti-globalization, anti-"free trade" and anti-war movements have an anti-imperialist content? Under what conditions and in what geopolitical locations can AIMs emerge and expand? What is the class base of the AIM and which classes, states and regimes defend imperialism? How do diverse classes become activated in anti-imperialist struggles? Do heightened economic crises and the emergence of new organizations and leaders make a difference? Under what conditions do AIMs emerge within the empire? What are their potentialities and limitations? And what strategies and tactics advance or limit the growth of the AIM?

Answers to questions such as these provide the framework for the following discussion about anti-imperialist politics today.

Anti-imperialist Movements (AIMs)

Opposition to imperialism takes a great variety of forms. There is no internationally dominant organization that is fully opposed to imperialism as a system of power. Rather, what predominates are a variety of single-issue movements opposing imperial policies and institutions. For example, throughout Latin America, significant demonstrations, movements and referendums have opposed the US-sponsored Free Trade Area of the Americas (FTAA, or ALCA in Spanish). For many opponents, resistance to ALCA is based on the destructive effects that free trade has on jobs, and on farmers and peasants. For others, ALCA is seen as a part of a US global strategy to conquer and dominate the economies and politics of Latin America and the rest of the world. The anti-ALCA movements oppose an important aspect of US imperialism — its attempt to dominate trade and investment in the region through formal control of the legal-political framework governing economic relations.

The anti-globalization movement and anti-(Iraq, Afghanistan) war campaigning contain both anti-imperialists and "imperial reformers" (groups that generally support US imperial power but oppose the particular way power is exercised or the specific location in which it manifests). Others oppose the behaviour of the multinational corporations but not the imperial state and system in which they are embedded. These movements are anti-imperialist to the degree that they mobilize popular forces to oppose an important manifestation of imperial expansion, raise popular consciousness about the motives of the US and some EU regimes and open the possibility of extending resistance to imperialism as a system.

However, the potentialities of these single-issue political movements are frequently unrealized; the struggle over a single issue remains isolated from a general rejection of imperialism, and the victory or defeat of imperial power usually ends the mobilizations. The anti-Vietnam War mobilization, the biggest and longest opposition to an imperialist war, declined when military conscription ended, the Vietnamese won the war and the US withdrew its troops. The after-effects were to limit the use of massive US ground troops for fifteen years (until the Gulf War), to increase the recruitment of mercenary armies (in Afghanistan, Nicaragua, Angola, Mozambique, etc.) and to increase reliance on intelligence agencies and special forces to overthrow anti-imperialist regimes (Chile 1973, Uruguay 1973, Argentina 1976, etc.) and on small-scale forces to invade small countries (Grenada, Panama). In addition, the single-issue anti-imperialist movements did not prevent or even mobilize to end the economic blockades of Cuba, Vietnam, Cambodia, Laos, etc. Finally many single-issue anti-imperialists joined the liberal wing of the pro-imperialist Democratic Party in the US, and the reformist pro-NATO parties of Europe — the Socialist Party of France, the Communist Party of Italy, etc.

The historical record of single-issue anti-imperialist movements is very ambiguous. In some cases they have medium-term residual effects, in others they dissolve into traditional politics and in a few cases they feed into larger social movements. In the latter case, the anti-colonial struggles in France and Italy fed into larger anti-systemic movements: Paris 1968 or the hot autumn of Italy in 1969.

The key to identifying the dynamics (forward or backward) of single-issue anti-imperialist movements is politics: the ideology, leaders and programs around which these movements are organized. Most of the short-term impacts are the result of the leaders' ideology of pragmatic lowest-denominator politics, focusing exclusively on the most immediate issue (imperial policy), dissociated from imperialism as a system of power, eschewing any political challenge for regime or state power, and accommodating or subordinating the mass movement to opportunist "dissident" politicians from the major imperial parties, who seek to capitalize on the mass protest for electoral purposes.

Single-issue anti-imperialist mobilizations, like the anti-globalization movement, erupt, extend and then become routine and decline, as they fail to connect with popular mass struggles to challenge for power. In the case of the anti-globalization movement, the false premises of its ideologues, that is, the idea that multinational corporations are autonomous powers divorced from the imperial states, has failed to anticipate imperial wars and colonial occupation. The reorientation of many former anti-globalization activists to the anti-Iraq War movement led to a massive increase in protests on the single issue of the war followed by a collapse after the US conquered and occupied Iraq. No mass movement has emerged to oppose the US colonial regime or support the Iraqi resistance.

Single-issue mass movements opposed to specific anti-imperialist policies do not necessarily lead to an advancing, radicalizing and consequential anti-imperialist movement, unless they go beyond single issues and develops a program and leadership capable of linking anti-imperialism to system transformation.

Conditions for the Emergence of AIMs

Under what conditions do AIMs emerge and expand? Almost all the most important and consequential AIMs have taken place in Latin America, Asia or Africa. In the present period we can identify several contexts in which significant AIMs have emerged.

Colonial Invasion and Occupation

Iraq has seen the regrouping and resistance of mass anti-imperial movements organized against colonial-military rule. The colonial regimes pillage the economy, appoint colonial rulers, destroy the infrastructure, kill civilians and torture suspects. The everyday humiliations of millions provoke hostility, rejection and resistance. The same is true in Afghanistan, with armed resistance to the US-EU occupation force and its puppet (Karzai) regime.

Military Intervention

Long-term US military involvement as advisors, arms suppliers and financial backers of the Colombian oligarchy has provoked a large-scale and long-term anti-imperialist guerrilla and civilian opposition. The most recent phase of imperial military intervention (Plan Colombia) has polarized the country, impoverished urban workers and heightened the killing of peasants, human rights activists, journalists and trade unionists. The direct involvement of US mercenary subcontractors in combat and coca eradication has further contributed to the growth of anti-imperialist politics in the rural areas.

Privatization and Declining Living Standards

Most of the privatized banks, telecommunications, public utilities (light and power), mineral and petrol enterprises have ended up in the hands of American and European MNCs. The result has been massive firings, higher prices, a reduction in regions served and large-scale transfer of resources overseas, legally and illegally. The very process of privatization was not transparent, as bribes and payoffs led to buyouts at below market value. This has led to massive protests against the particular foreign enterprise, against state policies and against the negative consequences. Massive anti-privatization protests have taken place in Peru (state-owned electrical companies), Bolivia (water), Ecuador (petroleum and electricity) and many other countries. In Argentina a mass popular uprising took place on December 20/21, 2001, after foreign-owned banks transferred depositors' savings abroad. The bulk of anti-privatization activity has focused on IFI sponsorship of privatization, and US and EU backing of the IFIs.

Unequal Trade and Investment

The US and EU subsidize their agricultural products to the tune of over $50 billion in direct payouts, and several billion more in state funded irrigation systems, export subsidies, technical assistance, favourable electrical and power rates, marketing promotion, infrastructure, networks and "tied aid." In addition, both the US and EU impose tariff barriers, quotas and non-traditional trade barriers on agricultural and manufacturing exports from the Third World. In contrast, the US and EU imperial states demand the lowering and elimination of tariffs and subsidies in the Third World. As a result, the Third World loses an estimated $200 billion in trade income a year, more than double all the loans, investment, grants and transfers from the imperialist regimes. The US proposes, through ALCA, to consolidate and deepen its unequal trade relationship with Latin America by establishing a legal and political framework under an ALCA commission, which it will control, thus converting Latin America into a colonial mercantile zone.

Throughout Latin America, millions have protested against the signing of the ALCA agreement. In Brazil, in an informal referendum, 95 percent rejected ALCA — a total of eleven million voters. The key to the advance of ALCA is found in the vassal regimes in Latin America, particularly in Bolivia, Brazil, Chile, Colombia, Ecuador, Mexico and Peru.

The defeat of Washington's recolonization agenda requires the overthrow or ousting of collaborating vassal regimes. The major social forces opposing the US agenda are the indigenous communities, peasants and small farmers who cannot compete with subsidized US agricultural products that sell at lower prices due to imperial-state export subsidies. In Bolivia, peasants have been put in a bind, squeezed by the US state from two directions. On the one side, they have turned to the production of an alternative crop, coca, since they cannot compete with subsidized US agricultural imports that have saturated local markets. On the other side, the US state (in the form of the DEA — the Drug Enforcement Administration) is exerting considerable economic, political and military pressure to force the same peasants to turn away from the production of coca, the raw material for the cocaine trade, towards what in Bolivia is termed "alternative development" (alternative crops?). In Mexico, Ecuador and elsewhere, producers of staple goods such as corn have been marginalized even in local markets, their economies decimated by the forces of global competition (imports of highly subsidized surplus corn from Texas, etc.). However, in Mexico, Bolivia, Colombia and Peru, rural movements of peasant and independent producers defend the right to produce alternative crops and oppose ALCA, rightly seen as the "death knell" of their economies and livelihoods. In Brazil the Landless Rural Workers Movement (MST) is the leading force opposing ALCA.

Insofar as ALCA, in substance and symbol, embodies the US imperial conquest and colonization of Latin America, the anti-ALCA movements represent a key element in the anti-imperialist struggle.

The transition from free trade to colonial mercantilist imperialism has heightened conditions for the emergence and expansion of anti-imperialist movements. Equally significant, ALCA has broadened the scope of opposition to US and EU domination. During the first phase of neo-liberalism, opposition to imperialism was based on a specific policy — privatization — and focused on particular industrial sectors (or even particular firms) affected. The protests were directed at specific grievances, loss of employment, lowering of salaries, increases in prices, etc. These particular struggles persist, notably by the Ecuadorian petroleum workers against the privatization and denationalization of the oil industry and by the light and power workers in Mexico. Increasingly these particular struggles are explicitly linked to opposition to ALCA and the US imperial conquest.

The AIM in Historical Perspective

The current anti-imperialist movement is the most recent of a series of struggles that go back to the original conquest of the Third World. Nevertheless the goals, social classes and programs of the AIM are vastly different from what they were in earlier times.

It is possible to distinguish several types and sub-types of historical and contemporary AIMs.

1. Traditional
The earliest movements against imperial-colonial conquest frequently resisted genocide, extermination, enslavement, displacement and serfdom. The goals of at least some of their leaders were to restore pre-colonial

systems of hierarchical rule by local emperors, councils or communities. The rebellion, defeat, re-enslavement and dispersion of colonized peoples created two parallel economies: the dominant colonial economy and the subsistence communities of anti-colonial peoples in remote regions of the conquered countries.

2. Modern

Modern AIMs can be divided into those that struggled for political independence from overt colonial rule (Latin America in the nineteenth and early twentieth centuries, and Asia/Africa in the mid-twentieth century) and those that struggled for political and economic independence through national and socialist revolutionary struggles in the mid-twentieth century (China, Cuba, Vietnam, Yugoslavia, etc). These anti-imperialist revolutions in turn laid the basis for new confrontations between nationalist-capitalist and socialist-populist movements. The modern AIM succeeded in establishing "hybrid" economies and regimes, mixed state, private and collective property forms, and popular hierarchical regimes. These hybrid regimes and economies served as the terrain for new confrontations with imperialism. The new nationalist and communist elites, divorced from mass socio-economic realities and subject to imperial influence or intervention, evolved over the decades into a new class or were overthrown and replaced by imperial vassal regimes, particularly during the last decades of the twentieth century. Nationalist regimes in Africa and Asia were overthrown and replaced by tribal warlords, colonial vassals and clerical reactionaries — all initially linked to the US and/or EU. The conversion of collectivist regimes to pro-capitalist/pro-imperialist regimes in the ex-USSR, Eastern Europe and Southern Asia was based on both external and internal social forces. In Eastern Europe, US financial and ideological support of nationalist politicians, intellectual elites and trade union bosses facilitated the shift of their regions from Russian satellites to US vassal states, extending the US empire from the Baltic to the Balkans. Military intervention and support for surrogate paramilitary forces extended the US empire from the Balkans to the Middle East. In the twenty-first century the US expanded to the Middle East and Southern Asia through war in Afghanistan and Iraq. The ideology of imperial conquest varied from the traditional colonial "humanitarian" rhetoric to "liberation" rhetoric in Iraq, and to the modern "anti-terrorism" subterfuge in Afghanistan.

By the end of the twentieth century there had emerged three variants of these anti-imperialist movements: (1) *right-wing anti-imperialism,* articulated by US client dissidents in Eastern Europe, the Balkans and Caucasus as an instrument to shift allegiances from Soviet domination to the US empire, (2) *clerical anti-imperialism,* based on religious (Muslim) opposition to US military aggression, political conquest, cultural influence, economic depredations and racial hostility, oriented toward "restoring" traditional clerical views and in some cases combining them with modern nationalist values, and (3) *modern anti-imperialism,* opposed to imperial wars and conquests, the MNCs, the WTO and ALCA, and supporting liberation struggles in the Third World. The profound class and political differences in these three anti-imperialist or nationalist movements — between pro-US empire movements, clerical-nationalist and modern liberation movements — has important theoretical and practical consequences. The US war against Yugoslavia based on an alliance with Muslim terrorists in Bosnia and Kosova, the clerical-rightists in Afghanistan and a colonial regime in Iraq indicate the way in which imperialism articulates with reactionary rightists against secular regimes. US support for and influence over the dissident elites in Eastern Europe and their conversion into US vassals demonstrates the capacity of the empire to co-opt anti-influential ideology and its propagators in order to secure military bases and political vassal states. The selective use and disuse of Muslims, secular intellectuals and ethnic extremists is a central part of US imperial strategy to weaken anti-imperialist regimes and divide imperialist opponents. This is particularly effective in the case of critics in the AIM, who lack a class perspective on the nature of imperialism, the multiple forms it takes and the flexible allowances it adopts: supporting Muslims against leftists in one moment, attacking Muslim nationalists in favour of secular or Muslim vassals in another moment. The current wave of AIMs contain both secular and clerical forces, socialists and nationalists, and progressives and restorationists.

Anti-imperialism in the US

Anti-imperialist movements have been weakest in the United States. With the exception of the height of the US invasion of Indochina between 1965 and 1972, there have been few sustained anti-imperialist mass activities. Nevertheless, US public opinion and electoral protests directed against particular US imperial incursions have not been infrequent. We can identify several periods of US public opposition to aspects of imperial policy.

1945–1947: US public opposition and overseas troop demonstrations forced post-World War II imperial planners to significantly reduce US troop deployments in the occupied countries and to limit US intervention against the Chinese, Indochinese and Yugoslav socialist revolutions.

1951–1953: US public opposition to the Korean War led to the defeat of the pro-war Democratic presidential candidate and pressured Eisenhower to negotiate an armistice that denied Washington military victory.

1965–1972: US public opposition (mass demonstrations and acute sociopolitical polarization) and large-scale discontent within the military in Vietnam undermined the political and military

bases of imperial power and contributed to the defeat of the
US military.

Subsequently there was sustained public protest over US intervention
in Central America, American support for the apartheid South African
regime and the US invasion of Iraq. These protests had a very limited
influence on US policy. Equally serious, the US interventions in Angola
and Central and South America between 1973 and 1983, in support of
mercenary and/or military coups, elicited little public response except
from small activist groups. The "anti-globalization" demonstration of
50,000 people in Seattle in 1999 was a singular event with little effective
follow-up, except for the flare-up of anti-war demonstrations in January/
February 2003.

What accounts for the rare but successful mobilizations of anti-imperialist protests in the US? In both Korea and Vietnam, US military forces
were defeated or unable to win and suffered heavy casualties (several
hundreds of thousands dead or wounded) over a prolonged period of time
(three to ten years) at the hands of the national liberation forces. The
imperial defeats and casualties brought the war back into the communities, neighbourhoods, workplaces, families and social organizations of the
US. Second, the earlier wars were fought with conscript armies, which
included or threatened to include the sons of the middle and upper middle
classes in combat situations, thus affecting an important electoral con-
stituency. The threat of conscription into a military already suffering
heavy casualties in a prolonged war motivated many draft-age men and
their parents to actively oppose the war. Third, prolonged and costly
imperial wars, while stimulating the economy, led to a loss of shares in
world markets and strengthened US imperial rivals, while limiting Washington's ability to intervene and control other regions of the world. Sectors of the ruling and political classes began to put the strategic interests
of the empire ahead of prosecuting a hopelessly stalemated war, leading to
inter-elite divisions over how best to build a world empire.

The combined factors of sustained popular resistance, US military
casualties, fear of conscription and inter-elite divisions led to organized
mass movements and sustained opposition. Nevertheless, even in the
mass protests against the US invasion of Indochina, the great majority did
not oppose the entire US imperial system but only particular aspects of it,
such as the war, conscription and US military casualties. With the ending
of the war, the success of the movement was relative; it led to a temporary
reduction of military spending (1974–78) and to resistance to new massive
commitments of ground troops in overt interventions. Subsequently, from
the 1970s to 1990s, when the US switched to covert CIA-led interventions
(in Chile, Argentina, Uruguay) and used mercenary armies (in Angola,
Mozambique and Central America), there was little protest. There was

also no significant opposition to US invasions of the tiny countries of Grenada and Panama in the 1980s, which entailed very few casualties among US enlisted soldiers.

Subsequently, the US invasions and occupations of regions such as Yugoslavia and Afghanistan — both being largely aerial wars with ground support from Muslim fundamentalist warlords and terrorists — elicited significant public support in the US. The US invasion and conquest of Iraq confirms this analysis. The successful invasion and conquest was largely the result of massive military force and bombing, an aerial war accompanied by a covert surrender of Iraqi military commanders, which led to a rapid and successful military conquest with a minimum of US casualties. However, the occupation and subsequent colonial rule has led to large-scale popular opposition in Iraq and sustained urban guerrilla warfare, leading to dozens of US casualties each week (over four thousand injuries and over one-hundred-fifty deaths) in the first six months (May–October 2003). As the Iraqi guerrilla resistance and popular opposition grew and US casualties mounted, US opinion shifted from outright support for imperial wars to growing opposition. This coincided with calls for congressional hearings and electoral campaign criticism of the war. At the time of writing (June 2005), a majority of Americans (58 percent according to a poll reported on by CNN, June 29) opposed the war, although opposition was muted (no mass mobilizations), notwithstanding almost daily reports of war casualties (attributed to terrorists) and the apparent belief by a majority of Americans that the Bush administration lied to them about the need for war in the first place.

Equally significant, the US invasion in Iraq was the first imperialist war not combined with socio-economic gains for the mass of wage and salaried classes. The empire expands and oil company and other corporate profits jump to double digits, as unemployment increases and reductions in health and educational benefits increasingly erode living standards for the mass of the labour force. Despite the extremities of imperialist aggression and the severity of the attacks on living standards, there has been little "movement" against imperialism from the working and salaried classes. In official and semi-official opposition circles, opposition is aimed at "misleading propaganda" (the lies of the state), not the substantive issue of the imperial wars. The progressive dissidents criticize the particular policies leading to war, but not the structures of power that generated the policies; they criticize the Bush regime, but not the imperial state. What "solidarity" exists is directed centred on US soldiers ("Bring our boys home"), not on the anti-colonial peoples' resistance to an occupation army.

The historical record tells us that it will take extreme conditions to move significant forces in the US to oppose imperial aggression, such as a major economic crisis, significant loss of lives or prolonged wars of attrition. We must look elsewhere, outside the US, to locate the dynamics of anti-imperialist movements, precisely in those regions and among those classes who have suffered the greatest impact of imperialist conquest.

Imperialism and the Class Structure

The new class-based AIM emerges from the vast transformation brought about by the penetration and takeover of Third World economies, particularly in Latin America. Imperialism, with its economic policies and successes in taking over strategic financial, commercial, mining and petroleum sectors, has had major effects on all social classes in Latin America. In addition, economic policies imposed by the self-styled "international" financial institutions (the IMF, World Bank, Inter-American Development Bank) have been instrumental in transforming the class structure. Equally important, the selective enforcement of "free trade" policies has been a crucial factor in restructuring the urban and rural classes. All the changes brought about by imperialist classes and institutions have been instrumental in shaping the nature of the emerging anti-imperialist movements. In the countryside, imperialist policies and class have

- undermined small and medium-sized farm producers through "free market" policies that allow the massive influx of subsidized US farm exports;
- concentrated ownership and displaced subsistence and landless peasants via loans and assistance to agro-export firms (both Latin American and US) that specialize in production of export products such as soybeans, coffee and orange juice;
- increased polarization in the countryside by ending constraints on foreign ownership and ending communal titles to land, encouraging internal stratification; and
- lowered prices paid to local producers and increased the cost of credit, mostly by denying formal credit and forcing small producers to borrow at exorbitant interest rates in the informal lending market.

The net result is to increase the number of landless rural producers, bankrupt family farmers and force rural migrants to the periphery of regional urban centres. Imperially induced mass impoverishment, land concentration and peasant displacement have been key factors igniting rural social movements that have been at the forefront of struggles against ALCA, the IFIs and neo-liberalism. Equally important, imperial policies have adversely affected countries with high concentrations of Indian and Black peasants and farm workers, via mechanization, job elimination, the takeover of pasture land and the use of illicit or legal coercive mechanisms to seize land with proven mineral reserves. IFI funding of infrastructure almost exclusively links large agro-exporters to markets, ignoring the needs of rural communities. Probably most important for small producers in Bolivia, Peru and Colombia, imperially designed chemical "eradication" programs have destroyed the livelihood of millions of households without providing any viable alternative crop to coca production. The result has been the mobilization of mass social movements of peasants in support of their land, homesteads and communities, and a sharp increase in anti-imperialist consciousness.

In the cities, imperially promoted privatizations of firms and budget cuts to pay foreign creditors has had a severe impact on employees and wage workers. Millions of public sector employees, particularly in social services and public administration, have lost their jobs and job security, and most had suffered income declines of up to 40 percent by 2003. The new owners have fired industrial workers as they consolidate enterprise operations or pillage newly acquired public resources. There has been a "proletarianization" of public sector workers as a result of low income, job insecurity and diminished status. There has been a major increase in public-sector-organized protest directed against imperially promoted "structural adjustment programs" (SAPs) and beyond, to the intellectual authors in the IFIs. Imperial policies and institutions have undermined these two pillars of "political stability" for imperial hegemony: small rural property owners and middle-income professionals in the public sector. The urban unemployed and displaced rural producers have been concentrated into the "informal sector" and the poorly paid and highly exploitative *maquiladora* (assembly plants). Increasingly organized as unemployed workers movements, as barrio-based self-employed street vendors, or in distinct markets, the leaders and activists in Bolivia, Argentina, Peru, Venezuela and some other countries have been in the forefront of opposing imperialist policies of privatization. For example, they have opposed the privatization of water in Cochabamba, Bolivia, and of electricity in Arequipa, Peru, and the increase in public utility rates charged by recently privatized and formerly state-owned firms now run by foreign monopolies. University, secondary and primary school teachers and students have opposed budget cuts and deteriorating public schools and salary reductions mandated by the IFIs to pay foreign debt holders.

Occasional protests have emerged among the tightly controlled *maquilladores* production workers, but the traditional private sector industrial trade unions have demonstrated either a lack of interest or ability in supporting unionization of imperialist-owned firms. In fact, industrial workers and their trade unions have been the least active and militant components of the anti-imperialist movements. Many workers fear the loss of employment, faced by a mass of unemployed workers. Equally damaging, most of the trade union officials have consolidated control and become closely linked to tripartite pacts with the state and employers, and reject independent class action, let alone active anti-imperialist solidarity.

Apart from formal denunciations of ALCA, neo-liberalism and SAPs, the industrial unions have been minor actors in the new wave of anti-imperialist struggles in Latin America, far less engaged than the progressive sectors of the Catholic Church. Exceptions exist, but they represent a minority in the Brazilian, Uruguayan, Chilean and Argentine confederations.

Imperialism has restructured the capitalist class. Hundreds of thousands of small and medium-sized manufacturers have been bankrupted or have switched to commercial activity, as the high cost and meagre availability of credit has cut off cash flow, cheap imports have undermined profits and MNCs have squeezed profits from subcontractors. A similar pattern has taken place in the commercial sector: large foreign-owned department stores and supermarkets have sharply reduced the share of small and medium-sized businesses in retail trade and food services. The net result is a substantial increase in low-paid, non-unionized service workers employed by giant foreign-owned emporiums. Large bank takeovers by US and European bankers has led to massive layoffs of bank employees and to a vast increase in speculative capital and the legal and illegal flow of billions of dollars in tax-evading earnings and illicit gains.

Instead of radicalizing the bourgeoisie, imperial policies have created imperial associates, linked to financial and commercial networks — an army of local consultants, publicists, legal and tax advisors and local political promoters who serve as intermediaries in facilitating lucrative privatizations, state contracts and monopoly market controls. A minority of productive small and medium-sized entrepreneurs (PYMEs) are active in seeking cheaper credit, protection, subsidies and lower public utility rates, but their opposition is tempered by their support for the anti-labour, anti-social legislation promoted by the IFIs and therefore they play a minor role in the new anti-imperialist movements.

Imperialism has also transformed the nature of the state, through military intervention, economic blackmail, coups, corrupt electoral processes or mass media manipulation of elections. The state in Latin America, namely the central bank, military, police, intelligence services and senior officials in the "permanent institutions" of government administration are trained, indoctrinated and networked by the imperial state, with some notable exceptions. The state buttresses the imperial vassal regimes, which have replaced the populist-nationalist regimes of an earlier period. Imperialism has established the parameters of vassal-regimes policies: imperial subordination in foreign policy, free markets and SAPs in economic policy, reconcentration of income upward and outward in social policy, and the primacy of debt payments to foreign creditors over reactivation of domestic consumption and investment.

This imperial-centred accumulation regime requires large-scale and long-term state intervention to reallocate resources to imperial enterprises, regulations to facilitate the free flow of profits and interest payments outward and intervention in civil society to repress, co-opt or eliminate anti-imperialist leaders and activists, among others, as occurs in Colombia, Bolivia, Guatemala and Peru, and in the countrysides of Brazil, Paraguay and Mexico.

Imperialism has moved toward overt political control via ALCA, a so-called "trade and investment treaty," which will convert the vassal states into outright colonies in a new, formal empire-centred politico-economic model.

Class Organization and Anti-imperialist Policies

On the surface it appears that the anti-imperialist movements include a multitude of classes, identities and strata that extend from the bottom to near the top of the social hierarchy. This impression reflects the views of those active in the US and European anti-globalization movements. This imagery is far from reality in Latin America. Today, as in the recent past, the bulk of the anti-imperialist movements are made up of wage workers, the unemployed and sub-employed in the cities, students, the self-employed and particularly peasants, Indian subsistence farmers and landless rural workers. There are no undifferentiated "multitudes." Rather, the participants are organized and/or convoked by class-based social organizations whose leaders and organizers have histories of involvement in class struggle and in class politics either in the workplace or neighbour-hoods.

The contemporary anti-imperialist movements are substantially different from those of the past, insofar as the composition of the movements, the leadership and their political forces have taken on the specific characteristics of the present period. First of all, there is an absence of any "progressive bourgeoisie," either as a hegemonic factor or participant. The bulk of the local bourgeoisie has subcontracted with imperial firms, converted to marginal associates, been bought out or benefited from the regressive labour legislation that lowers labour costs, even as it has been adversely affected by lowered tariffs.

Second, the popular base of the modern AIM has shifted from the industrial trade unions to the peasant and rural movements, as many of the trade unions are involved in collective bargaining agreements with the MNCs and prefer to negotiate contracts rather than raise issues such as nationalization. In contrast, peasant and farmer livelihoods and households are directly and adversely affected by the large-scale entry of subsidized food products, imperially dictated eradication programs and the expansion of foreign-owned agro-export corporations.

Third, the current anti-imperialist movements are not influenced by external states, such as the USSR and China, as was the case in the past, and thus have greater tactical flexibility and a clearer notion of the internal class dynamics of imperialist exploitation. In the past the anti-imperialist agenda was in part influenced by the priorities of the external "allies."

Today anti-imperialist priorities are determined internally, and international actions are based on open consultations. Finally, the leadership of the modern AIM are much more prone to direct action and sustained class struggles linked to anti-imperialism and less to big symbolic demonstrations. Social forums, whether global, regional or national, are meeting places for movements and others to exchange ideas, but they do not provide leadership or programs; nor do they provide resources for the daily anti-imperialist struggles within the nation-states.

Some Unsettled Theoretical Issues

The key to the modern AIMs is found in their theoretical analysis that locates the central contradiction as between classes and not states. The new AIMs link class exploitation to imperialist plunder, unlike in the past where the conflicts were perceived as the conflicts of blocs, such as socialist versus capitalist states, or Third World versus First World. The new AIMs clearly see that internal class differences and inequalities are linked to, and reinforced by, the coalition of imperial MNCs and states. Imperial penetration of the nation-state, particularly of its cupola, and regime and financial hierarchies means that imperialist classes and local collaborator classes are the initial point of conflict between capital and labour. In other words, imperialism does not merely influence and control national economic, cultural and political structures, but it also operates at the macro and micro political and socio-economic levels. The result is that anti-imperialism is expressed at both the national level, in the form of major demonstrations in the principal cities, and at the municipal/village level. Moreover, the different anti-imperial movements frequently become interconnected and escalate upward from the local to the national, and vice versa.

For example, in Bolivia, in the Chapare region and in Cochabamba, major anti-imperialist struggles took place at the micro city/country level. In the case of Cochabamba, it was over the privatization of water to a foreign company, and in Chapare it was over the US policy of coca eradication. These local struggles were linked to larger struggles against the imposition of neo-liberal policies, which undermined local agricultural and manufacturing employment and public sector financing, and in turn led to movements against ALCA, the IMF and US imperialism.

The key to the modern AIM is the direct link between macro-imperialist policies and their sectoral and local class impacts, which serve to raise worker and peasant consciousness from the level of simple economic demands to that of national political struggle. For example, the structural adjustment policies imposed by Euro-US financial institutions on the Peruvian and Argentine economies led to massive layoffs and salary reductions of public employees, particularly teachers and health workers. This led to massive public demonstrations for pay raises and attacks against the regime implementing the SAPs, the IFIs dictating the policies, US imperial policymakers and bankers benefiting from interest payments secured through state surpluses.

The biggest and most widespread protests against US imperialism are linked to the wide range of classes affected by the macroeconomic policies of US imperialism and the specific classes and public sectors affected by SAPs, "free trade" doctrines and the imperial decision-makers who impose these policies.

The high visibility of imperial policymakers, their clear identity with the imperial state, and the direct and sustained negative impact of imperial economic policies provide the mass of exploited classes a very clear target for their opposition and mobilization. It does not take great effort for the popular classes to identify the sources of their adversity when the IMF dictates a SAP that results in lower public funding, loss of public employment, termination of clinics in the barrios, overcrowded classrooms, teachers' strikes and children begging in the street. AIMs are no longer middle-class nationalist movements; they are class-based because imperialism is embedded in everyday work and household survival.

Anti-imperialist Movements and Regimes

Notwithstanding the triumphalist rhetoric from the US, the UK and Israel after the military invasion and occupation of Afghanistan and Iraq, anti-imperialist movements are gaining ground on several fronts. In Afghanistan the anti-colonial movement is regrouping and has launched several attacks, particularly against the civilian agencies of the colonial occupation. Even more striking, the Iraqi resistance movement has inflicted daily causalities on the Anglo-US occupation forces. Massive civilian protests and the daily hostility of millions of Iraqis have severely eroded the morale of ordinary soldiers of the occupation and forced the US government to beat a strategic retreat in the form of returning sovereignty back to the Iraqis. Israeli efforts, backed by US Zionists in Washington, to spread the Mideast war to Iran, Syria and Lebanon, and to provoke a renewal of the war against the Palestinians, is heightening anti-imperialist activity and raising consciousness throughout the Middle East. But it is in Latin America where the intersection of US imperial expansion and rising popular discontent with declining living standards is the most intense. After years of negative growth (1999–2005) and massive transfers of wealth to the US and Europe, Latin America represents the clearest symbol and most substantive illustration of the evils of the empire.

In order to analyze anti-imperialist movements, it is important to distinguish between anti-imperialist events and ongoing organized struggles and movements. For example, the anti-ACLA referendum in Brazil in July 2002 involved a coalition of movements, progressive church groups and leftist parties. Eleven million people voted in the referendum, making it an important event that highlighted the active opposition to US colonial pretensions. The referendum was a coming together of social forces at a specific moment in time. Similar but more amorphous events were the "World Social Forums" that met, approved resolutions and then disbanded or returned to organize national social forums. In contrast, the organizations of the *cocaleros* in Bolivia are in a continuous struggle against the policies, institutions and agencies of US imperialism deeply implicated in directing the country's agrarian policies and controlling the executive and military branches of government. In discussing anti-imperialism it is important to focus on the sustained movements and not merely on a recitation of international events that have received the bulk of the publicity but have had less effect on changing imperial rule.

The anti-imperialist movements in Latin America have developed unequally. One can identify three levels: (1) sustained large-scale movements; (2) movements that are large but not sustained over time; and (3) movements that are sporadic and of lesser dimensions. We can also distinguish between movements that are consistently anti-imperialist and those that combine anti-imperialism with conciliation with imperialism.

Sustained, Large-scale Movements

It has been argued by Amartya Sen, the first non-neo-liberal economist to win the Nobel Prize, and others, that electoral regimes (termed "democracies") generate greater equity, development and political stability than dictatorships. This argument is fallacious for several reasons. Despite having elections, many of the key socio-economic decisions of electoral regimes are made by non-elected foreign and domestic elites and have resulted in greater inequalities, declining living standards and negative or regressive growth. The four countries where anti-imperialist movements are strongest are all electoral regimes and all are economic vassals of the US who have been pursuing empire-centred policies since the 1980s.

The longest standing electoral regime, Colombia, has been under quasimartial law over the past half-century and receives the greatest amount of US military aid, advisors and contract foreign mercenary forces in Latin America. Colombia is also the site of the biggest, most combative and sustained anti-imperialist movement in Latin America. It includes two popularly based nationwide guerrilla armies and significant social movements. In Colombia the guerrillas are the most important component of the anti-imperialist movement. The Revolutionary Armed Forces of Colombia (FARC) number approximately twenty thousand combatants and almost ten thousand active supporters among their urban militias, commandos and rural support units, covering over half the municipalities of the country. The National Liberation Army (ELN) has approximately 4,500 combatants and probably another five thousand civilian sympathizers in the cities and specific provinces. The regime's military and para-military death squads have over the years decimated the legal civilian anti-imperialist movements. Over 250 trade union leaders were assassi-nated between 2002 and August of 2003, by far the highest figures in the world.

In contrast to anti-imperialist movements elsewhere, FARC is directed at overthrowing the vassal regime and taking state power to end imperial-ist control over the economy, military and state. They have a comprehen-sive multi-sectoral program that includes opposition to ALCA but extends to opposition to foreign ownership of natural resources and finances, payment of foreign debt and the US strategic Plan Colombia.

If socio-economic conditions in Colombia are similar to those in the rest of Latin America, what accounts for the growth of a revolutionary anti-imperialist movement in Colombia and less so in the rest of Latin America? We can hypothesize several factors. The highly repressive Co-lombian political system physically eliminates political critics of imperi-alism, such as the Patriotic Union, the electoral movement in the 1980s that suffered five thousand deaths at the hands of the regime and its paramilitary allies. There is a long tradition of popular armed rural resist-ance to centralized control by a government with ties to local landlords and narco-traffickers. Finally, the organization of the rural-based guerrilla movement and its leadership headed by Manuel Marulanda, who have close ties to the peasantry, with 65 percent of the guerrilla fighters coming from the countryside, have retained independence from urban reformists and electoral parties. The long-term presence of US counter-insurgency forces and their tactics of mass displacements of peasants, eradication of lucrative crops of family farmers and alliance with Colombian military/paramilitary forces and key landholders has radicalized the countryside. The overdetermined role of the US in military strategy and intervention for over forty years, the historic traditions of rural insurgency linked to rural leaders and the lack of democratic space have been key elements fostering the most powerful anti-imperialist movement in Latin America.

The second most important mass anti-imperialist movement is found in Bolivia. Once again, large-scale and long-term US military, political and financial intervention, US support of military regimes and coups, crop eradication and mine closures have produced a deep-seated and widespread anti-imperialist consciousness. From the US intervention in the post-1952 nationalist revolution, to the promotion of pro-US military juntas in the 1960s, 1970s and 1980s, to the closure of the tin mines, and to the massive and violent coca eradication campaign of the past twenty years, US policy and direct intervention in Bolivian politics has had a long and large-scale negative impact on urban miners, manufacturing workers (via "free trade" doctrines) and peasants. The second factor is the long tradition of anti-imperialist revolution and struggle, from the 1952 revolution and formation of worker militias, to the mass-based popular assembly of 1970–71, to the history of repeated general strikes, to the present massive road blockages by militant peasant groups, to the popular rural-urban uprising of February 2003 against US-IMF policies, Bolivian popular movements demonstrate a capacity for sustained struggle. The third factor is the mass-based political and social leadership of the coca farmers and their disciplined and democratic social movements and syndicates. The popular leader Evo Morales has combined rural-based direct action with urban electoral politics to build a nationwide anti-imperialist movement that links local demands to end US-directed coca eradication to opposition to ALCA. In Bolivia the anti-imperialist struggle has popular support based on the links to daily household and work survival.

In Argentina, Brazil and Ecuador there are large anti-imperialist movements that combine a conscious rejection of IMF and empire-centred development policies with mass events protesting foreign debt payments, ALCA and other manifestations of imperial power. These movements, however, are not linked to a project for political power and lack a unified political leadership and organization. Nevertheless, they have demonstrated a capacity to oust incumbent regimes (in Argentina and Ecuador) and to register mass opposition to ALCA (the referendum of eleven million in Brazil in 2002). In the rest of Latin America there is widespread opposition to ALCA, empire-centred neo-liberal policies, Plan Colombia and more specifically pro-imperialist regime initiatives like the privatization program of Toledo in Peru, which ignited national mass protests.

In addition to the anti-imperialist movements, there are two governments that oppose or are partially independent of imperialism: Cuba and Venezuela. Cuba has been in the frontlines, fighting imperialism from southern Africa to Latin America and beyond. Unlike other leftist and nationalist regimes in the past, such as those of Salvador Allende in Chile (1973), Joao Goulart in Brazil (1964) and several others, Cuba's revolutionary regime has successfully defeated US efforts to overthrow it. Unlike leaders of other ex-leftist and ex-nationalist regimes such as the Socialists in Chile, the Peronists in Argentina and the Workers' Party in Brazil, Fidel Castro has refused to retreat to pro-imperialist politics.

What accounts for Cuba's long-term trajectory as an anti-imperialist country in the face of the overthrow or decay of other leftist regimes? Basically there are several factors, both internal and external. First, the Cuban regime is the product of a revolutionary process and leadership that destroyed the old state apparatus and has successfully built a sophisticated homeland security organization to neutralize terrorists and saboteurs. Second, Cuba has large, professional and highly motivated armed forces closely linked to the mass of people, subordinated to the revolutionary leadership and capable of defending Cuba from a frontal invasion from the US (in simulated "war games" the Pentagon has estimated US casualties in the tens of thousands from a ground invasion of Cuba). Third, the original Cuban revolutionary leadership has been successful in reproducing a new generation of revolutionary cadres and technicians who, assuming the reins of power, defend the original social gains of the revolution. Fourth, the great majority of Cuban workers and farmers are significantly better off than their counterparts in Latin America and retain social welfare benefits that are not available to Cuban exiles in the US. Fifth, the Cuban leadership was successful in securing favourable trade, military and economic agreements with the USSR and China in order to resist US military attacks and economic embargoes. Subsequently the Cuban leadership was successful in restructuring its economy in the post-Soviet period and developing trade and economic relations with Europe, Asia and Latin America. More recently it has developed mutually beneficial ties with Venezuela, securing strategic energy sources. Finally, the US policy of unremitting hostility and military threats has undermined any groups in Cuba oriented toward conciliating with imperialism. In other words, for Cuba, anti-imperialism is a necessity as well as an ideal.

Venezuela under President Hugo Chavez presents a more ambiguous picture, similar to those of past Latin American nationalists. He pursues an independent foreign policy, opposing imperialist wars such as the invasion of Iraq and counter-insurgency programs like Plan Colombia, promoting solidarity and fraternal relations with Cuba and criticizing ALCA. In domestic policy, however, he has followed a neo-liberal policy, privatizing public firms, offering oil concessions to American MNCs, paying the foreign debt and following fairly orthodox monetary and budgetary policies. The key to Venezuela's ambiguous or contradictory policies is found in the process by which Chavez came to power, the class alliances and programs which he envisions in ruling the country and his liberal view of the political and social structure of the country. Chavez formed alliances with a broad array of social and political forces, and his majority included a substantial number of neo-liberal and pro-imperialist groups and personalities, who subsequently defected toward the coup-oriented opposition. Unlike Cuba, Chavez has not organized a coherent mass socio-political movement to support his regime. The outpouring of mass popular support reinstating him to power following a coup attempt was mostly spontaneous. It is only after three years into his term of office that a pro-Chavez trade union federation was being organized and neighbourhood organizing via "Bolivarian Circles" was taking place. Chavez still depends on "institutional" military officers and their personal loyalties to defend his regime. Most of these officers have not been part of any social revolutionary experience, save opposition to two US-orchestrated coup attempts. Chavez's ideology has never called into question class-based inequalities or the property and wealth of the upper classes. His reforms build around these obstacles to social justice. Given this complex situation of a political economy of the right, a public administration of dubious loyalty and competence, and a foreign policy of national independence, the limits of Chavez's anti-imperialism becomes clear: it is political, not economic; it tolerates a pro-imperialist bourgeoisie and American MNCs in strategic sectors of the economy and mobilizes the radicalized urban poor, who are more consequentially anti-imperialist in relation to ownership and control of the domestic economy.

The anti-imperialist movements and states have built large numbers of politically conscious supporters, who are activated for local, national and international struggles. All the successful movements and regimes have developed powerful leaders who have had long-term links to mass struggle. More important, the biggest and most successful movements have grown in direct conflict with the US. In Cuba, Colombia, Bolivia and Venezuela, failed armed interventions or military coups have radicalized mass supporters. Equally significant, these anti-imperialist movements are fundamentally class movements, not simply made up of an amorphous multitude. The mass bases of the guerrillas in Colombia are the peasants; the urban anti-imperialist movements are based on salaried and wage workers. In Cuba the mass of wage workers and peasants, and in Venezuela the urban poor, are the base of the modern AIM. What is striking is the absence of any significant sector of the bourgeoisie, despite the fact that imperial control of markets, credit and state policy has prejudiced many groups to the point of bankruptcy. The pivotal groups in Colombia, Brazil, Argentina and Peru are the public employees who have been hammered by empire-dictated budget cuts. In the case of Venezuela, Paraguay and Mexico, the public sector employees have been divided; significant sectors who owe their jobs to political patronage have sided with their pro-imperialist party patrons.

The popular class base of the anti-imperialist movements has influenced the direct action tactics of the movements and has been engaged because of the use of those tactics.

Tactics and Strategies of Modern Anti-imperialist Movements

The growth and extension of modern AIMs to all parts of the world is a result in part of the success of "direct-action" politics, which in turn is a response to the failures and betrayals of ex-leftist electoral parties. To understand the direct action politics of the AIMs, it is important to place it in context. Two factors stand out: the increasing aggressiveness of US and European imperialism, in both their economic and military faces, and the active collaboration of the traditional social democratic and ex-Communist parties and trade unions with regimes engaged in imperial conquests. In the case of US imperialism, the absence of any significant electoral or trade union alternative forces opposition into the street.

The approaches of modern AIMs in the US and Europe differ substantially from the AIMs in Latin America, even though there are points of similarity and a convergence of activists. In the US and Europe the major tactic and focus of organization is the "big event," like Seattle, Genoa, Davos or Barcelona, where huge numbers of NGOs, trade unions and anti-globalization groups converged to protest against meetings of the imperial powers, such as the WTO or G-8. These events demonstrate the scope and depth of popular opposition to imperialist policies, educate the "passive public" and force imperial rulers, particularly in Europe, to become more circumspect in their support of US plans for world conquest. These mobilizations also provide a means for the AIMs to exchange ideas, coordinate future activities and create networks of solidarity against repression, particularly in Latin America.

In Latin America the major focus of the AIMs is on the day-to-day struggles against imperialism: mobilizations against recurring privatizations, the countless series of SAP and IMF austerity programs and demands on debt payments, and the deep penetration of the US military in counter-insurgency, crop eradication programs and orchestrated coup attempts. While these confrontations receive far less publicity than the "big events" of the northern countries, they involve more workers and peasants and have generated concrete results in blocking privatization, sustaining struggles and educating the local population. Big events, like the World Social Forum (WSF) and its national and municipal offspring, do take place in Latin America. They serve an educational function but have more of a symbolic or inspirational impact on the participants than any direct impact on imperial conquests. In fact, over time the WSF has evolved from being a critic of imperialism into a much more ambiguous enterprise, especially as one of its key sponsors, the Workers' Party of Brazil, has become a pro-imperialist party.

There are more profound differences between the tactic of "big events" in the North and the sustained popular struggles in Latin America. Northern movements are a mixture of progressive reformers of imperialism, anti-capitalist radicals and chauvinist protectionist trade unionists, which makes on-going activity and mobilizations difficult. Moreover, the "big events," though creating scattered street barricades, a few broken windows and burnt garbage dumpsters, have had little sustained impact on the political structures or daily economic activities of the imperial powers, even those of the countries in which these events have taken place.

In Latin America, AIM movements have paralyzed nationwide transport and economic activity with sustained mass street blockages, takeovers of public buildings and general strikes against privatization. These actions have forced regimes to withdraw privatization decrees, limit US eradication programs, counter US military intervention and defeat US organized military coups. In short, the tactics of the Latin American AIMs are far more political than social, more anti-capitalist than reformist and more tuned to power than to symbolic protests, and they provide guidance through the practice of political leaders rather than the public lectures of overseas notables.

The profound disjuncture between the anti-imperialist struggle of the FARC, the *cocaleros* and the Venezuelan masses and the movements in the North is evident in the abundant media publicity and solidarity that the latter receives and the minimum attention and solidarity of the former. When sixty Bolivian anti-imperialist activists were killed between January and February 2003 there was hardly an outcry from northern NGOs, trade unions or progressive intellectuals, but when one Italian activist was killed in Genoa, there was a global outcry and calls for a parliamentary inquiry, and he became a reference point for the northern movement. In short, despite its claims of being "internationalist," modern AIMs still reflect profound differences in their degree of reciprocal solidarity.

The tactical differences reflect the contrasting strategic goals of the AIMs in the North and Latin America. The bulk of the northern movement (the NGOs in particular) is profoundly reformist; they attack "speculative capital," war preparations or the excesses of the MNCs, and they call for the Tobin tax and codes of conduct for the MNCs, and support UN resolutions against the wars. In Latin America the AIMs struggle to transform the capitalist system, replace the power holders and express solidarity with the colonized people of the Third World.

More significantly there are deep political differences between northern and Latin American intellectuals concerning imperialist intervention and solidarity with Cuba. US and European "progressive" intellectuals (Noam Chomsky, Susan Sontag, Immanuel Wallerstein and Howard Zinn among others, even Domingo Saramiento) condemned Cuba's arrest of US-financed agents posing as dissidents and the application of capital punishment to terrorists who had pirated a Cuban vessel and threatened the lives of its passengers.[1] In Latin America the great majority of anti-imperialist intellectuals and movements declared their solidarity with Cuba, recognizing the US funding and control of the "dissidents."

The ambiguities and inconsistencies among northern intellectuals and NGO anti-imperialists may be partly explained by the powerful media, peer and government pressure to label Latin American anti-imperialists as "terrorists," "authoritarians" or "narco-traffickers." Northern progressive intellectuals temper their criticism of imperialism with condemnation of Latin American anti-imperialists who don't fit their preconceived model of opposition. This policy of making moral equivalences reaches its lowest point in the US colonial war against Iraq, where the leading intellectual critics of the US war refused to support the Iraqi anti-colonial resistance either during the invasion or in the post-Saddam Hussein period.

Despite a lot of internationalist and solidarity rhetoric, the northern opposition (particularly in the US) has a murky record: many sectors supported the US invasion of Yugoslavia and Afghanistan, many criticized the US invasion of Iraq but equally condemned the Iraqi resistance; and most criticize ALCA, while also criticizing the leading regimes opposing it in Latin America, namely Cuba and Venezuela.

In Latin America almost all the major AIMs, leaders and leading intellectuals support the Cuban revolution and publicly express their solidarity in most of the mass mobilizations against imperially organized coups, ALCA and other acts of imperial conquest.

Behind the differing attitudes toward Cuba is a more profound strategic difference — the movements and intellectuals in the US are still mostly tied to the pro-imperial institutions of civil society (the "left wing" of the Democratic Party, or the AFL-CIO, a pro-imperial, pro-coup trade union confederation) and have always drawn back from supporting successful social revolutions in Latin America. The lack of common vision demonstrates the limits of any strategic alliance between US and Latin American AIMs.

Reflections on the AIMs

Most AIM supporters in the US are middle-class professionals, students or NGO affiliates. The great majority of AIM supporters in Latin America are workers, urban poor, peasants, public employees or lower-middle-class students from the provinces. The movements in the US are strongly tied to ecology movements, protectionist trade unions and peace and progressive citizens movements. In the US, imperialism is seen negatively because of its effects on the environment and civil liberties, loss of jobs, immoral overseas interventions and deceptions, and its degradation of democratic politics in the US. In Latin America the AIMs are based on the direct negative impacts on living standards, jobs and agricultural production and control over economic policy.

The connection between imperialism and repressive states and paramilitary organizations is a key point of confrontation in Latin America. The result is a far deeper and more comprehensive anti-imperialist consciousness that crosses the "sectoral divides" found in the US and European AIMs. The point is that class relations and different locations in the class structure in Europe, the US and Latin America have a direct impact on the emergence of different levels of anti-imperialist consciousness. The uneven impact of imperialist politics — its direct impact on the lives of Latin Americans and its indirect effects in the US and Europe — has resulted in an uneven development of militant action, scope and sustainability. Religious and secular AIMs in the Third World converge in their opposition to US dominance but diverge in their strategic goals, particularly in the Middle East.

The emergence of AIMs on a world scale, despite their fluctuations in the US and Europe and their repression in the Middle East and Latin America, demonstrates the vulnerabilities of US and European imperialism. Besides being part of the drive to impose colonial rule, the transformation of NATO into a colonial occupation army and the rapid development of imperial armed forces are largely a response to the new anti-imperialist resistance.

In Latin America, the class configurations of the new AIMs, their pre-eminent popular character and linkage to resistance against overt colonial rule (whether in Afghanistan and Iraq, or via ALCA) ensure that these struggles are not likely to be betrayed by defecting bourgeois nationalists. In other words, the class forces involved are those most likely to be prejudiced by the abandonment of the anti-imperialist struggle. The inherent class interests embedded in the movements provide a basis for sustained struggles. The vulnerability of imperialism is clearly evident in the series of tactical defeats: the reversal of the Venezuelan coup of April 2002; the regrouping of anti-colonial resistance in Afghanistan; the anti-colonial guerrilla resistance in Iraq; the failure of Plan Colombia to defeat the FARC, ELN or civic movements; and the growing continental resistance to ALCA. Imperial rule is based on class relations. As resistance grows in the Third World, and the human and economic costs grow in the US and Europe, they will engender political and social conflicts within and among the imperial powers of the US and Europe, and in the not-too-distant future could result in a unified challenge to imperial power.

8. DYNAMICS OF INTER-IMPERIALIST RIVALRY

In the aftermath of World War II, Europe was ideologically divided and economically devastated. The US was an economic superpower, accounting for close to 50 percent of the world's industrial production and up to 80 percent of global capital reserves (Maizels 1970). It was also a hegemon, dominating the world capitalist system set up in 1944 at Bretton Woods. In the context of an emerging east-west ideological conflict and a "cold war" with the USSR, whose industrial capacity and socialist system constituted a major strategic threat to "the cause of freedom" (capitalist democracy), the US embarked on a strategy of worldwide capitalist development. Its strategy was predicated on a program of economic recovery, reconstruction and development, above all in Western Europe, but also in Japan and, for ideological reasons (to prevent the inroads of a socialist alternative), in Taiwan, South Korea and the economically backward countries of the "Third World," especially those recently liberated from the yoke of European colonialism and prey to the lure of communism.

By 1961 the capitalist democracies of North America, Western Europe and Japan were well into what historians have termed "the golden age of capitalism" and formed an Organisation for Economic Co-operation and Development (the OECD) to advance the process. One of several ironies in these developments was that they were led by Germany and Japan, former enemies of the US and its allies, who are now major challengers to US economic power and serious competitors in world trade. By 1960, Germany and Japan together accounted for only 6.3 percent of world trade, but by 1970, after a decade of unprecedented growth and export expansion, their share of world trade had increased to 18.8 percent (Table 8.1). Over the same period the US share of world trade fell from 20 percent to 15 percent, a situation reflected by a rapidly growing deficit on its national trade account. By 1971 this deficit had assumed such proportions as to unleash various efforts by the US government to reverse the growing trade imbalance and offset related trends of sluggish productivity growth, falling profits and economic stagnation.

There were various dimensions to the system-wide crisis of world capitalism in the late 1960s and early 1970s. By most accounts it was a

Table 8.1 Shares of World Export Trade: Percentage of World Trade by Value of Exports, 1951–2003

	1951	1960	1970	1980	1993	2000	2003
United States	20.0	18.0	15.0	12.0	12.3	12.3	9.7
Germany	4.5	9.9	12.0	10.5	10.1	8.7	6.9
Japan	1.8	3.6	6.8	7.0	9.6	7.5	6.6
Asia (without Japan)	9.0	7.0	5.0	6.5	-	19.9	20.6
Latin America	8.0	6.0	4.7	4.4	-	5.6	5.0

Source: Created with data from IMF (1981, 2004, 2005).

crisis of overproduction (producing too many goods for the market to absorb, i.e., lack of purchasing power). According to Robert Brenner (1998), an economic historian who has extensively studied the dynamics of global capitalist development in the post-war period, the most critical factor remains inter-imperialist rivalry and world market competition. This competition, particularly between the US, Germany and Japan, creates downward pressure on prices and thus profits, pushing the whole system, which is geared to private profit, into crisis.

As Brenner constructs it, the period from the 1960s to today can best be understood in terms of the dynamics of this inter-imperialist rivalry, and the quest for economic dominance and political domination (imperialism). In the 1970s the major contending economic powers were the US, Japan and Germany, each of which constituted a growth pole for economic development, the US in North America, Japan in Asia, and Germany in Western Europe. By 1965 the economic rivalry among these countries had unleashed a process of cutthroat competition, saturating the world market with manufactured products and threatening to destabilize the whole system. By the early 1970s a crisis of overproduction, brought on in part by this inter-imperialist competition, sent the whole system into a spin, putting an end to twenty-five years of rapid economic growth and capitalist development and giving rise to an equally long downturn. Table 8.2 provides a schematic overview of this process, from the long upturn (1950—73) to the onset of crisis (1968—73) and the long downturn (1974—93).

The problems of overproduction/underconsumption generated by economic competition among the US, Japan and Germany for export markets led to a wide-ranging search for a strategic response that would prevent the collapse of the system and show a way out of the global crisis. One response involved the US Council for Foreign Relations (CFR) and an offshoot policy forum, the Trilateral Commission, founded by David Rockefeller, chair of the Chase Manhattan Bank, and Zbignew Brzezinski, national security advisor to President Jimmy Carter. The trilateralist

Table 8.2 The Long Upturn and Downturn, 1950–93 (annual change, percent growth)

	Output (GDP)		Labour Productivity	
	1950–73	1973–93	1950–73	1973–93
US	4.2	2.6	2.7	1.1
Germany	4.5	2.2	4.6	2.2
Japan	9.1	4.1	5.6	3.1
G-7	4.5	2.2	3.6	1.3

Source: Elaborated by Brenner (1998: 5) from diverse sources.

solution to inter-imperialist competition and systemic rivalry was what might be termed "international liberalism" — collective management of the world economy in the shared interest to preserve the system as a whole.

That was then and this is now. In the 1970s and 1980s, the structure of world trade was reconfigured into a new international division of labour that brought about a new growth pole in the global economy: a group of newly industrialized countries (NICs), all but one (Brazil) in East Asia (Hong Kong, Singapore, Taiwan and South Korea); and a second generation of NICs (Thailand, Malaysia, Indonesia, Vietnam), which, in pursuit of Japan's lead (and sparked by its economic progress), formed a "flying geese pattern" of rapid, export-oriented growth. In 1970 this group of eight "rapidly growing countries" in Asia accounted for 6 percent of world trade (Table 8.1); by the mid-1990s their share of world trade had doubled, while the US's share was reduced from 20 percent to 15 percent and Latin America's share over the same period rose marginally from 4.7 percent to 5.0 percent.

In the 1990s the "Asian Miracle" stalled, and Japan's lead began to sag and fell into a decade of virtually no growth. In this new world situation, within the macroeconomic policy framework of a "new world order" (neo-liberalism), the picture had radically changed. System-wide economic and productivity growth still lagged behind the 1950s and 1960s, but the US economy had recovered some of its former dynamism, as had Western Europe. Both Latin America and Sub-Saharan Africa had undergone a process of radical policy reform and experienced a "decade lost to development" (no economic growth). But the most significant change in the world economy — apart from the collapse of the socialist bloc and the Comintern, and the sweeping change in its underlying structure (globalization) — was the consolidation of the European Union and the emergence of a new economic power centre (China). Together the EU and China command the world's largest trading bloc and emerging market, accounting for a third of global production and 50 percent of world trade.

EU and China trade had doubled in just four years (from 1999 to 2003), and now China is second only to the US in exports to the EU and constitutes Europe's third largest export market. This situation is a serious challenge to the US imperialist ambition and drive for world domination, particularly if and when Europe and China come to a strategic understanding and mutual agreement. It is likely that a high-level strategic agreement along these lines will be reached by Chinese and European authorities soon. Such agreement might very well augur a new round of inter-imperialist rivalry and new forms of superpower politics within the US.

A united Europe represents a challenge to the US and a threat to its plan for world domination *from within*; China represents a challenge from without. The dynamics of the challenge from a united Europe are explored in this chapter. The dynamics of China's challenge to US imperialism are explored in the next, as is the significance of recent developments (capitalist transformation) in Russia. China, according to one analyst (Mearsheimer 2002), is becoming the most "formidable rival" to the US; a "rising China," he argues, "is the most dangerous potential threat to the United States in the early 21st Century." However, at least one other analyst (Rogoff 2004) argues that both the US and China should watch their backs. In the rising tide of Europe's "quiet leap forward," a new economic juggernaut is in the making that may very well come to dominate the twenty-first century.

The Dynamics of Inter-capitalist Competition

Fuelled by unprecedented rates of economic growth and the expansion of domestic markets in the capitalist world, the post-war period from 1948 to 1973 witnessed the restoration of international trade to pre-1930 depression levels. Most economies within the world capitalist system, particularly those that made up what in 1961 became the Organisation for Economic Co-operation and Development (OECD), participated in this growth of production and trade, and did so though the overseas global operations of multinational capitalist corporations, the major operating units of the system. In the 1970s, however, the system began to fall apart, with the onset of a system-wide production crisis that was reflected in a slowdown in productivity growth and growth of national and global production, and a profit crunch on invested capital.

The cause of the crisis has been hotly debated, generating diverse schools of thought and theories. In retrospect, if not in theory, it would seem that there is no single cause for the crisis but instead a combination of diverse factors: a built-in tendency for the average rate of profits to fall; limits to technological conversion or mode of labour regulation; pressures on capital exerted by a powerful working class demanding higher wages and improved working conditions; saturation of markets for manufactured goods; and pressures deriving from intra-capitalist competition.

Each of these presumed contributing factors to systemic crisis gave rise to actions or policies designed to offset the crisis. Capitalists launched a counter-offensive against labour, seeking to reduce labour's share of national income and thereby increase the pool of capital available for productive investment (Crouch and Pizzorno 1978). The MNCs relocated production overseas, closer to sources of cheap labour (Fröbel, Heinrichs and Kreye 1980). Some industrial capitalists turned towards new technologies and mode of labour regulation (Lipietz 1982 and 1987). On the advice of the Trilateral Commission, the big commercial and investment banks expanded operations overseas in the developing countries, particularly in Latin America, aiming to find more profitable outlets for their surplus capital and, via the extension of credit (debt financing), to open up new markets for excess industrial production, thus relieving overproduction pressures on producers in the OECD.

The major concern for the US was the competitive pressure on its industrial production from Germany and Japan, defeated enemies, but at that point (1971) rapidly winning the battle for the world market. At the end of World War II the US was hegemonic, accounting for over 50 percent of world industrial production and trade, and up to 80 percent of development finance and productive investment. However, after two decades or so of rapid capitalist development — the so-called "golden age of capitalism," according to historians (dubbed the "thirty glorious years" in France) — the US was running a substantial deficit on its international trade account and US-based MNCs were losing markets to their competitors, particularly Germany and Japan. Table 8.3 provides a schematic overview of this process.

The decline of the combined trade balance with Germany and Japan was the dynamic factor determining the collapse of the US trade balance. Between 1960 and 1964, merchandise imports had increased by 27 percent and exports by 29.7 percent; and between 1964 and 1971, imports grew by 144 percent and exports by 66.5 percent (Brenner 1998: 119). By 1966 the trade balance had already declined 50 percent with respect to its 1964

Table 8.3 US Trade Balance with Germany, Japan and the World, 1963–73 (US$ billion)

	1963	'64	'65	'66	'67	'68	'69	'70	'71	'72	'73
Germany	0.6	0.4	0.3	-0.1	-0.3	-1.0	-0.5	-1.6	-3.3	-3.9	-6.3
Japan	0.3	0.2	-0.5	-0.8	-0.3	-1.2	-1.6	-1.4	-3.3	-3.9	-1.3
Germany/Japan	0.9	0.6	0.2	-0.9	-0.6	-2.2	-2.1	-1.8	-4.1	-5.3	-2.9
World	5.2	6.8	4.9	3.8	3.8	0.6	0.6	2.6	-2.3	-6.4	0.9

Source: Elaborated by Brenner from various sources (1998: 119).

peak; by 1968, undercut by accelerating inflation, it had fallen to new post-war lows. In 1971 the US experienced its first trade deficit in the twentieth century, leading the government of Richard Nixon to unilaterally take the dollar off its fixed rate of exchange against gold, one of the pillars of the Bretton Woods system.

The US's merchandise trade balance went into the red by $2.7 billion in 1971, and by $7 billion the year after — down a spectacular $13.7 billion in the eight years from 1964 (see Table 8.4). These trade imbalances at the time were far too large to be counterbalanced by surpluses on trade in services and returns on foreign investment, although both of these would make a big jump in subsequent years. By 1971 the balance on the current account, including the flow in financial and business services, turned negative, by $1.4 billion. Table 8.4 indicates that in subsequent years this process has steadily advanced despite a massive growth in services and the rate-of-profit repatriation.

The first response of the Nixon government to these problems of foreign competition was to abandon the Bretton Woods fixed exchange regime, hoping via a currency realignment to lower the relative costs of US production and promote the export of industrial goods. As Aglietta (1982) has detailed, this initial response of the US state in backing up its MNCs was followed by a decade or more of diverse strategies and actions designed to offset competition from its rivals in Europe and Japan. By Aglietta's account, these diverse shifting strategies, through the manipulation of exchange and interest rates, the two macroeconomic variables under state control, did little to halt or reverse a systemic tendency towards crisis (sluggish growth in productivity and production) or change a slow but persistent trend towards a declining US share of global industrial production, reflected in a growing imbalance in the US trade account. Table 8.5 tells the tale, showing among other things that despite a sustained economic recovery from the mid-1980s to the mid-1990s, and an overall higher rate of export growth in the 1990s, the EU remains the

Table 8.4 Global Merchandise Trade Balance, 1995–2004 (billion US$)

	% GDP (2001)	'95	'96	'97	'98	'99	'00	'01	'02	'03
World	0.0	116	104	123	85	41	5	3	20	-23
EU	1.4	143	171	176	152	107	57	107	180	194
US	-4.3	-174	-189	-197	-249	-349	-458	-433	-484	-561
Japan	1.7	134	83	102	123	123	116	72	97	96
China	2.9	18	20	46	47	36	35	34	38	-
Latin Am.	-0.1	2	4	-15	-36	-8	5	-1	25	27

Source: World Bank 2004: A15, p. 194.

Table 8.5 Global Merchandise Total Exports (2001) and Export Growth, 1981–2003 (average annual growth in percent)

	Total Exports (2001) (trillion US$)	'81–90	'91–00	'97	'98	'99	'00	'01	'02	'03
World	6.02	6.4	6.8	4.1	-2.5	3.6	12.1	-3.8	4.3	13.7
EU	2.25	7.1	5.0	0.8	2.3	0.1	3.0	0.2	6.2	19.5
US	0.73	6.2	7.2	11.4	-1.1	2.3	12.6	-6.5	-3.9	7.3
Japan	0.38	8.1	5.0	2.4	-8.6	7.6	13.8	-16.1	1.7	7.1
NICs	0.44	13.2	9.2	3.0	-9.2	4.0	19.0	-11.0	4.9	10.6
China	0.27	11.8	17.1	20.9	0.5	6.1	27.9	6.8	20.4	-
Russia	0.10	1.0	9.5	-1.7	-15.9	1.0	39.5	-3.8	6.3	-
Latin America	0.35	5.4	10.1	11.1	-1.2	5.7	19.6	-3.6	0.8	5.8

Source: World Bank 2004: A13, p. 192.

dominant force in the global economy of production for export, accounting for over one-third of the world market. Although the US economy is larger than the EU's, its merchandise exports are dwarfed by those of the EU, being barely a sixth in total volume and value.

It is difficult to predict the long-term, or even short or mid-term, trend in these figures, given that they show a growth rate in European exports of 6.2 percent in 2002 and a phenomenal 19.5 percent in 2003, versus rates of -3.9 percent and 7.3 percent for the US. However, the figures for the first quarter of 2004 pointed in a different direction — 4.7 percent for the US but only 1.3 percent for the EU (euro area).

Economic Productivity and the Welfare State

Although it could not escape a propensity towards crisis, the US economy rebounded somewhat in the 1980s and sputtered haltingly towards a period of slow but persistent recovery in the 1990s. No doubt this development resulted from a combination of factors related to diverse restructuring strategies that were designed to reactivate the capital accumulation process.

One such factor was a restructuring of the relation of capital to labour within the US, which resulted in a decline of at least 10 percent in the value of wages from 1974 to 1984, and another 5 percent since, and a dramatic concentration of national income in the hands and banks of the corporate rich. Another response to crisis was a global restructuring of industry, which did not help in any way to balance the US merchandise trade account but did restore profitability to many American MNCs.

A technological conversion of industrial production in key sectors had a similar effect, as did the proceeds of economic imperialism facilitated by the new world economic order that liberated the forces of trade and finance. The system as a whole was still in crisis, caught up in sluggish productivity growth, but new poles of dynamic growth had emerged in certain industrial sectors and certain countries, particularly in East Asia, which dramatically increased its contribution to world trade. Industrial relocation, the expansion of world trade and the export of capital had also begun to show benefits (new markets, profitable returns), as did the projection of imperialist economic power via the battering down of the barriers to free trade and the unhindered global movement of capital.

There was also some improvement on the productivity front, although this seems to be more the result of a process of productive transformation (technological conversion) than of pressures on labour, which had to bear the brunt of the various restructuring strategies implemented by capital and the state. The evidence for this is provided by indications of a growing productivity gap between US and European capital — from 10 percent to 15 percent and up to 30 percent in some sectors. The technologies employed in these sectors are virtually the same in the US and Europe, so an explanation of the productivity gap is to be found elsewhere. According to research conducted by the Centro Studi Trasformazioni Economico-Sociali (CESTES) in Rome, and reviewed by Vasapollo (2003), it can be almost entirely explained in terms of the models of capitalism in Europe and the US, specifically the relative differences in worker welfare and conditions of work in the two locations. American workers work harder and longer — up to 360 hours a year longer — while many European workers, as in Germany and France, have achieved a 35-hour week, enjoy all sorts of benefits such as a four-to-six-week annual paid vacation, maternity and paternity leave, unemployment insurance and decent pensions, and generally command a significantly greater share of productivity gains than their American counterparts.

The productivity gap between American and European labour is essentially in the scope of the welfare state, which is to say that there is no productivity gap. Welfare always has been more advanced in Europe, with workers receiving, in addition to their paycheque, benefits (a social wage) that add about 30 percent to the remuneration of their labour.

This became so in the aftermath of the World War II, with the evolution of the welfare state. In addition, both the US and the UK have advanced much further than continental Europe in dismantling the welfare state and implementing deregulation and privatization. However, recent developments suggest that the situation of European workers may soon change, a result of inter-imperialist economic competition. Already workers in Germany's automotive industry (Daimler-Chrysler) have been forced in their negotiations with capital to accept a deal that calls for an increase in their work week from thirty-five to forty hours, the standard in the US (in the UK it is 37 hours), and a reduced wage rate (*Economist*, 31 July 2004: 51). Indications are that this deal, which Daimler-Chrysler workers were forced to concede as a condition of keeping their jobs (under the threat of moving them abroad), will become the wave of the near future. In the context of global competition, declares Gerhard Schroeder, Germany's chancellor, these and other such indications of "greater flexibility" on the part of organized labour are a "victory for common sense." The unions, understandably, see it as "blackmail," "terrorism" or the "revenge of the bosses," while an economist at the Bank of America calls it "pure capitalism" (ibid).

On the privatization front, continental Europe (particularly France and Germany) continues to lag behind the US and the UK, and behind recent developments in Latin America and in Eastern Europe (in countries undergoing a process of transition from socialism towards capitalism). However, the process of economic and political unification in Europe is generating pressures for further privatization, even though these pressures are being actively resisted by public sector workers (electrical workers in France, for example).

As for deregulation, the "apparent" lower productivity of European workers is blamed on the relative rigidity of labour markets in Europe. This rigidity, it is argued (by proponents of globalization and neo-liberalism), reflecting as it does the superior power and organizing/negotiating capacity of European labour, leads capital to withdraw from the production process, placing European capital at a distinct competitive disadvantage relative to US capital. Although the evidence for this is rather mixed, this argument nevertheless provides grist for the mill for proponents of a US-style capitalism based on greater freedom for management and flexibility on the part of workers — the victory of "common sense," to quote Schroeder.

This argument is also a factor in the ongoing offensive against the welfare state, not only in France and Germany but elsewhere in Europe. The decision of the Swedes not to join the euro zone is in good part related to their fear that European institutions provide a framework for increased pressures on the welfare state and a slow adjustment of European capital and the state to the form prevailing in the US. Membership in the EU would facilitate a final assault on the welfare state which has been under considerable pressure to adjust to the requirements of the new world order — to redress the problem of rigidities and the lack of freely functioning markets in key economic sectors. This assault on the welfare state is currently conducted under the pretext, if not the pressure, of global competition.

The Political Dynamics of European Union: The Attack on the Welfare State and the Erosion of Progressive Politics

If we look at Europe's recent history, we cannot but be struck by how much the unification process — from economic union to political unification to monetary union — has accelerated after the fall of the Berlin Wall and the dissolution of the USSR. For forty years the European capitalist establishment had functioned and acted within the borders of a common market approved and facilitated by the US. The class struggle, a strong workers' movement and the existence of the USSR forced European capitalism to adjust to and accept a program of social reforms, income distribution and international relations. An advanced welfare state system and the space created by a bipolar world allowed "Europe" to assume a somewhat progressive role as an East-West mediator and conciliator, as a more humane form of capitalism and as a geopolitical "equilibrating factor" at the level of international relations. In this connection, Tierry de Montbrial, an advocate of the old trilateralism, notes that, "Nowadays... the very concept of equilibrating factor has lost its meaning... weakened by the growth of the two blocs: NATO and the European Union" (2003).

The end of the balance of power between the US and the USSR had a major impact on Europe. On the one hand, it speeded up the process of economic, monetary and political "union" and centralization, awakening, at the same time, Europe's push for greater independence from US constraints on socio-economic and foreign policies. On the other hand, it seems to have not only increased the pressure on the welfare state (as a factor of economic competition) but also provoked a growing disillusionment with the idea of Europe as a progressive force in social reform and international politics. Behind this disillusionment, and at political issue here, is the construction of a European pole within the global economy and global imperialism. In the words of Romano Prodi, president of the European Commission, the idea of Europe means "a great power that can play a relevant role on the world's chessboard.... The Euro zone is a good starting point to stand up to the United States, which are, and will continue to be, the greatest competitors on the international markets" (1999).

However, for Europe to assume this role, there is no room for a welfare state or a more humane state-reformed capitalism à la Europe. Nevertheless, there is some room for various European governments within the union to manoeuvre on the global stage of politics and international relations, and to devise and use the institutions of European unity as instruments for advancing the singular economic and political interests of "Europe" and to contest the hegemony of the US over the imperialist system. The agenda of France and Germany vis-à-vis the construction of a non-NATO European military force can be viewed in this light, as can the pre-election announcement by George W. Bush of a redeployment of US troops out of Germany, with its anticipated negative economic impacts.

Prodi envisages a Euro-Mediterranean area in which high technologies coexist with reserves of cheap labour to be used to compete against the US-dominated NAFTA and against the Asian area in which China is emerging as a potential economic superpower (1999: 79). The concern behind this idea of Europe is the same as that which led to the creation of the United Nations after World War II. The concern then, as now, was to establish an institutional framework that would prevent a unilateral approach towards managing the global economy and inhibit, if not prevent, the impulse of any state towards world domination.

In the current context of an aggressive US state seeking world domination and hegemony over the system as a whole, this concern is reflected at two levels: (1) establish the institutional structure of a united Europe to constitute the world's largest economic union and trading bloc; and (2) strengthen rather than abolish the Bretton Woods system and to increase European representation and influence within these institutions and the broader system that includes the entire security and institutional apparatus of the UN — the Security Council, etc. (Young 2003).

The Conservative "Neo-liberal" Attack on the Welfare State

The idea of a progressive European Union has been battered from both right and left. On the socio-economic front, it is evident that the European establishment has opened up an offensive against the residues of the welfare state prosecuted by all manner of governments, regardless of ideological complexion. There is no "Blair politics," "Schroeder politics," etc. At issue in each form of politics (as well as in article 3 of the proposed European Constitution) is the same concern: how to deal with the questions of competitiveness and growth, and the prospect of global competition with the US.

Notwithstanding the evidence of dynamic growth in some sectors and emerging markets, the world economy overall has failed to respond to a major multi-faceted restructuring of the system and a heavy dose of neo-liberal medicine. System-wide productivity growth is still lagging and the rate of growth in world production has remained stagnant. Each year over the past decade the World Bank and the IMF forecast an economic recovery (see Table 8.6). Each year ended in sober recognition of a persistent trend towards stagnation and continuing crisis. A recent forecast is for a system-wide growth rate of 3 percent, following an average growth rate of 2.6 percent in the 1990s and 2.3 percent since 1998. The average rate of growth over the past two decades of globalization and neo-liberal "structural" reform was 2.7 percent (versus 5 percent in the 1950s and 1960s, and 3.5 percent in the 1970s in the throes of a system-wide economic crisis).

Thus the neo-liberal model has even failed to deliver on its fundamental promise of economic growth. And this is looking at the upside, without any consideration of the way the fruits of growth are socially distributed. On the downside of neo-liberalism is a drastic reduction in labour's share of national and world incomes — from close to 40 percent in the 1960s down to and below 20 percent in the 1990s — increasing polarization and social inequalities in the distribution of income and a deepening and extension of poverty.

According to the UNDP (1996), today just 358 individuals dispose of as much income as the 1.4 billion people at the bottom of the income hierarchy, in what Lewis (2004) terms "the lowlands" of the economic landscape. Over five billion people live in countries where the GDP per capita is 25 percent or less (for the majority, barely 10 percent) than it is in the US, a situation that has dramatically worsened after two decades of neo-liberal "reform," or structural adjustment. In 1970 the income ratio of the richest quintile of individuals and households to the bottom quintile was 32; by 1989 this ratio had doubled to 59 and by 1987, after fifteen years of neo-liberal "reform" and economic recovery at the centre of the system, the richest 20 percent received 74 times the income of the poorest. The world's richest one percent receive as much income as the poorest 57 percent and the income of the world's three richest individuals is greater than the combined GDP of all the least-developed countries. It is estimated by the World Bank, the institution with the major responsibility for structural adjustment, that under these conditions of global divide, over 1.4 billion people are forced to subsist on less than one dollar a day, which is to say, in conditions of extreme or abject poverty. The UNDP understandably classifies these and other such "facts" of market-generated income distribution as "grotesque," even though it fails to point its finger at the obvious cause.[1]

Over the course of two decades of structural adjustment and policy reform, the Anglo-American system of capitalism has burnt all its available reserves in the public sphere, privatizing all that could be privatized and making precarious all forms of employment that could be made precarious, pushing workers and their families into conditions of debt, unemployment, low income and poverty. The dysfunctionality of neo-liberalism as a model, and its failure to deliver either development or improved welfare, is now so glaringly obvious as to make it virtually impossible, from the viewpoint of labour, to complete the transition towards an Anglo-American type of capitalism in Europe — a transition that Europe's capitalist establishment deems necessary in the context of inter-imperialist competition.

Considering the resistance of the working class, the option available to Europe's capitalist establishment is to intensify class warfare, turning against the remaining vestiges of the welfare system — the health and social security systems, and the remaining corporations in the public sector; existing rigidities ("lack of flexibility") within the labour process and the labour market; and, above all, the social wage, in the form of benefits, annual four-to-six-week vacations, etc. — that make European capital uncompetitive with US capital.

Margaret Thatcher initiated the neo-conservative offensive against the welfare state. On the continent some time later the offensive against what remained of the welfare state was launched in France by the "right-wing" Jean-Pierre Raffarin, and in Germany by the "left-wing" Gerhard Schroeder. Behind these assaults was the fundamental concern that the European capitalist enterprise was losing ground to its competitors on the world market, particularly the US. For one thing, economic growth in the EU was weaker than forecast (see Table 8.6).[2] For another, productivity growth, and thus profitability, in the EU seemed to be losing ground relative to the US. While a number of analysts argued that US capital and labour in manufacturing exhibited levels of growth equal or superior to those of the US, studies by the neo-liberal Mckinsey Global Institute (Lewis 2004), using a purchasing power parity (PPP) as opposed to market exchange rate approach, showed that industry in the EU was losing ground to the US. In fact, according to Lewis, it still is. In each critical industrial sector, US productivity and productivity growth was higher than in the EU — up to 30 percent higher (Lewis 2004: 51).[3]

In the shadow of this debate on the relative productivity (and thus profitability) of the EU and US capitalist enterprises,[4] the competitiveness of Europe came under scrutiny as did the EU welfare system, seen as largely responsible for the problem. Another part of the problem was deemed to be government intervention in the economy — the excessive size and weight of the public sector — which created "distortions in the way markets would naturally work" (Lewis 2004: 56). These concerns led to another attack on the welfare system and the social wage, which via government programs, it was estimated, added up to a 10–15 percent greater cost to European labour relative to the US.[5] Privatization of the social security and health systems, it was argued, would help address these problems. It would "free" huge pools of public and private capital in support of global competition, reinforce the euro relative to the US dollar and help finance strategic projects such as the Galileo satellite system and the "European Army."

To generate financial resources for productive investment, it was necessary to reduce the weight of the public sector and change the structure of the labour-capital relation, reducing the share of workers and households in national income, transferring this income to that class of individuals with a greater propensity to invest their savings. At the moment labour in Europe still commands a respectable share of national income — somewhere between 30 percent and 40 percent — a share that, according to neo-liberal theorists, provides an inadequate pool of savings for productive investment. The relative rate of productive investment or capital formation is critical. It is higher in the US than the EU, but the

Table 8.6 Global Real GDP Growth, 1981–2003 (GDP in 1995 prices and exchange rates, average annual growth; percent)

	GDP (2001)	'81–90	'91–00	'97	'98	'99	'00	'01	'02	'03
World	33.9	3.0	2.6	3.4	2.1	2.9	3.9	1.2	1.7	2.3
EU	9.8	2.4	2.0	2.5	2.8	2.7	3.6	1.5	1.0	1.5
US	9.0	3.2	3.2	4.4	4.3	4.1	3.8	0.3	2.4	2.5
Japan	5.7	4.1	1.4	1.8	-1.2	0.2	2.8	0.3	-0.3	0.6
NICs	0.6	7.4	6.1	6.3	1.1	5.1	7.8	-1.4	2.8	3.3
China	1.1	9.3	10.1	8.8	7.8	7.0	8.0	7.3	8.0	-
Russia	0.4	1.5	-4.0	0.9	-4.9	5.4	9.0	5.0	4.1	-
Latin America	1.9	1.1	3.3	5.2	2.0	0.2	0.5	3.5	0.3	-0.9

Source: World Bank 2004: A8, p. 189.

average rate in both places cannot compare with the rate of investment in East Asia, particularly in China, where it has reached the extraordinary level of 44 percent of GDP. Lawrence Summers (2004) sees the low rate of national savings (and productive investment) as *the* fundamental problem of the US economy today.

According to Lewis (2004), their difference in the savings and investment rate explains the relatively superior performance of the US economy in the 1990s and the unprecedented growth rate of the Chinese economy — averaging 10 percent during the 1990s (Table 8.4). The purported engine of this growth is world trade, fuelled by exceedingly cheap labour, but this cheap labour reflects and is another facet of the increased concentration of national income in the form of a higher rates of savings and investment. In the case of China the exceedingly low cost of labour also reflects strong government control over development finance and sources of credit, allowing the government to stimulate a national savings rate that exceeds 40 percent and the productive investment of these savings. This government control over finance is undoubtedly a critical factor in the high rates of economic growth achieved by China. Thus the US economy has been outperforming the EU's precisely because of the excessive rigidity of European labour, protected as it is by unions and coddled by governments. Under these conditions, European workers work shorter hours (up to 360 hours a year less) than their American counterparts, and receive more benefits, such as a high minimum wage that is intended to aid income distribution, but, according to Lewis (2004: 56), provides a substantial "economic penalty relative to the US" and results in the high unemployment of low-skilled workers. Actually it is this difference in work per person rather than productivity that almost entirely explains the apparently superior performance of the US economy.[6] Thus, the better conditions experienced by European workers do not so much affect productivity as militate against rates of investment. Profits are constrained by these rates of investment, which in turn are constrained by the rate of national savings.

According to Lawrence Summers (2004: 47), treasury secretary in the second Clinton administration, the US government's "spending addiction" (foreign borrowing) and "savings crisis," reflected in a current account deficit that has reached a "startlingly large" 5 percent of GDP, is undermining the "virtuous economic cycle" that has for so long characterized the US economy. It means that the American engine of the global economy has begun to "run on fumes," with a potentially crippling effect on the country's global reach. The "national savings crisis" could also very well ignite trade wars and spell an end to policies of "globalization" that have been such a "boon to the US economy." The low level of national savings in the US relative to China and Asia, and its concomitant increased dependence on borrowing from abroad is putting at risk the entire US economy and the prosperity of its people. According to Summers, the US economy remains the most important "engine" of growth in the world economy, but "the world economy [cannot] fly forever on a single American engine" (2004: 47). Thus its position of dominance is being seriously challenged, a challenge which the US will ignore at its own peril if it wishes to maintain its global dominance.

With lagging production inside the EU, sluggish productivity growth and saturated or weak markets for European products, it would be a mistake — from a European perspective — for the EU to count on an "American recovery" to help its own economy. In fact, as is argued by Mario Deaglio and Robert Solow (Baily 2001), Europe cannot count on the possibility of an American economic recovery, which might even inhibit a European recovery. In any case, economic recovery in both Europe and the US will depend on emerging markets and developments elsewhere, particularly in China. Both the US and the EU will have to settle accounts with China.

What's the Matter with the Euro — and the Dollar?

From the beginning, the US government opposed the advent of the euro, as a currency that might replace the dollar as the fundamental means of exchange in the world economy. The idea of a European single market was accepted and indeed welcomed, but US policymakers have always feared European monetary union because it would weaken the US dollar and reduce its role as *the* reserve currency for the global economy.

From 1985 to 1995 the US government turned towards the currency exchange rate as its major weapon in the battle against competitors on the world market (Brenner 1998). It had also done so in 1971 when it took the US dollar off its fixed rate of exchange against gold, unilaterally abandoning a pillar of the Bretton Woods world order. However, as Aglietta (1982) analyzes in considerable detail, manipulation of the exchange rate and periodic "devaluations" to boost exports did not seem to make much of a difference in inter-imperialist commercial competition. However, after 1985 the policy, combined with other structural changes, particularly a reduction of labour costs (0.5 percent annual growth versus 3 percent in Germany and 2.9 percent in Japan) and an associated increase in productivity, provided a considerable boost to US production and exports (Tables 8.2 and 8.3). As a result, from 1985 to 1995 the US recovered some ground against its major competitors (Japan and Germany), notwithstanding growing deficits in the national trade account. This recovery is reflected in the evidence of some productivity growth, closely associated with a return to profitability.

In connection to this issue of monetary competition — at first with the deutsche mark and the yen, but in the late 1990s with the euro — William Clark opined that "Saddam signed his own death sentence when, towards the end of 2000, he decided to shift to the Euro, converting Iraq's $10 billion reserves." At that point, "Bush's second Gulf war became inevitable [as]… the capacity of the dollar to hold its ground was seriously jeopardized…. If the US had not found a remedy quickly, the fire would have spread to their whole economy and to world trade" (Clark 2003).

In February 1996, former German chancellor Helmut Kohl, in a speech at the University of Leuven, had addressed the same concern in the following terms: "The politics of European integration are in reality a question of war and peace in the twenty-first century." Eighteen months later, an American neo-con economist and advisor to George Bush Jr., Martin Feldstein, in an essay for *Foreign Affairs*, addressed the issue again, but from the perspective of US foreign policy. As Feldstein (1997) saw it, the introduction of the euro "will lead to discord and war among the European countries themselves as well as between the European countries and the United States." In an interview in the most important Italian economic daily, Feldstein reaffirmed this thesis: "I am convinced that the danger of war will increase, rather than diminish… with the introduction of the Economic and Monetary Union. It is for this reason that I recommend the American government to modify its whole approach to foreign policy in view of serious destabilizations and clashes with Europe" (Vasapollo 2003).

Since the institution of the Bretton Woods world order, the world economy has relied on the dollar as a means of controlling financial flows. With the emergence and enlargement of a euro zone the centrality of the dollar cannot but come to an end, making room for a system that will be at least bipolar and within which the US and Europe will have to find a new point of equilibrium, or conflict. In this context, the division of the world into several economic and monetary areas (the FTAA and the EU, above all), and a weakening of the role of the dollar in the global economy, is taking shape, in part as the result of a push to deregulate capital markets and a consequent propensity towards financial crisis (as in Europe in 1992, Mexico in 1995, Asia in 1997, Russia in 1998 and Brazil in 1999).

In an interview for *US News and World Report*, former American Secretary of State Madeleine Albright (2003) stated that "the new economic (and monetary) groups will be in the next century the equivalent of the military alliances in the past." If she is correct and this is in fact the case, the US and Europe cannot and will not be part of the same military alliance. What is happening within NATO and the competition between, on the one hand, the project for a European Army and, on the other, NATO's Reaction Force, proposed by the US and the UK at the Prague Summit, confirms that the strategic cleavage between the US and Europe might also very well widen in management of the stability and material interests of a region as vital as the Middle East. The "New American Century" decreed by Wolfowitz, Rumsfeld, etc. cannot but be built on the ruins and possibly even the blood of its strategic competitors.

Unfortunately for the Bush regime in Washington, an awareness of this possibility seems to have emerged within parts of Europe, spurring on a major competitive struggle, particularly in production technology, which is regarded as the driving force, if not the fundamental motor, of economic growth. At the same time it is important to appreciate the limits of this competitive struggle and the US drive for hegemony. Neither is likely to tear the system apart. In fact, reports of the demise of the transatlantic relationship between Europe and the US have been greatly exaggerated. The George W. Bush phenomenon notwithstanding, the European and US powers' mutual international interests far outweigh the conditions of transatlantic inter-imperialist conflict. Having long shared the spoils of global dominance, the US and the EU will undoubtedly find a way to bridge their differences and maintain the larger North Atlantic hegemony that has dominated the world for over a century.

Technological Competition: A Two-edged Sword

The EU is seeking to become independent of American technological supremacy. Competition is already keen in satellites, the space industry and military goods' production. This is a decisive aspect of global competition.[7]

In early March 2002, at 2:07 a.m. Italian time, a satellite produced by European technology — *Envisat* — took off from the equatorial forest that surrounds the launching pad in Kourou, French Guiana — the last remaining French colony in Latin America. *Envisat* is the biggest, heaviest and most expensive satellite that the European Space Agency (ESA) has ever sent into orbit. Technicians and scientists were very worried at the time because a previous launch with the same type of rocket had failed.

Envisat has since been orbiting around the globe. Its official mission is civilian and scientific, monitoring the environment,, etc. In reality, its data, collected by stations in Scandinavia and Italy, can also be sold to the private sector. But, above all, *Envisat* will have repercussions for US-EU relations. For one thing, "the satellite is the only one capable of providing in real time the data requested by institutions to control the enforcement of the Kyoto Treaty," says one of the top technicians working on the project. The Kyoto Protocol on the global environment, and the refusal of the US to sign the agreement to enforce it, is one of a growing number of bones of contention in US-EU bilateral relations.

Thanks to *Envisat*, Brussels will be able to document — and denounce to the world — the consequences of US non-compliance with the Kyoto Protocol, and it will be able to do this independent of data provided by the American satellite system. As admitted by the director-general of ESA, Antonio Rodotà, for the 2002–2006 period, the ESA has planned a vast strategic European program *"in order to exploit space in a more thorough and synergetic way and to make of these technologies one of the strong points of industry and research."* Rodotà added that Europe now holds 50 percent of the launch market and 50 percent of the satellite market; that Europe's technological competence is by no means inferior to that of the US; and that the success rate of satellite-launching is greater for Europe than for the US ("La grande sfida europea allo spazio," *Sole 24 Ore,* November 28, 2001).

Inter-imperialist competition for new advanced technologies is well under way. Around the same time that *Envisat* was launched, the EU also launched the Galileo, a satellite project whose explicit aim was to "reduce the European dependency upon the US in the field of satellite communications" (*Il Corriere della Sera,* September 19, 2003). News about the project was sensational enough, given that it was designed as a strategic weapon aimed at the US, but what really caught the attention of the world, and the US, was an agreement between the EU and China that provided for China's "participation."

On March 26, 2002, EU transport ministers of transport gave the green light to Galileo and in March 2003 its offices were located in Germany. It was originally to be located in Italy, but these plans were abandoned because of Berlusconi's pro-Americanism, which raised serious questions about whether that government could be trusted in the competition with the US.

Up to now, the world's satellites were either American GPS satellites or Russian Glonas. The latter, whose performance in the Soviet era had been superior to the American, is now in a rather bad state. Both systems were designed to guide nuclear missiles to their targets. The GPS (Global Positioning System) is managed by the American military and relies on a system of twenty-four satellites. Given that it is managed by the military, access to or use of it can be closed or limited, which is what happened during the bombing of Yugoslavia and, more recently, during the Iraq War. Thus it cannot be considered to be solely a civilian system of satellite navigation. In the words of Alenia Spazio's managing director, "GPS has been made by the military for the military. We can only use it on request and the [US's] kind authorization [which can be extended or not]. GPS is [also not suitable and] inaccurate for civilian use. If a nuclear head is launched, how important can a difference of 100 metres be?" ("La sfida di Galileo, un GPS mondiale in mano agli europei," *Affari e Finanza*, January 21, 2002).

As for Galileo, the editor of the journal *Rivista Italiana Difesa*, Andrea Nativi, points out that it "is the outcome of European technologies and designs." As such, Galileo "will not only break GPS's undisputed monopoly, but it will be more efficient and accurate. No wonder that the US can't bear the sight of it." In this context there was considerable talk in European circles about a heated letter written by US Secretary of Defence Rumsfeld in the first months of 2003 in which he expressed strong opposition to the project ("Gli USA in guerra contro Galileo," *Affari e Finanza*, April 14, 2003).

Galileo, then, is set to challenge and replace the US technological monopoly in the satellite field. Not only will Galileo "do more and better" than the GPS system, but it will be more cost-effective and efficient. According to European experts, by 2020 Galileo could earn about $17.8 billion against a cost of $3.9 billion. Private and public interests are thus invited to come forward and finance the project with the prospect of a considerable return spread over a fifteen-year period.

A specialized magazine reports that Europe is viewed with hostility in the US, and not only on the political and diplomatic plane. "After September 11, a political movement was born aimed at redefining the US-EU relations in the light of an increased economic, industrial and political competition…. Contrary to the previous decades, the transfer of technologies from the US to Europe is neither guaranteed nor taken for granted any longer" ("Potere tecnologico," supplement Alfa, *Sole 24 Ore*, March 22, 2002).

CETES in Rome has reported the existence of a confidential Pentagon document that rules out any form of cooperation in military technologies with many European countries (and in particular with France). For this reason the Galileo project has fallen like a boulder on transatlantic relations. This boulder is much heavier than the conflictual issues of agricultural subsidies and steel import duties.

Some idea of what is at stake can be inferred from the reaction of the US administration, which opened fire against the Galileo project well before Rumsfeld's threatening letter. A letter of "dissuasion" had already arrived on the eve of the European Summit in Laeken of December 2001.

In it the State Department explained to the European partners how point-less it would be to proceed with the Galileo project, given the existence of GPS, and invited the Europeans to participate in the management of the US system. Some results were obtained. Under the pretext of excessive costs, the faithful UK, and then Germany, Denmark, Austria, the Nether-lands and Sweden withdrew from the project. But in early March 2002, Germany and the Netherlands reversed their positions and gave their support to the project. Vienna and Copenhagen, always sensitive to Ber-lin's wishes, reconsidered the matter.

Three days later, on March 6 to be precise, a new letter arrived from the US administration to all foreign offices. In this letter, the US "asked" that Galileo be used only for civilian purposes. The day after, George W. Bush in person piled it on by completely rejecting the Galileo project, stating publicly that the GPS system would offer the same services for free.

On March 8, Jonathan Faull, the spokesperson for the European Commission, replied by stressing the usefulness of the Galileo project and restating that it was not in Europe's interest to have only one system: "We don't like monopolies," declared the functionary ("Bush contro Galileo," *Il Manifesto*, March 10, 2002).

But the US did not desist and demanded that a commission of mili-tary experts be formed to jointly control the creation of Galileo. Faced with this ultimatum, European unity began to show cracks, thanks to Spanish and Italian "fifth columns," an operation in which Group Finmeccanica played a determinant role (Vasapollo 2003).

In spite of strong American lobbying, on March 16, 2002, the EU gave Galileo the go-ahead, choosing Germany as the head office for the project. The thirty-satellite system will be operational by 2008, making Europe independent of the US in the sector of satellite navigation, something that, as an Italian newspaper said, "will break the American monopoly in navigation."

The president of the European Commission, Romano Prodi, summed up the political, strategic and epochal significance of the Galileo project in statements made over ten days. First he said, "the problem is not the costs; rather, we must decide whether we want to be independent or not." And then he said, "the American position on this theme too, as well as on steel, is hardly justifiable; we are asked to be dependent upon them, upon a system we do not control, which has often been suspended and modified, and which is in any case controlled by the military authorities." Finally Prodi stressed that the process of European emancipation had already started and that, as an important Italian newspaper reported, "it is a process with which the birth of the single currency has certainly some-thing to do" ("Galileo, la sfida europea agli Stati Uniti," *Il Corriere della Sera*, March 27, 2002).

Aerospace and Military Industries:
Global Competition with a Vengeance
Thanks to the 550-seat "superjumbo" A380, the European consortium
Airbus has managed to outdo the monopoly of US aircraft builder Boeing.
In fact, in 2001, Airbus was commissioned to supply 367 airplanes, 32
more than Boeing. Moreover, this historical overtaking of the US by the
European aircraft industry took place in a phase of drastic reduction in
global commercial orders, due both to a global crisis in the sector and the
effects of September 11. In 1998, Boeing was commissioned to produce
630 aircraft; in 2001 orders were almost halved, and orders for 2002 bore
out the trend. The overtaking by Airbus of Boeing — which had taken
over the other US giant of aeronautics, McDonnell-Douglas — consolidated the growth of an EU aeronautics industry, forcing Boeing to cut its
labour force in the civilian jet aircraft sector and direct its efforts towards
the building of military aircraft. Orders in the military sector are on the
increase, thanks to Pentagon procurement. The American monopoly in
civilian aeronautics, which had lasted for fifty years, suddenly became a
thing of the past (*Affari e finanza*, June 30, 2003).

In 2002 the European Commission submitted an openly protectionist
provision against American airline companies. The provision provides for
the levying of taxes on access to European airspace as compensation for
the unlawful subsidies granted to American airline companies after September 11. These subsidies provided support to the crisis-stricken industry in the face of a 20 percent drop in air traffic.

Other indications that US-EU competition is becoming generalized
with no holds barred is provided by the example of Italy's Alenia (Group
Finmeccanica). In December 2001, Finmeccanica's board of directors
gave the go-ahead to joining the European Airbus A380 program. With its
4 percent quota, it would have become a risk-sharing partner, together
with the European EADS and the English BAE-Systems. Finmeccanica and
these two companies also have a 25 percent partnership in the world's
second-largest missile group, MBDA. MBDA's French representative, Brégier,
in introducing the agreement, also made no secret of its intention to
penetrate the US market, "which is rather impermeable to European
products while the Americans sell copiously in Europe" ("Alenia sale sul
superjumbo," *Sole 24 Ore*, December 20, 2001).

The US Wants to Put a Stop to the "European Decoupling"
Towards the end of September 2002, news broke that China was set to
invest heavily in the Galileo project. The *Financial Times* wrote of 230
million euros that would consolidate the very important and emerging
strategic alliance between China and the EU. Obviously, the US was
concerned. US officials consider their global positioning satellite system
to be the only efficient one and hold that Galileo is a simple duplication.

But the EU agreement would have considerable advantages for both China and European MNCs, because it would greatly improve China's civilian and military communication systems, and these improvements would lead to profitable orders for European companies.

In short, the EU has shown that it intends to be autonomous in its expansion within the process of capitalist globalization, while China intends to fully exercise its power as an emerging market, independent industrial giant and economic power. Thus the emerging axis between the EU and China could have a strategic geopolitical and economic significance and would be strongly competitive with the US. Another significant finding is that competition among the highly technologically developed industries in defence and aerospace takes place within a context of blows below the belt, deals in shares, co-optation in industrial projects, government pressure and protectionist measures. What emerges very clearly is that the US-based MNCs and the US administration are trying with all the means at their disposal to prevent the formation of a European industrial-military complex independent of American technology and military policy.

Will the Europeans succeed?

Considering the determination with which the Europeans are pursuing the Galileo project, satellite systems and certain niches in military technology, they could succeed. But considering the stakes involved for US hegemony, it is conceivable that Airbus carriers could crash, satellites could inexplicably break down, propellant factories could mysteriously explode, as in Tolosa, or ministers and business owners could fall victim to "mysterious terrorist attacks." A careful review of recent events suggests that the competition between the EU and the US has become much sharper, and possibly more deadly, than the general public has been told and generally understands.

Is Europe a Growing Threat or Falling Behind?
A Question of Productivity

By 1990, analysts were seriously debating the question of whether or not the US economy was going down the drain. Having vanquished communism and the post-war threat constituted by the USSR, the argument went, the US was in the process of succumbing to the forces of global economic competition, and the costs of maintaining its empire. Analysts like Paul Kennedy (1989) and Lester Thurow (1992) were engaging in what neo-con economists at the time and today considered to be "loose talk" about an impending decline and implosion of the US economy, unable to compete with the growing centres of economic power in Asia and Europe and the superiority of Japanese and German forms of capitalism. Europe was regarded as providing the major challenge, a threat not only to US economic dominance but to the American way of life.

Ten years later the debate was by no means settled but had acquired a number of twists, including a new and growing concern about the potential threat represented by China. Rather than viewing the twenty-first as the century of Europe, as Lester Thurow and Paul Kennedy did, and Rogoff (2004) does, much of the new "loose talk" about impending US decline has fingered China as the new threat to the US. The roles of Japan and Russia in this scenario were unclear, but the new generation of cynics and pessimists vis-à-vis US power (concerned about its "feet of clay," "propensity towards crisis," "imperial overreach," etc.) looked at both Europe and China to discern the future.

So what can we conclude? First, we should reframe the terms of debate. On the one side, analysts point to the relative performance of the US economy, the economies that make up the EU and that of China. At issue here have been three "indicators": (1) annualized rates of economic growth — year-to-year increases in the gross domestic output (GDP) and associated national income; (2) growth of GDP per capita — total "productivity"; and (3) share of world trade, regarded by neo-liberals as the basic engine of economic growth. However, the crux of the issue, the fundamental indicator of future prospects is productivity, which defines the ratio between total output (GDP, national income) and the input of labour and capital.

On the issue of productivity growth there is in fact a renewed debate generated by evidence presented by William Lewis (2004) with regard to Europe and the US. The argument in brief is that, as of the early 1990s, precisely when arguments to the contrary were advanced by Thurow and Kennedy, the US economy has outdistanced and outperformed the EU; that productivity in the EU is barely 70 percent of that in the US (80 percent for Germany); that the superior productivity of US capital is leading Europe to fall behind more and more; and that the relative performance of the EU economy (roughly the same size as the US) demonstrates the superiority of the American model of capitalism.

The conclusion drawn by Lewis from the evidence he presents is that not only is the US economy alive and well, rising above its presumed propensity towards crisis, but that US imperialism does not have "feet of clay," nor can we speak or write of an "imperial overreach" — stretching global economic power beyond its sustainable capacity.

How solid is the evidence, and the argument, presented by Lewis? Several conclusions can be drawn from available evidence and our discussion above. First, the alleged difference in US and EU productivity (output of GDP/input of labour and capital) is more apparent than real, a matter not of fact but of definition. Lewis defines and compares output (GDP) data in terms of "purchasing power parity" rather than the rate of currency exchange, thus discounting the effect of a strong deutsche mark in the early 1990s and the growing strength of the euro compared to the dollar in recent years. Also, Lewis stresses the productivity of capital, which is higher in the US, rather than labour, which is higher in Europe.

Considering this difference, in Europe the state plays a much larger role than the US state in redistributing market-generated incomes in the interest of general social welfare — what Lewis defines as the "politics of poverty." In the US the lion's share of productivity gains and growth of production are appropriated by the rich, high-income "earners," who have a greater propensity to invest their savings than workers and the poor, who generally have a low capacity to save, tending to consume their income rather than invest it. In Europe, policy-makers have a more humane approach towards capitalist development, placing greater priority on welfare. Thus, as mentioned, in Europe, workers receive a larger share of national income in the form of social benefits such as minimum wages, welfare security and paid vacations. A policy of minimum wages, it is argued (by Lewis and other neo-liberals) generates unemployment, a cost that European governments and workers are prepared to bear in exchange for greater income security. Longer vacations and shorter working hours are viewed in Europe as a "right," a defined benefit or social wage. In the US such social conditions or benefits, like a minimum wage policy (which distorts the working of the labour market), are viewed as an unacceptable cost to doing business; in fact — and this is the crux of the matter — these social benefits account for 100 percent of the productivity difference identified by Lewis. In other words, the difference in the performance of the US and the EU, by these criteria, has nothing to do with productivity. The difference relates to the preferred form of capitalism, with Europeans generally opting for a greater level of social welfare even at the expense of corporate profits.

Energy Resources and Geopolitical Control: The Possible Foundation of Inter-imperialist War

> The big game is Central Asia. He who governs Eastern Europe rules the central zone. He who governs the central zone rules the Eurasian masses. He who governs the Eurasian masses rules the world. —Harold Mackinder (2005)

In defence of its empire, the US is locked into a war on many fronts, with diverse theatres and battles. One of these fronts is the world market, where, in the aftermath of World War II and within the institutional framework of the Bretton Woods economic order, the US engaged its erstwhile "enemies," Germany and Japan, in a major battle for dominance of international commerce. In 1948, at the outset of this battle, the US absolutely dominated world trade, accounting for over 50 percent of all commercial transactions by volume and value, but by 1971, after two decades of rapid system-wide export-led growth, the US was on the losing end of a vicious cutthroat battle being won by Germany and Japan, which between them accounted for 20 percent of world trade, reducing the US's share by 25 percent. The dynamics of this inter-imperialist competition are reflected in data on world market share and the trend towards imbalance in the US trade account.

Table 8.1 provides data on this point. It also points towards a major realignment in the structure of world trade in the 1970s and 1980s — a new, international division of labour that brought into play a new dynamic pole of economic growth in Asia, that is, the emergence of what would become known as the "newly industrializing countries" (NICs). In the context of a system-wide neo-liberal restructuring in the 1980s and the collapse of the USSR and the socialist bloc in 1991, the battle of the market shifted, bringing in new players, a renewed round of competition and a continuing erosion of the position of the US in the global economy. The US, as the system's largest economy by far and enjoying renewed dynamism in key sectors, remained the centre of economic power. But it was losing the battle for the world marketplace. By 2003 the US share of world trade had been reduced by 15 percent, a trend reflected in a persistent trend towards growing deficits in the country's trade account. By 2004 this deficit stood at $573 billion (versus a positive trade balance of $180 billion for Germany and $125 billion for Japan).

Notwithstanding the continued erosion of its economic dominance, other indicators showed that the US economy in the 1990s managed to halt and to some extent offset, if not reverse, the propensity towards crisis. No doubt this was the result of multiple factors, including technological conversion of industrial production, a shift towards a new regulatory regime and economic advantages squeezed from a process of globalization and structural adjustment that allowed US MNCs to not only penetrate "emerging markets" but buy up profitable corporations and pillage the resources of its newly acquitted economic colonies (see Chapter 4 on these dynamics). Other aspects of the restructuring process included a drastic devaluation of the dollar in its rate of exchange against other key currencies and an increase in productivity based on a reduction of labour costs. As a result of this restructuring of the global economy and the place of the US within it, the US economy in the 1990s achieved a measure of economic recovery, outdistancing in the process both Japan, which began a ten-year economic decline, and the EU. Table 1 speaks volumes about this process and the underlying dynamics of inter-imperialist competition.

Competition for Energy Resources and the Assault on Eurasia

Harold Mackinder (2005), a father of modern geopolitics, holds that those who control "the central zone" control Eurasia, and those who control Eurasia control the world. Well, it would appear that as a result of the collapse of the USSR the US is moving for control of the central zone; in order to achieve world supremacy, it is necessary for the US to rule Eurasia. As Zbigniew Brzezinski, a political realist of the old trilateralist school of US foreign policy, has put it, "The capability of the US to gain real world supremacy will depend on how they will deal with the complex equilibriums among the powers of Eurasia, and even more on whether they will be able to prevent the emergence of a dominant and antagonistic power in that region" (1998: 8).

In 1993 the EU launched the Trans-European Caucasian Corridor. The aim was to bypass Russian control of transportation, pipelines and investments related to the strategic energy and mineral resources of Eurasia. At stake were not only European and American interests in these resources and related imperial aspirations, but also the geopolitical interests of other states in the region such as Turkey, a NATO member, a generally faithful ally of the US and a candidate for membership in the EU. In 1994 an article in the Turkish daily *Milliyet* revealed a project for a pipeline between Baku, Azerbaijan and Ceyhan, Turkey, that would take Russia out of the Eurasian game. Following the "contract of the century" signed by Azerbaijan and a pool of oil companies led by British Petroleum, the "race" to the black gold, gas and the markets of Central Asia had begun, and with it a fundamental shift in US geopolitical strategy in the region. Up to 1993 the US had sought to co-opt Russia via treaties related to the Trans-European Caucasian Corridor and pipeline construction. But around 1995 the US administration's policy regarding Central Asia and the Balkans changed radically as Azerbaijan, Georgia and Uzbekistan fell under the American sphere of influence. In the same year the Taliban began its triumphant march from Pakistan into Kabul, which it "conquered" in 1996 with considerable material support from the US.

As for the European countries formerly belonging to the East European Economic Community, such as Poland, the Czech Republic and Hungary, the US welcomed and facilitated their integration into NATO — against Russian opposition. A precondition for this integration into a continental military alliance was a process of economic and political reform (capitalism, democracy), which these countries undertook readily enough. By 2000 the "transition" of these economies towards "capitalism" (privatization, liberalization, deregulation, free markets) and "democracy" (the rule of law, respect for human rights and the prerogatives of private property, "free elections") was sufficiently advanced to allow for the integration of these states into the new world order, to join the US-led "forces of freedom."

In the former Asian republics of the USSR and in the Balkans, this process has not advanced as far, but in 1999 the Balkans were brought onside, "put in order," by means of two military interventions, first in Bosnia and then Kosova and the Yugoslav federation, paving the way for "western capital" investments and Euro-American imperialism. As a result of its Kosovo campaign the US can now count on a large military base in Kosovo (Camp Bondsteel) and neutralization of strategic Corridor 10, in which the interests in Russia, Serbia, Greece and Germany converge. In addition, the US has managed to open up the western side of Corridor 8, where US and UK interests converge. And the US can now count on an alliance with the three countries that are most functional in maintaining this corridor: Albania/Kosovo, Bulgaria and a somewhat unruly Macedonia. Thanks to reconciliation with the nationalist pan-Albanian movement in the region, US interests now control all of the area's strategic junctions in Kosovo, Albania and Macedonia.[8] The situation for the US has improved so much that the US State Department is now able to consider the possibility of withdrawing a part of the US armed forces in Kosovo, Macedonia and Bosnia, leaving only fully operational personnel at Camp Bondsteel and entrusting the Italian contingent with the task of military policing.

Power Relations in Eurasia

More problematic for US hegemony and control is the situation in western Central Asia, a region where Russian and Chinese strategic interests converge. In this area can be found hostile powers (Iran) as well as allies (Turkey). Another complicating factor for the empire is the proximity of two nuclear powers — Pakistan and India — that maintain a mutual standoff of antagonistic relations but are not disposed to allow any imperial power, whether Russian, European or American, to take diplomatic or political advantage. Even so, Pakistan has been brought onside by the US with offers of military and economic aid on a large scale. In the middle of this strategic situation is a no-man's land called Afghanistan, recently converted into a satrap of US imperialism thanks to a successful invasion, occupation and regime change engineered by the US.

At the point immediately prior to the US intervention in Afghanistan (and after the war against Yugoslavia and the "dismissal" of Milosevic) the Eurasian scenario was as follows:

1. The Balkans, the terminal point of Corridor 8, had largely fallen to US control. Europe's aspirations and Russian influence in the area were scaled down.
2. In the Caucasian region, Georgia and Azerbaijan (the middle part of Corridor 8), had come under US control. In Georgia, the Supsa harbour on the Black Sea is the oil terminal point of the Baku pipeline. This corridor provides an alternative route for a pipeline, which runs from Baku but is routed through Russia (and Chechnya) to Novorossiysk, the Russian oil terminal on the Black Sea.
3. Georgia and Azerbaijan had applied for NATO membership, increasing US influence in the area as a result. Pending their anticipated

status as NATO members, Georgia in 1997 set up GUUAM, a military assistance pact among Georgia, Ukraine, Uzbekistan, Azerbaijan and Moldavia, under American supervision (GUUAM's second meeting was held in Washington). Turkey, as an ally of the US, took it upon itself to become Azerbaijan's guardian, placing itself side by side against their common enemy, Armenia, which is tied to Russia and home to several Russian military bases. Azerbaijan in this situation has acquired a particularly important strategic value. As Brzezinski (1993) put it, "An independent Azerbaijan, linked up with western markets by pipelines which do not run through Russian-controlled territory, would be an important channel connecting the advanced economies, which consume energy, with the oil rich republics of Central Asia."

4. In 1999 the Baku-Ceyhan oil project in the southwest region had overcome the resistance of the American oil companies operating in Azerbaijan (thanks to the promise of tax allowances). This project was designed to bypass Russia in accessing the oil fields and outlets on the Caspian Sea. To the north the war in Chechnya was meant by "the West" to make it clear to potential investors that this route was "no longer safe." It followed months of "tappings" of oil from, and attacks against, the Baku-Novorossiysk pipelines (and the pipelines under construction that connected Kazakhstan with Novorossiysk) by Islamic secessionists who were "too close by far to Bin Laden."

5. To the east, the US had attempted to bypass Russia and Iran through an energy corridor to the south. Starting from the reserves in Turkmenistan and possibly Kazakhstan, this corridor was meant to run through Afghanistan and Pakistan, ending up in the Pakistani harbour of Gwadar. This would have become the eastern terminal of Corridor 8. This was the squaring of the circle. The hydrocarbon reserves would flow west and east, under strict American control, "jumping over" the rivals of Russia and Iran.

The "Silk Road Strategy Act"

In 1993 the US started a full-scale march to regain control over Eurasia. To speed it up, at the end of 1997 the US Congress discussed the "Silk Road Strategy Act," the first objective of which was to cut off Russia's relations with its former Asian republics. The second objective of the act was to start up a dialogue with Iran, taking advantage of possible divisions between "reformers" and "conservatives," as suggested by an article written by, among others, Brzezinski, Scowcroft and Murphy (which appeared in the May/June 1997 issue of *Foreign Affairs*) and a 1988 document edited by Bush's deputy secretary of defence, Paul Wolfowitz.

The third objective was to set up a permanent military base at the region's strategic junctions. This was in fact the purpose of expanding

NATO towards the east (Georgia and Azerbaijan). But on the eastern side there were no operational structures or systems in place comparable to NATO. For this reason the US deemed it necessary to operate directly in the field, equipping its forces as necessary. As stated in the US publication *Quadrennial Defence Review* (September 30, 2001): "the density of the fixed and mobile structures in the region is less than in other crucial regions. For this reason it is important for the US to secure further inroads into the region and to develop systems capable to carry out distant and challenging operations with a minimum of support in the theatre of operations itself."

The plan to build US military bases in Afghanistan, Uzbekistan and Pakistan fits well into the US strategy in Central Asia. Here too, as in the Gulf, the Balkans and elsewhere, once the confusion provoked by war and by the emergency situation has cleared up, what will be left will be permanent US military bases.

Competition and Rivalries in Central Asia

What problems stand in the way of the US imperialist project to penetrate and control the strategic Eurasian junctions? And how are power relations in the region being modified as a result of the imperialist war in the region? These questions can be provisionally answered as follows:

Relations between the US and Russia

At the end of 1999, Boris Yeltsin was forced to retire and Vladimir Putin came into power. With Putin a new perception of Russia's "strategic" interests came into play. With the backing of the bosses of the oil and gas companies, Putin adopted a more "aggressive" policy towards the former Soviet republics, a policy oriented towards assuring continued access to the oil routes that account for 70 percent of Russian exports. In this connection, however, it appears that US and Russian interests somehow converged in the form of strategic cooperation in regard to the supply of oil. An indication of this is given by the inauguration of a pipeline between Kazakhstan and the Russian oil terminal of Novorossiysk and the news of a joint venture between Russia and Kazakhstan for the supply of gas from the latter to the former. The US secretary of energy, Spencer Abraham, participated in the inauguration of the pipeline, which, according to *Sole 24 Ore*, is "a Russian victory," whereas in the 1990s it would have been perceived as a challenge to efforts by the US and Turkey to take from Russia its control over the supply of oil and gas in the area. In exchange for confronting the US on this issue, Russia ignored OPEC's request to lower Russian oil production, which was meant to trigger a rise in oil prices. The US administration "much appreciated" Russia's position (Sinatti 2001).

Relations among the US, Russia and China

In July 2001, Russia and China reached an agreement designed to last twenty years, the "Treaty of good neighbourhood, friendship and cooperation between the Russian Federation and the People's Republic of China." The treaty provides for "strategic partnership in order to face growing American hegemony." Around the same time, India signed a military-commercial agreement with Russia worth $10 billion. Clearly these initiatives could deeply damage US strategic interests in Central Asia, creating conditions for a rapprochement between the US and China, a strategic power with which the US perforce has to come to terms with. It turns out that the Afghan War and the broader war against "international terrorism" created conditions for a changed and multi-faceted relationship of strategic cooperation between the US and China. In October 2001 at an Asia-Pacific Economic Co-operation Conference (APEC) summit, less than three months into the Russia-China accord, China played host, allowing the adoption of a US political document against terrorism in a setting where normally only economic problems would be discussed.

China in this context sided with the international coalition put together by Washington in order to legitimize the "infinite war" and the military aggression against Afghanistan. In exchange it obtained two results. The first was similar to that obtained by Russia concerning Chechnya, i.e., an American and western acceptance of a violent solution to Muslim secession in Xinjiang. "China too is a victim of terrorism," declared Tang Jiaxuan, the Chinese foreign minister. "The group of Eastern Turkistan is certainly a terrorist organization and to hit it is part of the fight against terrorists." The second and perhaps even more desired result was that Bush accepted — at least at this point — the doctrine of "One China."

Full-scale Competition among the Oil MNCs

In the ruthless competition for Central Asia, which has been raging for years, Italy, through its multinational ENI, has also started to manifest ambitions of imperial grandeur. Recently, ENI "stole" from Exxon-Mobil a contract concerning the immense Kashagan reserves in Kazakhstan. It also signed a very big contract with Russia concerning the oil fields in Astrakhan. ENI has also commenced work on an underwater gas pipeline, Blue Stream, in collaboration with Russia. This pipeline, which will bring gas from Russia to Turkey, once again brings Moscow back into play in a project that actually supersedes the Baku-Ceyhan project, on which the US administration had placed its hopes. In 1998 the US openly declared its opposition to the Blue Stream project and during the year 2000 pressured Turkish members of parliament not to approve it. These pressures, however, were fruitless, indicating limits to the capacity of the US to control its allies.

In addition, ENI and FinaElf have expanded operations in Iran. Profiting from the absence of the US — the result of the US embargo against Teheran — they have signed contracts and concessions worth billions of dollars for the South Pars fields. Leaks have emerged about fiery telephone conversations between Madeleine Albright, and then Colin Powell, and Italian authorities. Despite the support of Italy under Berlusconi for the US war effort in Iraq, relations between Italy and the US also hit a snag over ongoing efforts by the Italian government to pursue its own economic interests in Iraq. As Brzezinski (1998) commented in this regard, "the divergence of opinions with Europe concerning Iran and Iraq has been considered by the US not as a quarrel between equals but as a manifestation of insubordination."

The clash between US and European MNCs for control of energy resources is now definitive and frontal. At stake is the capitalist development of their respective economies and the profit-making opportunities available to US and EU firms. At the bottom of this issue is the matter of low-cost energy, a matter of national policy and strategic interest and, as noted by China's minister of foreign affairs Tang Jiaxuan, of inter-imperialist competition (interview by *La Stampa*, September 2000, as reported in the US Army *Military Review*, November 24, 2001).

The Alliance with the Taliban and Saudi Arabia

More than one observer has documented the longstanding close relationship between the US, Saudi Arabia and the Taliban regime in Afghanistan (see, in particular, Chossudovsky 2004). The interest in common was a gas and oil pipeline from Turkmenistan, through Afghanistan, to Gwadar in Pakistan. The US company Unocal and the Saudi company Delta Oil had converging interests for this project. As *Le Monde Diplomatique* wrote: "in spite of its denial, Washington supports completely this project.... As soon as [Kabul] fell into Taliban hands, the State Department published a document in which their victory is considered "positive" and announces a decision to send a delegation to Kabul" (Roy 1996).

But the agreement between Unocal, Saudi Delta Oil and the Taliban regime fell through. Some say that the cause was the failure to reach an agreement concerning royalties on the oil and gas pipelines. Others such as Chossudovsky (2004) hold that the insistence of the Saudis that they run the whole operation was the cause.

In September 1998 the US launched some missiles into Afghanistan in retaliation against the bombing of the US embassies in Kenya and Tanzania; Unocal abandoned the project and Afghanistan did the same only four months later, in December 1998. In return, Hamid Kirzai, an advisor on oil interests and still on Unocal's payroll, was chosen by the US as president of the country and put in place as its puppet.

Afghanistan within the Eurasian "Great Game"

Even though it is a poor and inhospitable country, Afghanistan is located in the right geopolitical location for the US to enter forcefully and participate directly in the "Great Game of Eurasia." As noted by Lieutenant-Colonel Lester W. Grau, one of the most prominent military experts on the region, "Thanks to its geographical location, Afghanistan has always played an important role for the stability of the region and has often been at the centre of the great powers' attention" (Roy 1996). The campaign against Islamic terrorism fits well into this scenario. In 1998, Brzezinski wrote:

> Even a possible challenge of Islamic fundamentalism to US supremacy could be part of the problem in a region characterized by instability. A religious condemnation of American life style and the Arab-Israel conflict could be used to provoke the crisis of more than one pro-West government, i.e., it could jeopardize America's interests in that region, especially in the Persian Gulf. It is clear that, without political cohesion and without an Islamic state, strong in the true meaning of the word, a challenge from Islamic fundamentalism would lack a true geopolitical centre and would run the risk of expressing itself as diffuse violence.

Was Afghanistan a "strong" Islamic state — a geopolitical centre — capable of jeopardizing US interests? In the light of what we know now and of what we have seen of this inhospitable, poor country devastated by a twenty-year war, it is hard to believe. Yet the most powerful nation of the world targeted the Taliban regime as a major threat against "the free world," the "forces of freedom, democracy and free enterprise." Clearly, very serious US geopolitical interests were at stake. And the Washington gang of Wolfowitz, Rumsfeld and their neo-con associates targeted Afghanistan as the first step in a strategy of "infinite war" against the enemies of "freedom" — international terrorism and radical Islam.

Russia and China, it turns out, are beset by the same problem — in Chechnya and in Xinjiang, respectively, just as India is in Kashmir — a problem that Samuel Huntington (1996) views not in terms of a struggle for global supremacy but as a "clash of civilizations." Iran, in this context, even threatened to invade the western part of Afghanistan in order to protect the pro-Iran Shiites defeated and decimated by the Taliban. This in itself was enough to mark Iran as next in line after Iraq. What is interesting is that none of these contending Eurasian powers have hidden their support, both political and military, for the Mujahedeen of the Northern Alliance against the Taliban regime and Pakistan's ambitions in the region. Both the Northern Alliance and Pakistan up to a few years ago, and today, had the support of the US.

The various Eurasian "competitors" for Eurasia's resources were able for a time to accommodate US interests in the region but not for long. For its part the US needs to put an end to the Afghan War or risk getting bogged down in an endless and costly conflict. To this end, it is necessary for the US to come to some agreement with Russia and China as to their reciprocal limits and common interests in the area. But it is also strategically necessary for Washington to consolidate its military presence in the region within a framework of relative stability. The US strategic project in Eurasia would be crowned by settling down permanently in Afghanistan and in Pakistan, by penetrating into Uzbekistan and in Kazakhstan, the Eurasian giant, and by testing its relations with Turkmenistan and Tajikistan.

Target Kazakhstan

On December 5, 2000, the Russian business paper *Argumenty e Fakti* reported that the US planned to build military bases in Kazakhstan, Georgia and Azerbaijan. The first of these three former USSR republics is the "hen with the golden eggs." It has the greatest hydrocarbon (oil and gas) reserves, and access to these reserves is an indispensable condition for making the pipelines economically advantageous.

A war is already being waged for the acquisition of the Kazakhstan oilfields. This war has provoked a series of clashes between the US, Russia and China, as well as Italy, which is emerging as more than a bit player in the Eurasian game. In 2000, Shell lost its role as "operator" of the Kazakhstan oilfields. From December 2000 to January 2001 only the Italian ENI (already active on the oilfields of Tengiz and Karachay-Cherkess) and the French ELF/TotalFina were still competing for them. US-based Exxon/Mobil had been cut out of any deal. In fact, another American company, Chevron/Texaco, with Condoleezza Rice as an advisor and a rival of Exxon/Mobil, has entered into the fray in Tengiz.

On February 12, 2000, Kazakhstan signed an oil concession granting ENI the Kashagan oilfields. Exxon/Mobil protested vehemently, asking Secretary of State Colin Powell to put pressure on Italy, but the Kazakhstan government announced that the pipeline between Tengiz and Novorossiysk (preferred by Russia and sabotaged by Chechnya's rebels) would start operations in 2001. US interests and plans in this area were thus given a hard blow. The significance of this is that whoever comes to power in Kazakhstan, the second republic of the former USSR bordering on both Russia and China, will no doubt seize its strategic energy reserves and have Eurasia in their hands.

Around the Caspian Sea: A War in the Making

In the 1990s the Caspian zone was dotted with tension, conflicts and wars that have been generally defined as "low intensity" conflicts.

As noted, it seems that the planned pipeline between Baku (Azerbaijan) and Ceyhan (Turkey) has been abandoned, mainly because if it were not possible to link the oil of Kazakhstan to the project, the Baku-Ceyhan pipeline would be uneconomical. Uzbekistan has openly sided with the US for six years in this competitive struggle and strategic conflict. Turkmenistan, on the other hand, got by with an open declaration of its neutrality in the US campaign against Afghanistan. However, the problem for both countries is how to get their reserves of oil and gas to the world market. Economically, the Russian option would be more advantageous, while politically the "Afghan way," supported by the US and imposed through control of the territory by the Taliban, thus far has failed, leading the US administration to "push with its shoulder" in order to decisively step into the region.

For the US, Afghanistan was the first experiment in gaining permanent access to the "heart" of Eurasia. The acknowledgment by Secretary of Defense Rumsfeld concerning the construction of a military base in Afghanistan demonstrates this point. Similarly, at the end of the first Gulf War, after the confusion caused by the war settled down, three great military bases were left (in Saudi Arabia, Kuwait and Oman), in territories where previously there had been none.

Camp Bondsteel in Kosovo and Camp Rhino in Afghanistan are meant to be the two outpost "fortresses" for the control of the Great Corridor 8, which runs from east to west, following the "Silk Road." In between are countries allied to the US empire, such as Turkey, Georgia, Azerbaijan and Uzbekistan. Here is the heart of Eurasia and, according to at least one geopolitical theorist, the potential for world rule.

It is clear that the US, wanting to maintain and strengthen its hegemony, has found a way into Eurasia. The emergence of rival powers competing with the US, the failure to date of the US to cut off not only Russia and Iran but also China from these strategic routes — these are the dangers of which the 1992 Wolfowitz report and, more recently, Brzezinski have warned. The scenario for the US is becoming more gloomy because of the possibility that some of the most important oil-producing countries of the Middle East are on the verge of using the euro rather than the dollar for their international transactions. Preventing this from happening is one aspect of Bush's war against the "forces of evil." There are, of course, other aspects, which will be discussed in Chapter 11.

9. RUSSIA AND CHINA IN THE EMPIRE
Western Imperialism at Bay

THE GEOGRAPHY AND POLITICAL ECONOMY OF IMPERIALISM ARE COMPLEX and changing. At issue in these changes are the institutions of global domination and imperial power. In Latin America, as we have seen, the major agents of imperialism are the multinational corporations whose way is paved by the imperial states, both through various apparatus under their direct control and adjunct institutions such as the World Bank. Within this imperial system, governments in the region are put at the service of the imperial states. Where it matters, they are converted into client states, while their countrysides are converted into virtual colonies, ripe for the pillage of resources. Resistance to this process tends to be restricted to the social movements that enter the contested terrain of government policy. In other parts of the world, imperialism has not had such an easy time of it. In the European Union, and to a lesser extent in Japan, US plans for world domination have run up against economic competition and political demands for a sharing of resources and power. The end result is a bipolar, even trilateral (with reference to Japan, a waning power, and China, an emerging power in East Asia) system in which power and resources are shared, not equally to be sure, but somewhat "equitably," reflecting the unequal balance of economic, political and military power. In this context we should properly speak and write of Euro-American rather than US imperialism — an empire with more than one centre; a system searching for new forms of global governance.

Governance of the system is problematic and politically contested. For most theorists of global or international relations the problem is viewed as a matter of working in concert to collectively manage the new political system through the construction of international organizations. For the Bush regime in the US, however, the issue of governance is seen differently: it's either anarchism — a loose configuration of uncoordinated power centres — or domination by the US, the only superpower in the world today with the resources, will and power to take on the responsibility. Given that they expect to share in the benefits, allies in the US project, it is argued, should be prepared to assume some of the heavy costs of empire.

The economic structure of the empire has frequently been visualized and represented in the academic literature as a "centre" and "periphery" (and even, in the rather useless model advanced by Immanuel Wallerstein [1976], a "semi-periphery"). In this conception, the centre is constituted by states and multinational enterprises within the Organisation for Economic Co-operation and Development (OECD), a club of rich capitalist "democracies" that dominate and collectively manage the system. The "periphery" in the same conception takes the form of a multitude of "premodern" or "failed" states and "underdeveloped" or "developing" economies in the so-called "Third World" of Asia, Latin America and Africa. The states in this world are to be converted into "allies," their economies into virtual colonies. However, the real world bears little resemblance to this theoretical simplification. For one thing, there are entire regions of the world that do not fit easily, if at all, into this structure. And the notion of a "semi-periphery," used to group countries that are somewhere in the middle — middle level powers such as Canada that are neither rich nor poor, neither dominant nor dominated — is, as already noted, a rather useless analytical concept. So the question is how to conceive of countries such as Russia and China, and regions such as the Middle East — how to fit them into the empire, not as conceived of by Hardt and Negri (2000) but in its reality.

Russia in the Eye of Imperialism: Strategic Considerations

One of the areas of greatest strategic interest for the imperialist states is the Middle East, particularly the oil-rich gulf coast and the Arabian Peninsula. Another area of strategic interest to the architects of US empire is Eurasia, a region encompassing what remains of the Russian federation and the former Soviet republics in Central Asia. It encompasses one of the largest reserves of strategic resources in the world.

The collapse of the USSR radically changed the strategic significance of Eurasia, because it opened the way for US and EU capital and associated interests to penetrate the continent. The collapse of the Soviet Union not only caused a loss of international prestige for Russia, the dominant power within the union of socialist republics, but it broke up the Soviet empire, converting Russia from a superpower able to challenge US supremacy into a medium-level power. It also brought about a change in geopolitics vis-à-vis the availability of strategically important energy resources, particularly oil and gas. Since1991, Russia has had to adjust to a radically changed reality: its rule over the Asian territories of the Russian empire has diminished in scope and is barely 20 percent of what it once was. The population in Asia subject to Russian rule has dropped from 75 million to 30 million, while millions of Russians living in the Caucasus are now separated from their "motherland." In addition to these changes, the dynamics of mass migration and ethnic movements for national autonomy, which somehow were kept under control by the Soviet regime, have provoked major conflicts and conflagrations, in the Caucasus and Chechnya, for example, which will undoubtedly be drawn into an impending inter-imperialist war for the region's strategic resources. These conflicts appear to be ethnic and religious in form, but behind and at the bottom of these internecine conflicts can be found a struggle to control access to the region's huge reserves of energy and mineral resources — the "greatest energy mine" of the world.

The present Russian Federation has some 150 million inhabitants (mostly Russians), half the population of the US. However, there are also millions of Russians living outside the boundaries of the Russian state, providing fuel to the smouldering idea of "restoring the empire" and defending those of the same blood who live outside Russia — an idea that clashes with the birth and consolidation of diverse ethnicities and nationalisms in the Eurasian region. The situation can be summed up as follows:

> Russia was up to recently the maker of a great territorial empire and the leader of an ideological bloc of satellite states which stretched out to the heart of Europe and to the southern Chinese Sea. [However] it has become a restless country without easy geographical access to the outer world and potentially exposed to devastating conflicts with its neighbours along its western, southern, and eastern borders. Only the empty and inaccessible spaces in the North, almost always in the grips of frost, seem to be geopolitically safe. (Brzezinski 1998: 132)

The Asian territory formerly contained within the Soviet Empire encompasses Tajikistan, Kyrgyzstan, Kazakhstan, Turkmenistan and Uzbekistan. These areas are going through a difficult economic phase characterized by continual internal conflict and political instability. The collapse of the USSR also caused a geopolitical earthquake of sorts in the Caspian Sea area, the location of one of the world's most abundant reserves of oil and gas, second only to Saudi Arabia/Iraq/Kuwait. Up to 1991, control of this territory was shared by the Soviet Union and Iran. But after the collapse of the Soviet Union, besides the Russian Federation and the Islamic Republic of Iran, three other countries have to be factored into any strategic empire-building considerations: Turkmenistan, Azerbaijan and Kazakhstan. Apart from strategic resource considerations related to outside economic interests, as well as the interests of these five coastal states in the reserves of oil and gas, the Caspian region is also a maelstrom of interests in conflict, a problem exacerbated by the lack of any centralized political control. For one thing the region is experiencing environmental degradation of devastating proportions. For another, local economies in the region based on traditional industries and occupations such as fishing and, more recently, tourism are under severe stress, putting at risk the livelihoods of many thousands of inhabitants and hundreds of communities. Given these difficulties international talk of the region sitting on a mine of strategic resources appears to local inhabitants as a cruel joke, much the same as the offer by the Bush regime "to advance the cause of freedom and peace" in the region (step one: invade Afghanistan and change the regime; step two: liberate Iraq and change the regime; step three — presently stalled — deal with Iran, the new potential centre of Islamic political power).

Since there is no definitive agreement among these five countries in the Caspian Sea region concerning the exploitation of energy and other economic resources, the conflict of interests is unresolved. And it is evident that this area, rich in energy resources but within a political vacuum, is a strong temptation to outside "interests," particularly American and European. From a geopolitical point of view, resource access and exploitation in this strategic area will most likely end up being regulated via an agreement among the five coastal states. But up to now such an agreement has not been in the offing, partly because of strained relations among the governments involved and partly because of the lack of a formula acceptable to the US, the EU and Russia.

From an economic point of view, the collapse of the Soviet Union and its transition towards capitalism has had grave repercussions. From 1992 to 1998, Russia's GDP shrunk 40 percent and at present is barely 20 percent of EU GDP. The rate of gross domestic investment also collapsed, reduced by 60 percent, to 13 percent of GNP (compared to 31–35 percent in East Asia and 44 percent in China). From 1992 to 1994, manufacturing production fell by 50 percent. A major cause of this economic collapse, one of several, was the virtual disappearance of purchasing power capacity in the working and middle classes. Under conditions of price liberalization implemented in 1992, the withdrawal of state subsidies and a near total collapse of the currency, widespread poverty accompanied a major contraction of the domestic market. This contraction, coupled with a major bottleneck in exports, brought about an idling of a large part of the production apparatus and a consequent rise in unemployment.

The situation began to improve in 1998, until the economy succumbed to the effects of a financial crisis that first hit Mexico in 1995 and then Asia in mid-1997. To some extent because of this crisis, but also for other reasons, the subsequent capitalist development of the Russian economy does not compare well with other so-called "transition economies," such as those of Poland and Hungary, which have managed a more successful "adjustment" to the requirements of the new world economic order. In 1997, business investments in Russia were below 13 percent of GNP and foreign direct investments did not even reach one percent of GNP (0.8 percent). Russia's "integration" into the world capitalist system in

1998 was rewarded with a financial crisis of devastating proportions, pushing a large part of its besieged middle class, which had been formed under very different economic conditions, into poverty and other conditions of low income. In this situation, Russia, like Asia the year before, succumbed to pressures exerted by the IMF and other "international" financial institutions to devalue its currency. It was also forced to restrict consumption (imports) and promote exports, and thereby generate hard-currency, foreign-exchange reserves in US dollars. (However, the Russian government has since turned towards the euro, to the consternation of US officials). Under these conditions, according to the State Statistical Committee (Goskomstat), imports were indeed reduced (by 45 percent) but exports in the first semester of 1999 also fell by 11.7 percent.[1]

Russia's situation improved in 2000, largely as a result of oil and gas exports and increases in world market prices for these energy resources. With the contribution of these exports, the GNP grew 10 percent in 2000, 5.5 percent in 2001 and 2002, 7.6 percent in 2003 and 7.4 percent in 2004 (with a 9.2 percent growth in industrial production) — a growth rate sustained almost entirely by increased oil and gas exports and increases in oil prices. Under these improved conditions, unemployment shrank from 7 million in 2000 to 5.7 million in 2004 and the rate of inflation was reduced from some 20 percent in 2000 to 10.2 percent in 2004, leading to a mild recovery in wage levels and incomes available to households (a 6 percent increase in real income in 2003). All this led to an expansion of the domestic market, fuelled by increased demand for consumer goods and machinery.

However, this improvement in macroeconomic conditions has not manifested at the micro-social level: the share of labour in national income is less than 50 percent of what it used to be, average wage rates are barely at the poverty line and access to government-provided free social services is unavailable, mainly because they no longer exist; public services have by and large been either privatized or eliminated, despite a major recovery in public finances due to state revenues from the export of natural gas and oil. The most striking indication of Russia's economic recovery is the growth in its trade surplus ($67 billion in 2004), by far the largest trade surplus of any "emerging market" country (China's trade surplus for the year was $15.3 billion) and in fact the third-largest in the world. Only Germany and Japan posted higher trade surpluses from mid-June 2003 to mid-June 2004 — $179.6 billion and $124 billion, respectively (*Economist*, July 31, 2004, p. 89). The euro area as a whole posted a trade surplus of $107.6 billion, while the US trade deficit climbed to $572.9 billion.

These trade balance differences play into the dynamics of inter-imperialist competition. However, for Russia, even though integration into the global economy has begun to produce some macroeconomic benefits, growing inequalities in the distribution of these benefits means that the economic conditions of the majority of working Russians continue to deteriorate. Most of the benefits have been appropriated by members of a rapidly emerging capitalist class, a situation not unlike the US, where the corporate rich, the top 10 percent of income "earners," have appropriated 90 percent of the economic surplus generated by the economy since the mid-1980s and the record-breaking economic boom of the 1990s, leaving a third of the population (15 percent officially) in poverty (Collins, Hartman and Sklar 1999).

In September 2001, in the midst of an economic upswing, the Russian Federation's foreign debt was $143.3 billion, $93.3 billion of which was inherited from the Soviet epoch. Of this debt, $17.6 billion was due to the IMF and to the World Bank and $39 billion to the Paris Club <www.ICE.it>. From 2000 to the first nine months of 2001, foreign investments grew by over 23 percent, attracted by the prospects of profit repatriation, an emerging market and the promise of legal security for any business set up or property acquired. The major investors are Germany, the US, Cyprus, France, the UK, the Netherlands and Italy, Europe's second-biggest importer of Russian goods.

In 2002 and in the first months of 2003 the macroeconomic "fundamentals" remained positive, showing a mild upswing, particularly in the growth of GNP and foreign investments. The Russian Stock Exchange also increased in value and volume of transactions, reaching a peak in September 2003, and the ruble acquired a degree of relative stability and strengthened its international exchange rate. The exchange rate of the ruble to the dollar in June 2005 was 1:27, a favourable situation for exports. These are all positive signals for foreign investors, who had left en masse after the 1998 financial crisis.

With an increase in its real value (between 3 and 5 percent in 2004), the convertibility of the ruble on international markets has become a real possibility. Russia has also begun to show increasing interest in the euro as a reserve currency. In addition to gold and dollars, the government has been shoring up reserves in euros, a fact that has not gone unnoticed in the US.

Economic growth in Russia is the result in part of a substantial increase in the world price for oil, which rose from roughly $24 a barrel in 2002 to more than $58 a barrel by June 2005. Russia, like China, hopes to join the WTO, signalling its integration into the new world order. This integration, it is thought, would bring about a considerable increase in its GNP, increasing the probability of the ruble becoming an international currency. Negotiations have gone on between the several countries of the former Soviet Union on the possibility of using the ruble as a common currency.

However, for Russia to become an economic power capable of competing with the "West," it must regain control over the Ukraine. In addition to having a population of over 50 million and thus a huge potential market, the Ukraine is a strategic junction endowed with underground resources of great quantity and quality, which controls the passage to the Black Sea. Control over the Ukraine would provide Russia with a presence in both Asia and Europe. If Russia could control Azerbaijan, also endowed with enormous energy and mineral resources, in addition to the Ukraine, it would gain access to Central Asia as well as the Caspian Sea (Brzezinski 1998).

Geological studies have estimated that oil resources in the area could be as much as 235 billion barrels — like a new Persian Gulf. In Kazakhstan there are enormous oil fields (in Kashagan) exploited by the Italian company Agip, the leader of a group of nine international companies that includes Shell, British Gas, and BP-Amoco. Azerbaijan has reserves of more than 20 billion barrels of oil, and Turkmenistan has 25 percent of the total gas reserves of the Caspian Sea area (i.e., 18 percent of world reserves) (Vasapollo 2003). And these figures do not take into consideration as yet undiscovered reserves.

Russia no longer considers oil as solely a raw material to be exported. It accords oil a strategic value for its own geopolitical and geo-economic position. Russia seeks to convert its reserves into a strategic alternative to the Persian Gulf reserves, particularly in the context of a forecasted increase in world oil production from 380 to 520 million tons. But to increase production it needs to attract infrastructural investments and international sources of capital to the tune of $500–800 billion (Vasapollo 2003). And it was in this context in September 2003 that the news broke that Saudi Arabia and Russia, the world's two major exporters of oil, were about to sign a five-year agreement for cooperation in the energy sector and collaborative initiatives in world markets.

Oil, gas and electrical energy constitute the flywheel of Russia's "national" development, allowing it to portray itself as a major competitive force on the world market, once again a (potentially) major economic power — and potential threat to US economic dominance. It is for this reason that Russia is trying to maintain a measure of political and military control over the whole area of the former Soviet Union, exploiting "internal conflicts" to this end. This obviously clashes with the expansionistic designs of "Western" imperialism, which favour the emergence of new states, precisely to prevent Moscow from installing military bases on its former territories.

How do Bush's and Russia's "wars on terrorism" play into these strategic geopolitical considerations? First of all, as long as the world is involved in a war on Afghan territory and its surroundings, Russia can keep using the pipelines on the northern banks of the Caspian Sea that run from Kazakhstan to the Russian coasts of the Black Sea. In this way, the Novorossiysk pipeline allows Russia to become the main country able to provide Europe with oil from the Caspian Sea. Thus it is that Russia seems to look favourably on the presence of the US in its former Asian territories. However, in the longer view, it is doubtful whether Russia would be willing to surrender a great part of Eurasian territory to the US or the West. On the internal political front, there are many Russians who, mindful of Russia's past geo-economic power, do not at all look favourably on the American presence on territories previously belonging to the Soviet Union.

It should be clear from all of this that, after the collapse of the Soviet Union, Middle and Eastern Europe have become strategic areas of fundamental importance for the geopolitical and geo-economic interests emerging in the global competition between the US and the EU. In fact, in spite of their diversification, fragmentation and economic and social depression, these territories have significant potentialities because of their energy resources and geographical positions to act as a bridge between Asia and Europe. For these reasons they have attracted outside interest in the investment and trade opportunities offered by the region — and its strategic value.

The situation for the US is summed up by Brzezinski in the following terms:

> The collapse of the Soviet Union not only creates possibilities for the penetration of American influence in the Eurasian void (especially by consolidating the non-Russian states); it has also very important geopolitical consequences in Eurasia's sub-western ramifications: the Middle East and the Persian Gulf have been transformed into a zone of evident and exclusive American influence... [even though] due to religious and nationalist conspiracies against a foreign hegemony in the region, the present American supremacy in the Middle East is based, literally, on sand. (Brzezinski 1998: 164–65)

As Brzezinski sees it, despite its distance from these territories, the US needs to control them, if not militarily, at least economically. As he sees it, "the basic choice... will be between a delicate regional equilibrium and... ethnic conflicts, with the ensuing political fragmentation and with a possible outbreak of hostilities along Russia's southern borders." To reach this "regional equilibrium" and its consolidation remains "the main objective of any general American geo-strategy for Eurasia" (Brzezinski 1998: 202).

The US's China Syndrome

China today exports up to one-half of its social product, but the basic motor of economic growth in China has been not the world market but the extraordinary rate of internal savings and domestic capital formation — 44 percent of GNP. Unlike Latin America, which has succumbed to the new economic model of neo-liberalism and its reliance on the importation of capital (termed "liberalization" and "integration"), China has financed its economic growth with internal savings, generated largely through the compression of wage costs, the lowest in the world. Foreign investments constitute barely 5.6 percent of China's GNP, a situation that contrasts dramatically with Brazil, whose economy was the same size as China's some ten years ago but today, according to the World Bank (2004), has a GNP barely 50 percent of that of China ($1.4 billion).

The pace of China's economic growth has been so phenomenal as to raise concerns about "overheating" and a possible crash landing for the fastest-growing economy in the world. Reflecting this concern, Chinese authorities have pursued policies designed to reduce the rate of annual growth, from up to 12 percent in 2002 to 9 percent in 2003 and an anticipated 8.5 percent in 2004. Most observers project a "soft" rather than "crash landing" for China's economy precisely because of the capacity of the Chinese Communist Party to control the speed and direction of economic growth.

There are those who saw the hands of imperialism in the Asian crisis of 1997, viewing it as a means employed by the US to reduce, if not destroy, the rate of economic growth and competitive edge of many Asian exporters in the world market. But China is a different matter. For one thing, its participation in world trade is so large (60 percent) that a collapse of this trade would have serious repercussions for all of the major economies in the world, not least for the US, to which China contributes directly to 21 percent of export growth. Chinese exports soared by 111 percent over five years to reach $82 billion in 2004, surpassing Mexico as the second-largest exporter to the US. At this rate of growth, in a few years China will also surpass Canada, whose annual exports to the US are valued at $100 billion. China also contributes to 28 percent of export growth in Germany (Rahme 2004: 16). More generally, China consumes 55 percent of the world's production of cement and 36 percent of steel production, an issue of vital concern for US producers in this sector. It is also estimated that two-thirds of Japan's economic growth is directly tied to the growth of Chinese exports. So all these and the other forces propelling its high and rapid rates of growth should make China an economic superpower in the coming decade.

One of several anticipated positive effects of what Alan Greenspan, chair of the US's central bank, "the Federal Reserve," in a conference on bank regulation, termed China's "successful de-acceleration" (slowing down its economic growth from 12 percent to 9 percent in 2003) is a lowering of pressures for higher prices in the world market for natural resources and raw materials. Another anticipated effect is a reduction of inflationary pressures, particularly in Asia's inflated stock market, a situation that will ultimately impact the large volumes of US treasury bonds placed there. However, slowing down the engine of China's economic growth has broader implications for the US vis-à-vis its ambition to dominate the world economy. If China were to continue its recent rates of growth, in a few decades it would surpass the US economy in size and importance, and become a threat to US economic power — a "formidable rival," according to John Mearsheimer (2002), even greater than the European Union. "[A] rising China," Mearsheimer argues, "is the most dangerous potential threat to the United States in the early 21st Century." Thus, he adds, "the United States has a profound interest in seeing Chinese economic growth slow considerably in the years ahead."

China is thus a critical factor in US strategic calculations. However, the China factor has also thrown a spanner in the workings of and/or support for "globalization," leading some "liberal" economists to underestimate the negative effects of global competition on the US economy and turning others towards protectionism. Cheap imports from China have dramatically increased consumption in the US, sustaining the growth of the home market, but at the same time they have seriously undermined US industrial production, with a consequent negative impact on the country's trade account, which in July 2004 was imbalanced to the tune of $573 billion (*Economist*, July 31, 2004). Only the continued capacity of the US economy to attract investments and finance from all over the world has allowed it to sustain a deficit on its trade account of this dimension. China, with a positive trade balance of $15.3 billion and a current account balance of $45.9 billion, understandably has resisted any pressures towards isolationism, pressuring instead for membership in the WTO, expanded trade, globalization and free trade, with open access to the US domestic market.

Precisely because of its capacity to draw on its comparative advantages in the new world order of global capital, China has become a major champion of globalization and "free trade," even opening up to some degree its own domestic market to foreign competition, by encouraging MNCs to set up shop inside China, allowing them to not only penetrate its huge potential emerging market but also to take advantage of its huge reserves of cheap labour. One reason why China factors so large is that 60 percent of US imports from China are actually manufactured in China by American MNCs. Thus US capital benefits from US trade deficits. However, these developments have also stirred up dormant protectionist forces within the US, even among circles that have been traditional champions of liberalism.

In the first half of the 1990s, DRI/McGraw Hill, a "prestigious" consultancy agency in world affairs, launched the "10 percent theory." According to this theory, one should not count on the whole market of the emerging countries; one should count on only the 10 percent with a purchasing power comparable to that of the top OECD countries. The strategic objective is one-tenth of consumers in China and other "emerging markets." In the case of China this means anywhere from 120 to 180 million people (10–15 percent) — attractive enough to awaken the salivating juices of Euro-American imperialism.

Within the context of a sluggish if not stagnant world economy — in 2003 the rate of growth system-wide was only 2.3 percent — the only country that has been on a consistent growth path has been China. The US economy is still regarded as the fundamental engine of the global economy, pulling along economies all over the world, especially Mexico and Canada, countries that are so closely integrated into the US economy as to be nearly totally dependent on it for both exports and imports. Similarly, economic growth in China has pulled along growth in other countries, not only in Asia but even in the US itself. It is seldom appreciated or sufficiently understood that China is growing not only on the supply side (exports), but also on the demand side (imports, investments, wages, consumption). China is leading the global demand for many goods and some services, particularly for raw materials — from energy to wool, from metals (such as aluminium and copper) to cotton. According to some estimates, from now to 2020, China's consumption of electric power will grow by 5.5 percent annually. Moreover, China consumes more than it produces and exports. This is an indication that China's internal market is starting to grow and absorbing its own output and that foreign investment is likely to accumulate in Chinese industrial cities ("La sindrome cinese sui mercati," *Sole 24 Ore*, February 3, 2003).

The acquisition of new technologies through the opening provided by foreign investments allows China not only to export but also to develop its own internal market, often according to the expectations of foreign multinationals. The cases of automobiles and cellular phones are paradigmatic. In the case of cars, for example, the Chinese government tries to aid the development of a competitive and wholly national automobile industry by stimulating, through incentives, the 120 Chinese car producers to purchase their component parts mainly within national borders. To this end it has raised import duties. In 2003 the number of cars sold for private use grew by 60 percent. It took China, whose present national fleet of cars totals ten million, forty years to produce its first million cars, nine years to reach its quota of two million, and just two years to manufacture three million automobiles ("La Cina protegge l'auto nazionale innalzando barriere fiscali," *Sole 24 Ore*, August 29, 2003). This policy of import substitution also has major repercussions on the global economy and on the market share, if not the very survival, of some of the biggest US and European multinationals.

China in the WTO

China joined the WTO in November 2001, and already the question posed by anti-globalizationist Walden Bello (1998) is pertinent: "Will the WTO hit China or will China hit the WTO?" The results of the failed Cancun Summit point towards the latter.

As a condition of joining the WTO, heavy costs were imposed on China. These included the reduction and phased elimination of 5,000 import duties (above all on agricultural products), the modification of 2,300 internal laws and regulations, and a reduction by 25 percent of import duties. As of 2004, foreign banks were allowed to operate in local currency in nine cities (there were five banks in 2003). Foreign companies will be allowed to hold up to a 35 percent ownership in the telephone sector and up to 49 percent in high value-added companies (those which need higher technologies).

Yet, according to *Sole 24 Ore*, within the framework of the WTO's ambiguous rules governing trade, China is already winning. Five years ago, China was "politely asked" by the US not to devalue its own currency in order to function as a source of stability in Asia, some of which had collapsed under the weight of the 1997 financial crash. Thus, while the currencies of the Asian tigers were suffering, in an attempt to give some breathing space to exports from these countries, China was compelled to endure competition from its neighbours — competition which China, unlike Japan, could cope with. China accepted the mechanism of tying the yuan to the dollar. But when the US decided to devalue the dollar in order to make life difficult for the euro zone and other trading blocs, the yuan followed the greenback, giving China an unanticipated competitive advantage in trade. Chinese exports skyrocketed, causing the wave of panic that led to Guilio Tremonti's and George W. Bush's protectionist counter-offensives. US pressure on China, somewhat diminished after September 11, resumed.

Politics or Economics: Who or What is in Charge?
China is now an important player in global competition. Unlike other "emerging market" countries, it is in a position to successfully exploit globalization in its national interest and reinforce its internal market. Clearly, this approach could not work without political support from within and above. Economics alone cannot explain and does not help us understand the Chinese factor.

It is unlikely that such important changes in the socio-economic structure of the world's most populous country, which is an emerging economic superpower and likely to overtake the US in the second or third decade of this century, could take place without a serious debate within the Chinese Communist Party (CCP). This debate is in fact ongoing, and, in the context of the country's sizzling growth rate, has developed a very sharp edge. The CCP sees socialism as not only "anything that works" (Deng Xiaoping) but also as a mixed economy in which public ownership will continue to predominate. A mixed economy comprises public property (with state, collective or cooperative ownership), enterprises combining public ownership with private ownership, and private ownership (national and foreign).

The Central Committee of the CCP elaborated this notion in September 1999. Its concluding document stressed that "the nationalized economy, which as a whole has been further strengthened, keeps carrying out a primary function in the national economy and has always been the main source of income, thus backing up in a decisive manner the reform and the building of the country.... The public ownership economy, including the state owned economy, constitutes the economic basis of the Chinese socialist system" (*Die Zeit*, July 27, 2000).

However, the same CCP asserted the need to bring about changes in the structure of state industry and in company ownership. It was decided that the government could relinquish control of non-strategic enterprises, making room for several forms of ownership and allowing the conveyance of big state-owned companies. At the same time the government retained control of four categories of state-owned enterprises: (1) enterprises operating in the arms and national security sectors, (2) natural monopolies (tobacco, the Mint), (3) enterprises active in infrastructure and in the water, energy, railways, health and school sectors, and (4) basic industries such as metallurgy, coal, high technology and new technologies. Thus industry's strategic heart remains firmly in the hands of the state.

The relationship between the public and private sectors is a critical issue. According to Yang Quixan, president of the Research Institute on Economic Restructuring, 30 percent of China's GNP is accounted for by state-owned enterprises, down from 84 percent in the 1970, 40 percent by collective enterprises (35 percent of total enterprises, up from 21 percent) and 30 percent by private national or foreign enterprise (up from 4 percent to 6 percent of the total). Even if the latter would be allowed to grow to 40 percent — a possible development determined not only by government policy but also, from the perspective of private enterprise, by greater legal security for private property and protection against what is considered to be "corruption" — the greatest part of the production of national wealth would remain in public or collective hands.

The Struggle within the CCP

At the 2002 congress of the CCP, several positions clashed. The old leadership of Jiang Zemin tried insistently to impose the "Three Representations" line, which would have made the CCP an interclass party also open to private entrepreneurs. This line was firmly opposed within the party, an opposition that culminated in the "Letter by the Fourteen," addressed to the Central Committee and signed by fourteen members:

> We oppose firmly and without any reservations the proposal that the owners of private enterprises be allowed to join the Party. We believe that the position of comrade Jiang Zemin is wrong, for several reasons. It contradicts the Marxist theory of the proletarian party... it contradicts the programs and the Statute of our

> Party... it violates party discipline... [and] it acts against the will
> of the Party and of the State. (*Monthly Review*, May 2002)

The signatories invited private entrepreneurs to join another party[2] or to participate in political life as deputies of the People's Congress. Later, Ma Bin and Han Yaxi, two signers of the letter, sent a second letter to Jiang Zemin and the Central Committee, thus bringing to light a political struggle within the CCP. A large part of this struggle is concerned with exactly defining the role of the "capitalists." At present in China, two million private enterprises employ 27.13 million workers (3.7 percent of all Chinese workers).

A sector of the CCP would prefer private entrepreneurs to be co-opted by the party in order to control them better. Another sector wants to safeguard the party's class nature and prevent the "capitalists" from becoming a veritable class with their own representation. And in 1999, when a debate was opened on Marxist value theory, one official article in the party press submitted the idea that entrepreneurs are "workers" rather than "exploiters."

At the 2002 congress, three tendencies confronted one other: the left, right and centre. The left wants economic reforms that place the plan before the market and rejects the political reforms as "bourgeois liberalization." The right wants reforms that increase the role and weight of the market and assign the state only a supporting function. The centre thinks that the plan and the market are equally important and wants to keep the country's political structure as it is. However, within the left itself there are three currents: those who oppose Deng's reforms because they distort socialism, those who do not oppose the reforms but criticize their extent and the pace of their adoption, and the "New Maoist Left," who demand greater workers' control and the democratization of the economy and state (Theuret 2002).

From the CCP congress emerged Hu Jintao, to replace Jiang Zemin, and eight new members of the Permanent Committee, practically a total turnover. The CCP itself was enlarged from seven to nine members. The Political Office too was enlarged from twenty-two to twenty-four members, of which no fewer than sixteen are new. It is difficult to understand exactly who represents or occupies what position, but one thing is for sure: the political situation in China is anything but frozen.

China and Asia: Surprises in Sight

Few have paid attention to a series of bilateral and multilateral initiatives undertaken by China in the Asian region. Yet a part of this dynamism is represented by important changes in the international equilibrium and by a multilateralism that is appealing to many as a way to contain the US's imperialist aggressiveness.

In November 2003, the Association of South-East Asian Nations (ASEAN) Summit was held in Phnom Penh together with China. The organization was originally made up of Indonesia, Malaysia, the Philippines, Singapore and Thailand but later was extended to include Vietnam, Brunei, Laos, Myanmar and Cambodia. Its set-up was pushed by the US, and during the Cold War it had had an anti-Chinese function.

At this summit, the ASEAN countries signed an agreement with China to start negotiations which within ten years would produce the greatest trade area in the world: 1.7 billion people, a total GNP of $1,500–2,000 billion and an inter-area trade valued at $1,200 billion.

One year earlier, China had proposed the creation of a free trade area that would have excluded Japan and South Korea. But this time round in Phnom Penh these countries participated in the proceedings. It was anticipated that a first comprehensive agreement would be signed in 2004 (Angela Pascucci, *Il Manifesto*, November 5, 2002). And indeed it was.

China set up in 2001 the Shanghai Organization for Cooperation, to which Russia, China, Tajikistan, Kyrgyzstan and, above all, the energy-rich republics of Kazakhstan and Uzbekistan belong. The US has tried to weaken this organization by various means, including intervention in Afghanistan, but Beijing's bilateral relations with these countries, especially with Russia and Kazakhstan, seem to be improving remarkably. High-level meetings have also taken place between China and India, another slumbering but awakening Asian giant opening up to the forces of globalization but under conditions that the US will find difficult to control; the tentacles of US imperialism will find India as hard to get a hold of as China.

After years of hostility and a bloody war fought more than forty years ago but still resonating in its after-effects (having encouraged India's anti-Peking and pro-Moscow orientation in the old world order), the two giants of Asia have discovered that they have many common interests. China has agreed to recognize the previously contested borders of Sikkim, and India has declared Tibet to be "Chinese land" (which should be viewed in perspective, given that India is also host to the Dalai Lama). Their economic agreements indicate a synergy full of potential between India's state-of-the-art software knowledge and China's industrial structure. Rapprochement between such significant demographic, economic and nuclear powers as India and China can mean many things, some of which were at work at the failed summit in Cancun, and others which are causing increasing concern on the part of the US administration about the structure of the global economy and its own prospects for world domination.

10. IMPERIALISM AS LOCAL DEVELOPMENT

OVERSEAS DEVELOPMENT ASSISTANCE (ODA), OR FOREIGN AID" IN MORE common parlance, is widely viewed as a catalyst of economic development. It provides a needed boost to developing economies to assist them in a process of industrial development and modernization that is already traced out for them by the more advanced countries that now make up the rich club of "developed countries" at the centre of the system. But it is possible to look at foreign aid in a very different way — as a means of advancing the geopolitical and strategic interests of the governments and organizations that provide this aid, i.e., as designed to benefit not the recipients but the donors. In 1971, at the height of the Bretton Woods world economic order, this view was expressed in the notion of "aid as imperialism" (see Hayter 1971).

In the early 1970s, however, this world economic order was close to falling apart as the "golden age of capitalism" (Marglin and Schor 1990) came to a close. As a result, the entire system had to be re-engineered to create the conditions for renewed expansion and the accumulation of capital on a global scale. But it was not until the 1980s that a strategic solution to the crisis was found in the neo-liberal model of capitalist development: a global economy based on the principles of free enterprise and the free market. This model would also be used by the US government as a means of re-establishing its hegemony — as a new way of ensuring its domination of the world system.

The dynamics of this change — the institution of a new world economic order and processes of globalization and neo-imperialism — have been the subject of considerable theorizing and analysis (see, for example, Petras and Veltmeyer 2001, 2003a). Less well studied is the impact of these structural (and political) changes, which some see as "epoch-defining" in their scope, on the project of overseas development assistance. This chapter illuminates critical features of this process.

Aid in the 1940s and 1950s:
Combating the Lure of Communism

According to Wolfgang Sachs (1992) and his associates, the idea of development was "invented" in the late 1940s as another form of imperialism, imposing new relations of domination on peoples (and countries) struggling to liberate themselves from the yoke of colonialism. Indeed, it is often traced back to the Point Four Program of overseas development assistance announced by President Truman on January 10, 1949. However, in its multilateral form[1] it goes back to projects funded by the International Bank of Reconstruction and Development (IRDB, subsequently known as the World Bank) in Chile in 1948 and in Brazil and Mexico the year after.

The US government was the major donor by far of both bilateral and multilateral forms of ODA, and the geopolitical and strategic considerations of the US government were the most relevant in shaping the form of foreign aid. From the beginning there existed an extensive policy debate within the US as to the value and possible uses of foreign aid. Central to this debate was the question of whether or not and how the US's economic and broader interests could be served. A number of voices were raised to the effect that it would not be in the economic interest of the US to promote development in the backward areas of the world and that efforts to contain the underdeveloped countries within the Western bloc would be "unrealistic" and not fruitful for US interests. The dominant view, and the one that would eventually prevail, was that ODA could be a useful instrument of US foreign economic policy in the achievement of the broad objective of containing Communism without, at the same time, damaging US economic interests.

The US's post-World War II doctrine and foreign economic policy of "global containment" (and indirectly "domination") is reflected in the following quote: "Since 1945 the foreign economic policy of the US has been used openly... to provide maximum support for our general foreign policy.... Today [both] commerce and finance are manipulated in the interests of diplomacy" (Cohen et al. 1968: 2). This doctrine, as Levitt (1985: 33) points out, was challenged within the US by a group of political "realists," including Hans Morgenthau, George Ball and George Kennan. However, the contrary position of John Foster Dulles, who shaped the foreign policy of the Eisenhower administration, prevailed. Dulles had no sympathy or tolerance of either socialism or Third World neutrality. Like W.W. Rostow, foreign policy advisor to subsequent administrations, Dulles also had no qualms about using overseas development assistance as a weapon in this "cold war" struggle between socialism and capitalism (and "democracy").

Aid in the 1960s and 1970s: Reform or Revolution?

In areas of the developing world emerging from decades or centuries of colonial rule, the emphasis of "aid" was on building the administrative capacity of the state and providing the infrastructure for both public and private enterprise — "nation-building" in the parlance of imperial policy. In Latin America, however, the main concern in the 1960s and 1970s was to stave off pressures for revolutionary change — to prevent another Cuba. To this end, USAID promoted state-led reforms and the public provision of credit and technical assistance to the mass of small and peasant producers in the region. A good part of ODA took a bilateral form, but increasingly USAID turned to nongovernmental organizations (NGOs) as their executing arm, bypassing governments in the region and channelling funds more directly to the local communities. The NGOs provided collateral "services" or benefits to the donors, including strengthening local organizations opting for development and weakening class-based organizations with an anti-systemic orientation. In this context, the NGOs were also used, almost incidentally — and somewhat "innocently" from the perspective of many of their personnel — not only to promote economic and social development (rather than social change and revolution) but to promote the values of democratic forms of organization as well as capitalism (the use of the electoral mechanism in their politics and the market in their economics).[2]

In effect, these NGOs served as executing agents of US imperialism, promoting values and behaviour that were deemed to be functional for the economic and political interests of the growing US empire. In this they resembled the missionaries in the old imperialism; they were commissioned to spread the gospel, in this case the good word about capitalism and democracy (elections, markets) and knowledge of the "evil forces" (Communism, revolutionary change) that were lurking on the land and challenging state power.

The difference between the new missionaries and the missionaries of old — or then again perhaps there is no fundamental difference — is that more often than not they were not in the least conscious of the broader political and cultural implications of their interventions. Generally, NGO personnel were not ideologues, concerned to spread the gospel, but rather well-intentioned individuals seeking to make a small difference in the lives of people they were able to touch with their "development projects."[3] Nevertheless, in their interventions and actions, mediating between the donor organizations and the grassroots, they could not help but promote an alternative to the politics of revolutionary change. Indeed it was to this end that USAID and other bilateral or multilateral donors financed them (Friedmann 1992); the donors used the "private voluntary organizations" as partners in the shared enterprise of economic and social development — to implement their economic development programs at the project level. In this partnership they helped turn local communities away from organizations seeking to mobilize for direct action against the system and instead promoted a reformist approach to social change. In this the NGOs of the 1960s and 1970s were no different from the thousands that emerged and proliferated in the 1980s under very different circumstances.

Foreign Aid in a System in Transition: 1973–83

The period 1948–1973 has been described as the "golden age of capitalism," with reference to unprecedented rates of growth, up to 5 percent on average, across the system, both North and South. In the late 1960s, however, cracks began to appear in the foundations of the system that had generated the conditions and dynamic forces of this growth, and the engine of growth began to sputter and slow down. The result was an extended period of crisis and an extended series of strategic efforts to restructure a way out of the crisis. One of these responses involved a direct assault by capital on labour — on its share of national income, hitherto pegged to productivity gains, its organizational capacity and its political power.[4] The aim of this counteroffensive (to a series of offences by labour in the struggle to increase wages and improve working conditions) was to increase the pool of investment capital. The effect was a compression of wages to the point where in the case of US labour, the average wage of workers in 2003 was at or below the average wage rate of 1973. The same story unfolded in other parts of the world, particularly in Latin America, which under a national-populist model, had experienced rapid growth, particularly in Argentina, Brazil and Mexico. In these and other countries, the share of wages in national income was dramatically reduced — from an average of 24 percent in Mexico and 38 percent in Chile to below 20 percent in many cases — and wage rates have been compressed to levels well below those achieved in the early 1970s.

Other strategic responses to the worldwide production crisis involved the following:

- a process of technological conversion and productive transformation — without the "equity" called for by the UN Economic Commission for Latin America and the Caribbean (ECLAC) in its benchmark 1990 study;
- the evolution of a new more flexible form of regulation — post-Fordism;
- a global restructuring of development finance — provided primarily in the form of official ODA, which at the time dominated global North-South capital flows ("international transfers of resources" in official discourse); and
- a restructuring of national macroeconomic policy on the basis of what the World Bank economists dubbed the "structural adjustment pro-

gram" (SAP, later, in the context of widespread criticism, renamed "structural," or "policy," "reforms").

In regard to financial capital flows, as mentioned, the dominant stream took the form of ODA, designed as a supplemental form of finance needed to stimulate a process of economic growth. Until 1983 such aid, provided through a variety of multilateral and bilateral channels, was used for development projects or to establish the infrastructure for economic activity. As of 1983, however, in the throes of a widespread debt crisis, official aid began to take a different form. Rather than project lending it became policy lending, that is, lending premised on policy reforms oriented towards the free market.

Until this point the World Bank and other international financial institutions took the position that aid would service national development strategies "owned" by the developing countries, which were expected to pursue their own development paths. After 1983, however, with the need for countries to refinance their debts as well as access new capital, lending by the World Bank, the IMF, and bilateral institutions such as the US government, which indirectly controlled them, was predicated on policy reforms set under the SAP.

In the wake of the global crisis, the commercial banks in the US and Europe — and later in Japan — initiated a policy of overseas lending that led to an enormous flow of capital in private forms. It was an explosion of loan capital, or debt financing, that in parts of the developing world such as Latin America would exceed the official ODA. It also exceeded the transfer of capital to MNCs in the form of foreign direct investment (FDI). Table 10.1 provides a picture of these relative flows of capital as well as the returns on private equity capital flows (returns on FDI) and payments on the external debt.

Table 10.1 reflects several global trends, including the eclipse by private capital of ODA in the 1990s; a dramatic decline of commercial lending in the 1980s (with the debt crisis) and in the second half of the 1990s (after the financial crises in Latin America and Asia); and the growth of FDI as the dominant capital flow (the "backbone of private sector external financial flows," as the IMF puts it) — largely used in the acquisition of privatized enterprises and mergers with other firms, leading to a global process of asset and income concentration. The table also points towards an enormous outflow of productive resources (thus, potential capital) from the developing countries to those at the centre of the system. It is estimated that over the 1990s in Latin America alone outflows of capital in the form of returns on investments (profit repatriation, interest payments on debt and equity investments) were in excess of $500 billion (ECLAC 2002).

These outflows represent a huge drain of potential capital, which could have been used to expand production in the developing countries.

Table 10.1 Long-Term North-South Financial Flows, 1985–2001 (billion $US)

	1985–89	'90–94	'95	'96	'97	'98	'99	2000	'01
ODA	200.0	274.6	55.3	31.2	43.0	54.5	46.1	37.9	36.2
Private	157.0	547.5	206.1	276.6	300.8	283.2	224.4	225.8	160.0
FDI	76.0	268.5	106.8	130.8	172.5	178.3	184.4	166.7	168.2
PI	6.0	111.5	36.1	49.2	30.2	15.6	34.5	50.9	18.5
Other	75.0	172.5	63.2	126.2	98.1	-10.7	25.5	8.2	-26.7
Net Resource Inflows	357.0	822.5	261.4	307.8	343.8	337.7	270.5	263.7	196.2
FDI Profits	66.0	96.5	26.5	30.0	31.8	35.2	40.3	45.4	55.3
Debt Payments	354.0	356.5	100.8	106.6	112.9	118.7	121.9	126.7	122.2
Net Resource Outflows*	420.0	453.0	227.3	136.6	144.7	153.9	162.2	172.1	177.5

* This figure does not include interest payments on portfolio investments, royalty payments, shipping, insurance and other service fees; nor does it include illegal outflows of financial resources, estimated in the billions, or the even greater "loss" of productive resources through the mechanisms of trade. UNCTAD (2003) estimates this loss (hidden and indirect transfer) of productive resources to be greater than the financial resources lost to developing countries through interest payments and repatriated profits.

Source: IMF 2002a; World Bank, *Global Development Finance, Country Tables 2002*; OECD 2003.

In themselves they adequately explain the "lack" of economic growth and development in a large part of the Third World, including Sub-Saharan Africa and Latin America, under regimes of globalization and structural adjustment. Even ODA has served as a mechanism of capital drain: in 2002, repayments by the developing countries to the World Bank exceeded outlays of new "financial resources." And these calculations do not take into consideration other, less overt, forms of capital drain, such as the loss of productive resources through the organization of trade and the exploitation of labour. On this, see in particular a revealing study by Saxe-Fernández and Núñez (2001) into the diverse methods used to expropriate and transfer productive and financial resources from Latin America to the United States.

According to ECLAC (2002), over $69 billion in interest payments and profits were remitted from the region to the US home offices of the multinational corporations and banks in just one year. Saxe-Fernández and Núñez 2001) note that if we take account of the billions in royalty payments, shipping, insurance and other service fees and the billions more illegally transferred by Latin American elites via US and European banks to overseas accounts, the total pillage for 2002 was closer to $100 billion. And this is for just one year in just one part of the US empire.

Aid in an Era of Globalization: 1980s and 1990s

With the debt crisis, bank loans dried up as creditors lined up behind the World Bank and the IMF, leaving it to these institutions to ensure that the debtors would not default on their loans. And they did indeed oblige by ensuring the debtors' capacity and disposition to repay their debts. Table 10.1 shows that from 1985 to 1989, $354 billion was diverted from development projects and programs in the developing countries (primarily Latin America) to the head offices of the commercial banks — a capital drain that led directly to a "decade lost to development" both in Latin America and Sub-Saharan Africa. From 1995 to 2001, another period in which virtually no new loans were extended to the developing world by commercial banks, another $800 billion was "lost to development" in the form of interest payments on the external debt. The context for this lack of development was provided by the implementation or imposition of the SAP — a set of policy reforms set by the World Bank as a condition for restructuring existing debts or providing further aid (Burnside and Dollar 1997; Kreuger et al. 1989; Mosley 1999; Rodrik 1995). These structural reforms were designed for the requirements of a new world order based on the organizational principles of free trade and the free circulation of capital — and the unfettered global operations of free enterprise.

In the context of the announcement in 1982 by the Mexican government that it would not be able to service its debt obligations, an announcement that triggered a regionwide and to some extent global debt crisis, the IMF similarly imposed a set of austerity measures designed to establish "macroeconomic equilibrium" — that is, lower inflation and balance national accounts.

These policy reforms are well known and have been subject to considerably study, particularly as regards their socio-economic and political impacts (see, for example, Collier 1997; Veltmeyer and Petras 1997 and 2000). They are based on what has become known as the "new economic model," or more revealingly, "neo-liberalism," an economic doctrine with policy prescriptions designed to integrate all economies into the new global economy within the framework of the "new world economic order."

These policies include the following:

- privatizing the means of production and associated enterprises;
- liberalizing trade and financial flows;
- deregulating product and labour markets; and
- downsizing the state in the context of the preceding three structural reforms i.e., substituting for them the institutions of private enterprise and "the forces of freedom" (Bulmer-Thomas 1996; Veltmeyer and Petras 1997; Veltmeyer, Petras and Vieux 2000).

Both in theory and practice these policies are designed to facilitate a process of globalization and structural adjustment, and thereby a renewed global process of capital accumulation.

The second half of the 1990s opened to a virus that first affected Mexico and then, in mid-1997, Southeast Asia. Caused by the volatile and uncontrolled (deregulated) movement of hundreds of billions of dollars in capital in search of short-term profit, the "Asian (financial) crisis" devastated economy after economy in the region, stilling any talk (and much writing, particularly by the World Bank) about the "economic miracle" of rapid growth in one part of the world system.

The financial crises in Latin America and Asia resurrected the spectre of a more generalized economic crisis, even the collapse of the system itself. Under these conditions the multinational commercial banks once again pulled out, leaving a vacuum partly filled by FDI, and leading to another half decade lost to development in Latin America and elsewhere (ECLAC 2002; UNCTAD 2003). Official aid flows in this context were minimal and largely unproductive (i.e., not used to expand production), and the much larger FDI flows were also by and large unproductive (i.e., used to finance mergers and the acquisition of privatized firms). The end result of these "developments" — implementation of neo-liberal macroeconomic policies; the expropriation and transfer of productive and financial resources; and the unproductive operations of capital in the form of FDI and ODA — are not hard to find. They are exemplified in the experience of Argentina, hitherto the strongest economy in Latin America but now (and for the past several years) in the throes of a far-reaching and devastating crisis.

Alternative Development and Imperialism in an Era of Globalization: 1983–2003

ODA was originally designed to meet the foreign policy strategic requirements and interests of the US state. It can quite properly be described as an imperial policy — in the service of the agenda to establish the dominance and hegemony of the US state. In its later form, as implemented with bilateral and multilateral funding and the agency of NGOs, the development project was pressed into the service of the US empire as a means of defusing pressures for revolutionary change within its client states. The history of US state (political and military) intervention in Central America — one of the more successful arenas for the projection of US power (versus the failures in Vietnam and the Gulf region) — is a testament to the fact that more often than not the development project did not work. True, there were no other Cubas in the region, but this was the result not so much of the operations and development projects of USAID as the projection of military force and the extensive "aid" provided to counterinsurgency forces in the region.

In the 1980s an entirely new context was created for ODA by a neo-liberal project of globalization based on the SAP. In this context the development project was restructured, designed to be initiated not from above and outside but from below and within. It became an alternative, more participatory, form of development based on the partnership of intergovernmental ODA organizations and NGOs, which would mediate between the donors and the grassroots in the execution of a new generation of development projects targeted at the problem of poverty.[5] The actual flow of funds channelled through these NGOs, many unwittingly converted into agents of the new imperialism, was actually very modest but yet enough to serve as an incentive for popular organizations to turn away from groups seeking to mobilize against the system and the neo-liberal policy program and to opt instead for a more participatory form of "local development." This development is predicated on the accumulation, not of natural, physical and financial assets, but of "social capital," which the poor are deemed to have in abundance and which does not require a political confrontation with the power structure or substantial structural change (Knack 1999; Woolcock and Narayan 2000).[6]

Foreign Aid as a Catalyst of Regression

Until the 1980s ODA was the dominant form of international resource flows. The assumption behind the official transfer of ODA was the incapacity of developing countries to accumulate sufficient capital to finance development. The rationale for foreign aid was that the provision of supplementary finance, and appropriate investment of this capital, would have a catalytic effect on the economies of these countries, generating conditions that would reduce poverty and stimulate economies to grow. However, over fifty years of experience have demonstrated that, in fact, aid serves the interests of and benefits more the donor country. In effect, as a form of imperialism, ODA functions — as do other forms of resource flow — as a mechanism of surplus transfer and as such a catalyst not of development but of regression.

The evidence is clear. After two decades of rapid growth within the Bretton Woods international order, the development process stalled precisely in the areas subject to structural adjustment and dependence on FDI, commercial bank lending, and foreign aid. Parts of the Third World — to be precise, a small group of newly industrializing countries (NICs) and eight rapidly growing countries of East Asia — continued to experience high rates of economic growth and with this growth a substantial improvement in social and economic conditions. However, as shown by Bienefeld (1988), these countries neither pursued a neo-liberal model nor were subjected to the SAP. In Latin America and Sub-Saharan Africa, policies of neo-liberal reform and foreign aid were (and are) associated with a decided deterioration in social economic conditions that includes a dramatic growth in inequality in the distribution of wealth and income and a substantial increase in the number of people living and working in conditions of extreme poverty.

By the end of the 1990s, an estimated three billion people, representing close to 44 percent of the world's population, were identified as unable to meet their basic needs, and an estimated 1.4 billion are forced to subsist on less than a dollar a day, under conditions of abject poverty and misery.[7] Some of this poverty is rooted in entrenched structures of social exclusion, but it is clear enough that a large part either originates in or is exacerbated by the policy reforms associated with foreign aid. In this context, aid can indeed be viewed as a catalyst of economic underdevelopment and social regression. The historic record on this point could not be clearer. In the neo-liberal era of globalization and structural adjustment, the conditions of this regression are the direct result of the policy conditionalities attached to the provision of foreign aid.[8]

Conclusion

The dynamics of foreign aid can be understood with reference to three strategic geopolitical and economic projects advanced in the post-World War II period: *international development, globalization* and *imperialism.* Under the conditions generated by the implementation of these projects, foreign aid is an instrument of US foreign economic policy and a catalyst of underdevelopment and regression. While, of course, regression is not the intended outcome of the development enterprise, it is the inevitable outcome of the policy conditionalities attached to the provision of aid. The problem is that economic growth and development — and the whole ODA enterprise — is predicated on the adoption of institutional and policy reforms that are designed to serve the interests of the donors rather than the recipients. The historic record shows that, in this sense, foreign aid and the development project generally have been eminently successful. Foreign aid, as Hayter pointed out over three decades ago, is a form of imperialism, nothing more or less.

11. IMPERIALISM AS WAR
The Neo-cons Take Action

The alternative to a single superpower is not a multilateral utopia but the anarchic nightmare of a new dark age. — Niall Ferguson (2004)

[Bush is] likely to learn the same lesson in the early 21st century that Theodore Roosevelt and Woodrow Wilson learned in the early 20th century.... When the United States goes out alone in search of monsters to destroy — venturing in terrain which imperial powers have already trod — it can itself become the monster. — John Judis (2004)

The United States has discarded pretensions to international legality and decency, and embarked on a course of raw imperialism run amok. — William Rockler, Nuremberg Tribunal prosecutor, quoted in Chossudovsky (2004)

The Neo-cons and US Global Empire

Some five years prior to Ronald Reagan becoming president of the US, the first wave of neo-conservatives (neo-cons) formed the infamous Committee on the Present Danger (CPD). Of its sixty-one original directors, twenty-nine eventually found positions in the Reagan administration. Some of the key members of this group were Defense Secretary Donald Rumsfeld, George P. Schultz, who became secretary of state under Reagan, Richard Perle, William Kristol and several other hawkish academics who personify the contemporary neo-con, such as Richard Pipes, a member of a secret team outside the CIA ("Team B"), organized by then-CIA director George Bush Sr. This coterie of neo-cons was later joined by Paul Wolfowitz, who would join Richard Perle as assistant to Dick Cheney as secretary of defence in the Bush Sr. administration and who shared Cheney's concern with the Middle East and the geopolitics of oil.

Media coverage of US policy towards Iraq and the Persian Gulf has always debunked the idea that oil had anything to do with it or, for that matter, with the Iraq War, but it actually had a lot to do with it, and so did various plans for global domination cooked up by the neo-con gang that has captured the apparatus of the US state. In fact the US and the Middle East have been embroiled in a tug-of-war over oil ever since the 1970s "oil crisis" and the formation of the Organization of Petroleum Exporting Countries (OPEC). But at the time the prospect of seizing control of Arab oil fields by force was considered out of line, and not politically feasible. Still, the idea of controlling Middle Eastern sources of oil was and remains very attractive to this group of hard-line Washington insiders. If Saudi Arabia erupted in turmoil, Russia turned off its pipeline, "representative democracy" continued to unravel in Venezuela's Bolivarian revolution and the US lost Iraq, the oil-dependent US economy might well collapse. And, as McQuaid (2004) among others has documented so well, this strategic national interest in securing a reliable supply of oil ties in directly with US corporate interests, represented, as it happens, by Cheney himself, not to speak of other ties that bind the neo-cons in Washington to corporations in the oil sector.

During the Clinton years the neo-cons were active in conservative think-tanks and projects such as Project for a New American Century (PNAC), which included plans for gaining control over the Middle East's oil fields, and to attack Iraq and Afghanistan, long before 9/11. But they had to bide their time — until the elevation of George W. Bush to the presidency.

With the added complement of Condoleezza Rice and Colin Powell, authors of "Defence Guidance Planning" (DGP), a document that outlined the need for the US to assert its power unilaterally "when collective action cannot be orchestrated" in the service of the global American empire, the neo-con noose around the neck of US foreign policy was set to be tightened.

The neo-con project of global American empire — its plan for global dominance, for a "new imperialism" that would not "hesitate to use [coercive] force if, when and where necessary" and for unilateral action if required — was at least a decade in the making and was hatched within George Bush Jr.'s presidency, if not earlier. In 1992 *The Washington Post* made public a secret Pentagon document — the infamous "Wolfowitz Report." The existence and paternity of the report was denied, but it did nevertheless arouse controversy, especially among US "allies." The report anticipated what would later be asserted by Martin Feldstein: "We must discourage the other industrialized nations from challenging American leadership and from bringing into question the economic and political established order. We must keep such a military supremacy that potential rivals will be dissuaded from aspiring to a larger regional or global role." The 1992 Wolfowitz Report explicitly asserted that the US had to maintain a military machine so powerful as to discourage local or global rivalries, and to maintain its supremacy, America had to forcefully terminate the proliferation of nuclear, chemical or biological weapons in Iraq and North Korea. Wolfowitz was also the lead author of the notorious "Project for a New American Century" document, drafted eight years later, which proposed the unilateral projection of US political and military power in the service of empire — to help the US carry out its global responsibilities and its imperial burden, to free the world and secure the new American world order. This document draws much of its inspiration, and its policy recommendations, from the earlier report and, like it, is saturated with a belief in the moral and military supremacy of the US.

By 2000 the neo-con cabal had found the perfect puppet for their plans of global domination in George W. Bush and were able to codify the 1990 DGP document into official US policy. Having seized state power, they began to plot in earnest the invasion of Iraq. The rest, as they say, is history.

The Bush Doctrine: Unrestrained Empire-building

The Bush Doctrine, set out in his US National Security Strategy report, and speech of September 20, 2002, promotes a "single sustainable model for success" on the basis of a unilateral projection of US power and unlimited offensive ("pre-emptive") wars. While couched in the language of "defence" and "liberty," the Bush Doctrine is an extreme departure from the previous Truman doctrine of "containment" (limiting Soviet influence) and even the Reagan doctrine of "rollback" (reversing Soviet influence). The Bush Doctrine is based on reference to undefined conspiratorial enemies — "shadowy networks of individuals" who "overlap" with "rogue states" that are opposed to US policy and power (an "axis of evil") and are planning an "imminent" attack on the US with terrorist tactics and dangerous technologies ("weapons of mass destruction") that threaten the "forces of freedom and good."

In most of Bush's speeches — and those of Rumsfeld and the rest of the neo-con gang — the imperialist starting point of US politics is made clear: "Today, the US enjoys a position of unparalleled military strength and political influence.... We seek... to create a balance of power that favours human freedom" (i.e., US empire). By definition, any country, big or small, that fails to accept or support US imperial conquest is an enemy. In Bush's words, "you are either with us or against us." The US will persuade countries to support US empire-building "by convincing or compelling states to accept their sovereign responsibility." Washington's vitriolic attacks on German Chancellor Gerhard Schroeder's opposition to the US war against Iraq was one example.

Washington's vision of world conquest through offensive wars is defended by a totally irrational logic: "Weak states... can pose as great a danger to our national interest as strong states." However, Afghanistan and Iraq did not bomb the US. It was the other way around.

The Bush Doctrine speaks of "emerging threats linked to dangerous technologies," citing 9/11 even though the hijackers used $2 plastic box cutters — $38 of high technology — to seize airliners and crash them into the Twin Towers and the Pentagon.

The doctrine does not target active terrorists with weapons intent on causing harm. Rather, it plans to destroy "plans" and "emerging threats." "Plans" refers to discussions, ideas, debate — not to actions or even the securing of weapons. In other words, US destruction of "emerging threats" means licence to assassinate any "international terrorist" associated with "dangerous technologies." Watch what you say when shaving.

More seriously, the Bush Doctrine states that "economic freedom" — the failed neo-liberal economic system — is one of the key "values" that the US will defend militarily through offensive war if necessary. This part of the doctrine has specific relevance for Latin America, where US "economic freedom" has devastated the lives of hundreds of millions of people. Instead of acknowledging that "economic freedom" in Latin America has led to poverty, authoritarianism and insecurity, the Bush Doctrine reduces "regional conflict" to a problem with "drug cartels" and "terrorists and extremist groups," referring to US military intervention in Colombia as a model.

But the resurgence of popular social and electoral movements in Argentina, Bolivia, Brazil, Venezuela and elsewhere that reject US domination and its client states puts the lie to Bush's assertion that "in the Western Hemisphere we have formed flexible coalitions with countries that share our priorities, particularly Mexico, Brazil, Canada, Chile and Colombia." Below the level of certain "foreign ministries," the great majority of Latin Americans reject US priorities, as do the ten million Brazilians who voted against ALCA, the majority of the Mexican Congress who reject support for the US war against Iraq, and the several hundreds of thousands who joined a general strike against the Uribe/IMF austerity plan.

The Bush Doctrine refers to "consultation," "allied cooperation" and "freedom," yet in the same document makes over a dozen assertions of the US "right" to unilateral action. It speaks of "allied cooperation," yet Washington venomously attacks France and Germany, and indirectly Canada, in fact all NATO allies and members of the same club of rich nations, the G-8, who do not support the US in its warmongering. Bush talks of "consultation," yet rejected the near unanimous voice of the UN insisting on the return of weapons inspectors to Iraq. The Bush Doctrine claims to support an "independent and democratic Palestine," while the administration abstained from a UN resolution calling on Israel to desist from bombing Arafat's headquarters.

The Bush Doctrine combines the rhetoric of freedom, coalition building, consultation and peace, with war preparations, unilateral action and military conquest. It explicitly warns European competitors and critics, as well as Russia and China, not to challenge US efforts to build a world empire in the cause of "freedom and peace." The Bush Doctrine warns China's leaders to make the right "choices about the character of their state" and not to seek "advanced military capabilities." In regard to the Russians and Europeans it "reaffirms the essential role of American military strength." It says "[the US] must build and maintain [its] defenses beyond challenge" — a warning directed against the "renewal of old patterns of great power competition."

The Bush Doctrine goes beyond flaunting US military power to presenting it as a form of political blackmail to keep competitors and allies in line and cow "the enemies of freedom and peace." In this cause the doctrine justifies not only the waging of war against any nation or group opposed to the self-appointed role of the US as the guardian of the new world order of freedom and democracy but also the need to strike without provocation, to take preventative action as it sees fit. The Bush Doctrine's extremism is found in its embrace of "defensive" (that is, offensive) war and its explicit commitment to not only defend the current boundaries of the empire though client regimes but to extend geopolitical, military and political boundaries to conquer and exploit new "strategic regions."

What has been the outcome of Washington's warmongering and paranoiac rhetoric about threats to national and world security, to the forces of freedom and peace?

Because of his initial defiance of Washington and because of Rumsfeld's vituperative attack, Schroeder won the German election. In Bolivia the US ambassador's intervention in the presidential elections led to a doubling of the popular vote for the Movimiento a Socialismo (MAS), almost elevating to state power the leader of a 30,000-strong movement of coca-producing peasants. Washington's unilateral war against Iraq has aroused worldwide opposition in the streets, parliaments and UN — more than any other event in recent history. Out of eleven top officials in the Bush administration dealing with Latin America, eight are Cuban exiles profoundly hostile to Cuba. Even so, seven hundred US business executives, agricultural producers and politicians participated in the Food Fair in Havana, and the US Congress narrowly failed to end the travel ban. Polls showed that two out of three US citizens regarded domestic economic issues as more important than the war. It was the prospect of losing the November 2004 elections that finally led Bush to beat a strategic retreat from Iraq to return "sovereignty" to the Iraqis (that is, to those willing to do the US's bidding).

The ultra-imperialist policies enunciated in the Bush Doctrine are a real threat to humanity. Apart from Israel and its lobby in the US, and the extreme warlords in and surrounding the US administration, there was limited support for the Bush Doctrine and the Iraq War largely because of fear that a war would have a negative and possibly catastrophic impact on the economy and provoke more violence. By June 28, 2005, CNN polls indicated that 58 percent of Americans opposed the war and believed that they had been misled by the Bush administration about the motivations for going to war in Iraq.

It is important to criticize and reject the immediate threats posed by the Bush Doctrine in particular, as well as the longer-standing imperialist agenda that can be traced back deep in US history and that certainly encompasses various Democratic administrations, including those of Kennedy and Clinton. But it is also important to recognize and oppose the imperialist system and militarist governing class that sustains it. In Canada George W. Bush has been described as a "moron leading a coalition of idiots." It is tempting to view him as a moron (his many Bushisms seem to proclaim it), and for the majority of Americans, who seem to have no problem with US assertion of its state power, to follow blindly or slavishly Bush's crusade against "the forces of evil" (the "enemies of freedom and democracy") can certainly be described as idiocy. But it would be a mistake to view Bush thusly. He should be viewed as the personification and political representative of class forces operating in the US and the world economy. These class forces need to be studied and understood.

The Middle East and the Geopolitics of Imperialist War

Against the background of the Iraq War, which has been more costly and more destabilizing than other wars waged by the US since Vietnam, another long-standing problem is threatening to move onto centre stage, dragging the US into the regional conflict between Israel and the Arab states over the Palestine question.

Palestinians are under threat of a "final solution." Many think that the Sharon government would like to take advantage of tangible and effective US support to eliminate the Palestine National Authority — to bring about a "final solution" to the Palestine question and fulfil the dream of "Eretz Israel," a "Greater Israel" whose constitution requires the expulsion of a great many Palestinians, confining those who remain to a Bantustan-type system. Sandro Viola stresses this point in a "Letter to a Palestinian friend," which sees the threat hanging over the Palestinians as symmetrical to the "violent shake-up in the Middle Eastern picture" that the US and Israel seek to impose within the framework of preventive war (*La Repubblica*, February 25, 2003).

Day after day, an endless string of selective murders and a process of ethnic cleansing continue to ravage the cities, villages and refugee camps of Palestine. Constant, almost daily, roundups and killings, aimed at militants but with enormous "collateral damage" (the death or maiming of countless innocent citizens, including women and children) entail the devastation of permanent refugee camps, bombings and mass arrests.

What took place in the Balkans could be a pale rendition of what will likely take place in Palestinian territories occupied by Israeli colonists and soldiers. The argument that pain and mourning affect Israelis as much as Palestinians because of suicide bombers and attacks against Israel would no longer hold if the real story of the military and colonial occupation of the Palestinian territories were come to light. At issue are resistance to foreign occupation by force and the historical complicity of European colonialism.

In March 1982, right before Israeli tanks and aircraft invaded Lebanon, the Israeli embassy in Italy gave parliamentarians "a document that summed up Israel's point of view on the political and security problems in the Arab-Israeli conflict" (Vasapollo 2003) The document was the text of a conference held in London by Israeli Ambassador Shlomo Argov. An attempt on his life was the pretext for unleashing operation "Peace in Galilee" and the invasion of Lebanon. In his speech, Argov asserted that "Israel's obsession with peace will be permanent and undeletable." He also spoke of "the determination to obtain new borders, more secure than the old, 1967 ones" and gave his assurance that "the view of a total withdrawal, as that from the Sinai Peninsula [following the Camp David accords], will not be repeated somewhere else."

These three strategic, almost theological concepts — security, new borders, no withdrawal — some twenty years later have taken shape as the project on which the Israeli government is betting in order to "solve" the Israeli-Arab conflict on its own terms. No serious peace negotiations and no "road map" are possible on the basis of these three concepts, but the Israeli government keeps thinking that it has to present the world with a *fait accompli*. In this context, the Oslo peace talks could not but fail because of the colonization brought about by a "critical mass" of 800,000 colonists from Russia. The ensuing boom of settlements on Palestinian territories forced the Palestinians into a desperate struggle for defence of their land, their water wells and their very survival. But the occupation and settlement by almost one million Israelis of Palestine land, water and settlements is not a process that can be easily reversed without risking a sharp and possibly terminal social conflict within Israeli society. The efforts of the Sharon regime to finesse a solution by closing down settlements in the Gaza Strip while extending them on the West Bank is likely to fail and unlikely to resolve the conflict.

Israel's withdrawal from southern Lebanon, after an occupation of almost eighteen years, highlighted the human, material and political costs exacted by the constant guerrilla initiative of the Lebanese and Palestinian resistance (which has cost the Israeli army hundreds of casualties). As told by Mordecai Richler in some of his novels, this cost cannot be borne indefinitely by a society such as Israeli, where the "Western" way of life coexists, albeit with difficulty and much conflict, with confessional obscurantism.

The second Intifada and its transformation into a liberation war (moving from street fights with stones to guerrilla initiatives) probably counted on this "Lebanonization" of the conflict — on a wearing-out effect to force the Israeli government to consider "abandoning its policy of colonial settlement" in Palestinian territories and accepting the thesis of "two peoples, two states."

A painful but objective accounting reveals that suicide attacks against Israeli occupation petered out in the 1990s and stopped altogether in 1999 and the first months of 2000. This means that the Oslo negotiations and the prospect of a durable agreement that would lead to an independent Palestinian state had weakened the strategy of suicide attacks. But it is just as clear that Sharon's provocation in the open space of the mosques and the escalation of Israeli repression brought about a resurgence of these attacks. In fact, suicidal attacks have targeted Israeli cities and colonies in reaction to the Israeli murders of Palestinian leaders. Thus, the nexus between cause and effect and the impossibility of reaching a military solution of the Palestinian problem vividly emerges. Moreover, in a document made known by Edward Luttak in the autumn of 2001, one year after the second Intifada began (Vasapollo 2003), the Israeli authorities stated their conviction that they could manage the repression of the Palestinian revolt with a very low loss of Israeli lives. But events took a different turn.

As reported by many correspondents, the sense of insecurity within the settlements and in the very heart of the Israeli state is causing considerable damage to the economy and the cohesion of Israeli society. The option of total war represented by Sharon was supposedly meant to avoid this situation. In reality it aimed at a quick and definitive repression, at the expulsion of as many Palestinians as possible from the contested territories, and the reduction of those who remained to the condition of a South African Bantustan.

To achieve this aim Israel needs US support and the conspiratorial neutrality and indulgence of Europe. The systematic activation of pro-Israel lobbies in all important countries has become a sort of general mobilization from which no "Jew" can escape, even at the cost of exaggeration or of the asphyxiating omnipresence of commentators, writers, experts, historians and Israeli or pro-Israel Nobel Prize winners in all the most important media.

This is the meaning of the attempt to paint the Israeli-Palestinian colonial conflict as a clash of civilizations where Israel is seen as the democratic stronghold of the Western model (the "best possible model" in that region, in spite of all its defects) as against the Arab-Islamic terrorism and barbarism that threaten Western civilization. The phobic campaign against Islam and the Arabs which burst out in the US and Europe after the attacks against the Twin Towers in New York coincides exactly — perhaps too exactly — with that orchestrated for the defence of the Israeli stronghold in the Middle East. But why does Palestine, this little piece of occupied territory, continue to be the unresolved contradiction of the Middle East?

The Middle East and the US Empire

> We have seen things that we had never dreamt of seeing: burning cars in Bahrain, half a million persons protesting in Morocco, other demonstrations in Egypt. This situation worries us and this preoccupation is due to the fact that we no longer face a conflict between the two sides of the occupied territories. Rather, we are faced with something that seethes and brims over as a cauldron and affects not only Israeli interests but also America's, in a lasting, long-term, way. —Colin Powell (quoted in Vasapollo 2003)

This evaluation by Colin Powell on one of his trips to the Middle East as secretary of state, reveals a new situation in the Middle East. The conflict unleashed by the Israeli military and colonial occupation of Palestine is the crux of both the Middle Eastern crisis and the not-so-hidden secret of what is at stake in the "war without end" unleashed by the Bush gang in the US administration. As Ugo Tramballi, a commentator on international affairs, says in *Sole 24 Ore*, after the war in Afghanistan, which paved the way for the US to move into Central Asia, the "heart of the problem" is not "that country far away (Afghanistan) but the Middle East, including that wedge of western civilization in Israel" (September 16, 2001).

Powell's apocalyptic scenario and Tramballi's assessment provide different perceptions of an inter-imperialist rivalry that can be traced as far back as the "Great 1973 Crisis," which presented capitalist democracies in Europe and the North America with a major set of challenges, including an oil shock.

Some time ago, in an extensively published comment, Henry Kissinger, a protagonist of this crisis, settled the Palestinian question rather peremptorily in the following terms: no international peace conference because it would "isolate America," no Israeli withdrawal from the territories occupied in 1967 "because no Israeli premier has ever thought that such a line could be proposed," and no support to the Saudi Arabian plan "because it would encourage Jihad fanatics roaming the world." The solution proposed by Kissinger was a division of the world between the US and its European allies in terms of "their own interests." In Kissinger's scenario the former should play the role of the main negotiator and the latter that of "contributing to interrupt the flow of peace initiatives aiming at improving their position in the Arab world but actually necessarily fostering the radicalization of the Arabs' expectations and position" (*Los Angeles Times/La Stampa*, May 9, 2001).

US officials and foreign policy strategists understand that the US must play hardball in the Middle East if it wants to avoid the scenario painted by Powell and to bring back under its influence and control the area's strategic states, with which relations have become strained, to say the least. On the list of "rogue states," those that reject US dominance, are already Syria and Iran, but Lebanon and Saudi Arabia could also be placed on this list if future political developments there turn against the US. Three of these countries account for half of the world's oil production, but four of them have built a privileged relationship with the EU and Russia rather than the US.

Events surrounding Bin Laden and al-Qaeda have shown that economic groups determined to compete with US hegemony have grown in the Arab and Muslim countries. In Saudi Arabia, Egypt, Pakistan, Indonesia and Malaysia, sectors of the "petro-feudal" bourgeoisie, with strong interests in the world of finance, seek to escape American control.

A document elaborated by Wolfowitz in 1998 argued that the Arabs should be forced to sell not only their oil to the MNCs but also their oil wells, and that it is necessary to prevent the destabilization of strategic countries such as Saudi Arabia. It is a document ahead of its time, but indicative of US preoccupations in the area.

According to the assessment by Kissinger as well as by the hard-core neo-cons in the Bush administration (Rumsfeld, Cheney, Wolfowitz), management of the Middle East crisis should dispense with not only the EU but the cooperation with the so-called moderate Arab countries. As Geoffrey Aronson writes in *Le Monde Diplomatique* (May 2002), "What advantage would there be in paying a political price for Arab cooperation if this is not essential and if the US are sure to be able to obtain it in case of an American victory?" The absence of any Arab allies in the war against Iraq (with the exception of Kuwait and some Gulf emirates) confirms this view as US policy.

Iraq as a Sacrificial Lamb to US Imperialism

George W. Bush's regime needed to settle scores with Iraq in order to send several warnings to the other players in the Middle East conflict. The first warning was to the Arab world's popular movements, which would like to topple their governments or force them to adopt a more hard-line policy towards Israel and the US, and to push to regain their national identity and independence.

The second warning was to Saudi Arabia which had, even before the quarrel over Osama Bin Laden and funding support of al-Qaeda, begun to show some signs of independence, threatening the presence of US military bases on Saudi soil and ready to convert its "petrodollar" capital into euros, depriving the US of a crucial fund of capital ("Doccia fredda sulle relazioni con Washington," *Le Monde Diplomatique*, May 2002). Behind

Bin Laden and al-Qaeda's challenge to the US are also the ambitions of a nascent Arab bourgeoisie, which, relying on oil and its capital deposited in American and English banks, has gradually come to the realization that it can become a new power pole, a fine line in the balance — if not in the world equilibrium — certainly in the regional equilibrium in the Middle East. The influence and prestige earned by the television channel Al-Jazeera is an indication of the changed cultural climate. The September 11 events have brought to light how much the US has feared this possibility. It is obvious that the game is played above all in the Gulf, and that Iraq is in this sense a "sacrificial victim" through which to send very serious warnings to Saudi Arabia, Iran and the Gulf emirates without having to bomb them.

The third warning of the Bush administration was directed towards Europe. One message was that the US would do whatever is required, and at whatever cost, to maintain world order and protect its national interest — the secure development of its economy, the fundamental engine of growth in the global economy. Another message was that the US has both the moral responsibility and the duty of leadership in the global struggle for freedom and democracy; and the will and resources to exercise this leadership.

The Irony of History and the Tragedy of Iraq

Among the most insidious lies and distortions that the Bush/Blair regimes and their mass media outlets spouted to justify this genocidal war is the notion that the Iraqi people would welcome the invaders as liberators and (especially the Shiites) would rise up to overthrow Saddam Hussein. When neither event took place — the Iraqi population was hostile to the invaders — the Anglo-US state media campaign claimed this was because of the Iraqi people's fear of the Iraqi army, Baath Party cadres and local militias. The media continued to picture the Iraqi people as "terrorized" (as they were) by Saddam Hussein and eager for the US to destroy his regime before expressing their "true feelings" of gratitude to the invaders, their tanks, missiles and fragmentation bombs. Even today with much evidence to the contrary, the media continue to advance this view, derogating forces of Iraqi resistance as solely "terrorists."

The theory of the Western media and the Anglo-US generals and politicians was that there was an unbridgeable gap between Hussein, the Iraqi state and "the people" that would lead to a collapse of the army once the US and British armed forces conquered the cities and villages. Needless to say this did not happen — far from it. The "coalition of the willing," in their crusade to defend the US and "liberate" the Iraqis (never mind imperialist aggression), were not welcomed as liberators but as the occupying force they are.

In the first instance the war did not lead to any division or defections within the armed forces or the political leadership, despite the fact that the military units were decentralized and frequently isolated from the Baghdad command.

Second, there was no popular uprising against the Iraqi regime during the first days of the US invasion, nor when the invaders entered the cities. On the contrary, the most effective and consistent resistance in southern Iraq to the US invaders were the popular militia and guerrilla forces, which included in their majority civilians and citizens unconnected to the elite Republican Guard or the regular army.

The heavy bombing of Basra and the British siege of the city was due to the fact that citizens, militia and soldiers fought together, not under the coercion of the repressive regime but because they were Iraqi patriots defending their families, communities and nation from invaders. Whatever opposition to the regime that may have existed disappeared in the face of the massive bombardment, which killed and maimed thousands of Iraqi children, women, elders and ordinary citizens. Rumsfeld's "total war" united the diverse political and social sectors of the Iraqi population in villages, towns and cities. Elderly peasants shot at convoys, pregnant women blew up US Marines, adolescents shot at helicopters from rooftops. In the south, Basra, al-Najaf and large parts of al-Nasiriya were taken only after weeks of aerial and artillery bombardment. The US-Anglo invading forces, finding almost universal hostility and rejection, began to shoot indiscriminately young men for wearing the wrong type of boots and women with their huge flowing robes. Above all, the general command directed the air force to use fragmentation bombs to decimate urban neighbourhoods.

The local militia were not merely Baath activists; they were mostly non-political Iraqis infuriated by the death and mutilation of friends and family, the destruction of homes, schools, factories, offices and their livelihoods. Baath activists mixed with thousands of volunteers from poor neighbourhoods and middle class exiles who returned to fight for the Iraqi nation. Of course, with the Islamic Shia the resistance assumed a different form, acquiring a different complexion — a struggle of liberation from the forces of US imperialism (falsely portrayed as the bearers of "Western" secular culture) against the puppet regime appointed by the US. This struggle continues as do efforts of the US to distort the nature of the resistance.

The distinctions that Western media have made in portraying Iraqi resistance under the conditions of war is false because bombs and missiles make no distinctions in their murderous assaults.

The Western state mass media have portrayed Saddam Hussein as a dictator, a tyrant hated by his people, particularly (and increasingly) in the wake of the war and occupation led by the US "coalition forces." This characterization might have been the apt in some sectors before the war — and few would dispute the tyrannical nature of Hussein's rule — but faced with terror bombing, the seizure of the country's oil wells, the occupation of the country and the destruction of the country's water, electrical and food supplies, the US-led invasion converted him in some circles into something close to a national quasi-hero. In any case, precious few Iraqis welcomed the invaders as liberators, a situation that might indeed have been otherwise if the objective of the war had been in fact to liberate the Iraqis from tyrannical rule. But most everyone, including the Americans, knows all too well (from the long history of US support for dictators, including Hussein himself) that this is far from the case.

Many well-meaning "progressive" Western journalists both before and after Hussein's capture by the occupying forces sought to "balance" their reportage of US-British atrocities with continued references to Saddam Hussein's crimes of one or two decades past as if his original sins still defined him and his political identity — even in the midst of a war against colonial invaders that had absolutely nothing to do with the reasons presented for going to war (international terrorism, al-Qaeda, 9/11, the national security of the US). These "progressive" or liberal reporters could not accept the notion that a politician like Saddam Hussein who had committed grave crimes in the past could redeem and redefine himself in new circumstances. Though a former war criminal, at that point he was engaged in fighting against a murderous invasion. These reporters felt instead that his heavy-handed tactics and repressive measures against political opponents, and the atrocities committed by his regime, somehow justified Bush's war. Even with indisputable evidence that the war was manufactured entirely with lies, the US mass media continues to soft-pedal and ignore the imperialist nature of an unjustified war, letting the Bush regime off the hook.

History works in strange ways. From being a client of the US against Iran, Saddam Hussein for a while became a leader in a revitalization of the pan-Arab movement seeking to overthrow corrupt, pro-US client regimes in the Middle East. For Arabs and Muslims in the region, it appeared as a choice between two demons, between the US cluster bombs raining on civilians and the Arab dictator Saddam Hussein arming the people and standing alone in defence of a Muslim nation from recolonization. In any case, with the capture of Saddam Hussein, this threat — to both US imperialism and Arab leaders in the region —subsided. Today it means Iraqi resistance in the form of suicide bombings.[1]

In the film, *The Battle of Algiers*, a young petty thief jailed by the French colonial authorities is released and joins the National Liberation Front, becoming a leader in the anti-colonial resistance and a hero of the Algerian masses. The colonial state propaganda machine would likely have described him as part of the "criminal-terrorist conspiracy" for challenging the symbols and presence of the French colonialists. But to the colonized people, he was a heroic symbol of a nation resisting the torturers and bombers, a man who, in the course of the struggle, transformed himself from a petty thief into a people's hero. It is possible, perhaps likely, that this might also have happened with Saddam Hussein had he not been captured. However, be this as it may, we should be clear on one point. Saddam may personify national resistance for many, as Muqtada al-Sadr does today, elevated from being a relatively unknown cleric to representing a powerful ideological force. But for the vast majority of Iraqis fighting US Abrams tanks, Cobra helicopters and B-52 bombers and armed with little more than rifles and rocket launchers, the struggle is over objectives that transcend both Saddam Hussein and Muqtada al-Sadr. Dubbed as "thugs and criminals" by Bush and his imperial entourage, the Iraqi resistance is a people fighting for their country, their nation, their five-thousand-year-old civilization and their dignity as an independent people.

This is why thousands, if not millions, of Iraqis are continuing to resist the invaders, why pregnant women and teenagers continue to attack the occupying armies. This obvious fact is something that the Pentagon experts, mass media commentators and Israeli advisers cannot and will not understand — that a proud and independent people will fight alongside a national tyrant turned courageous leader against a murderous conquering invader. *Armed force can conquer but will never rule.*

In years to come, Middle Eastern scholars will undoubtedly write of the irony of history when self-proclaimed "Western democracies" committed crimes against humanity while a one-time dictator defended his people. He will be more revered in death than in life, not for his tyrannical past but for what he defended.

The Meaning and Uses of Iraq: Assertion of Military Power, Oil and Corporate Interests

The real reasons for the US war on Iraq remain a matter of debate. On the one hand, the strategic concerns and economic interests of Wolfowitz, Cheney and other members of the Bush regime are well established and undeniable (McQuaid 2004). On the other hand, it would appear that one fundamental for going to war in Iraq was predominantly symbolic: to send a clear message to allies and enemies alike that the US intends to assert its claim to world power unilaterally if it has to and will not brook opposition in any form. This argument makes sense of the Iraq War not just in terms of Bush's psychology (the need to assert his will against resistance — what Nietzsche would have termed his "will to power") but also that of the US, which had experienced a series of defeats in the exercise of state power (from Vietnam to Bosnia and Somalia). However, the answer might best be sought in what the US has actually done in Iraq, besides secure regime change and gain access to Iraq's oil.

In this regard, Carmelo Ruiz Marrero, a Puerto Rican researcher with the Institute for Social Ecology and director of its Bio-Security Project, advances an interesting argument that warrants a closer look. He notes that oil is not the only booty sought by the US in Iraq. Apart from the economic interests directly served by the project to rebuild Iraq (after destroying its economy and social fabric), Ruiz Marrero (2004: 2) points towards the hundred or so directives given by Paul Bremer, the US's civilian administrator of its Iraqi protectorate, before turning over "sovereignty" to a puppet regime installed by the US. These directives have been given the force of law. Directive 81 is particularly revealing of the US agenda. It explicitly prohibits Iraqi farmers from harvesting seeds and thus sowing them for production of the next year's crop, as has been standard practice for millennia. In effect, the directive obliges Iraqi farmers to buy seeds from next year on from the agribusiness corporations that dominate the commercialization of seeds: Monsanto, Dupont, Syngenta, Bayer and Dow Chemical.

Directive 81 created a furor among defenders of the human rights of producers and biodiversity such as GRAIN and the Global South, which sent out an advisory warning that Iraq under this directive is one of several places where agribusiness multinationals seek (and are given license) to impose their monopoly property rights in seed production and thus maintain their control over world trade in agricultural products. Although Iraq in this instance is by no means a unique case in the privatization of seed production, what is unique about this circumstance is that Directive 81 was not the product of commercial negotiation. It was not approved by any sovereign legislature, and far less was there any consultation with the producers affected by this directive. It was instead imposed by a foreign government, the US.

UBINIG, an NGO concerned with promoting ecological agriculture in Bangladesh, has sounded the alarm to the effect that the implications of Directive 81 go well beyond the imposition of corporate property rights and the future dependence of farmers on the purchase of seeds from agribusiness conglomerates. In its report on the issue to the World Food Program and other UN development agencies, UBINIG argues that "the US is preparing to solve its economic problems at the cost of Iraqi dead and wounded" (Vasapollo 2003). It adds that the US, through Directive 81, is exploiting the hunger of the Iraqis, taking advantage of their vulnerability by forcing the acceptance and consumption of a genetically modified food product that governments in Sub-Saharan Africa have rejected under similar conditions: the introduction of transgenetically modified food products under USAID via the World Food Program.

Peter Russet, on the same point, argues that "with the war on Iraq and... military bases in countries of the South, the US seeks a comparative advantage over its competitors in the new war of colonization in the Third

World" (cited in Ruiz Marrero 2004: 2). Reflecting on this point, Russet adds that "free trade is nothing more than war by other means, a war waged against people in the North and the South."

Is Iran Next?
US negotiations with Turkey on military bases needed for the Iraq War, a certain hesitation by the executive of the Islamic Party and the open hostility of Turkish public opinion to the war introduced elements of uncertainty into the relations between Washington and its faithful NATO sentinel at the doors of the Middle East.

At this point the only true ally of the US is Israel. According to Geoffrey Aronson (2002), Israeli leaders have been trying for more than twenty years to attune the US to their perception of the non-conventional danger to the US represented by Iran, Iraq and Syria. The pacifist intellectual Uri Avnery explains very well how, after September 11, the Israeli establishment has tried to force the hand of the US against Iran. Avnery holds that the Israelis have been conducting this campaign for months. In his words:

> Israel exerts an enormous influence upon the Congress and the media. The following will happen: each day the Israeli generals will say that Iran is producing weapons of mass destruction and that it threatens the Israeli state with a second Holocaust. Sharon announces that the confiscation of an Iranian ship full of weapons shows that Arafat has ties with the Iranian conspiracy. Peres tells everybody that the Iranian missiles threaten the whole world. Each day an American newspaper writes that Bin Laden is in Iran or with the Lebanese Hezbollah.... Sharon has gotten a free hand to oppress the Palestinians, to apprehend Arafat, to assassinate militants, and to expand the settlements. The exchange is simple: you get me the support of the media and of the Congress and I will serve you the Palestinians on a silver dish. This could not happen if America still needed the support of the European or Arab allies. But in Afghanistan they have understood that they can do without it. (<www.Gush-Shalom.org>)

In an interview for *The New York Post* of November 8, 2002, Sharon stated that as soon as the war in Iraq was over he would pressure the US "to place Iran on the top of the list of the questions to be solved." He adds: "Teheran does whatever it can to get hold of weapons of mass destruction and ballistic missiles. It is a danger for the Middle East and for Europe" (Uri Avnery <www. Gush-Shalom.org>).

From Israel's point of view, Iran is a more serious problem than Iraq. Iran suffered neither the devastation of the first Gulf War nor the ensuing embargo, and up to now has not been subjected to the suffocating inspections of Washington, which had infiltrated the UN inspector system — even though the International Atomic Energy Agency (IAEA) in Iran lends itself to a rather ambiguous game. Iran has easily evaded the commercial embargo imposed by the Iran Act passed by the US Congress and has continued to do business with European and Russian companies (and also some American firms); it is a large country richly endowed with oil; it is well armed thanks to years of procurements from Russia, France and China; it has openly supported the Hezbollah resistance in Lebanon that has humiliated Israel by forcing it to withdraw from the southern zone occupied in 1982; and it supports Hamas and Islamic Jihad in the occupied Palestinian territories.

The images borrowed from American intelligence and broadcast by CNN in December 2003 showed what the IAEA already knew but has now made official: Iran has two nuclear plants, one in Isfahan and the other in Bushehr. But Iran has signed the Non-Proliferation Treaty and IAEA inspectors have verified the civilian character of the two plants. Neither is the case for Israel.

A media campaign was begun that aimed to show that Abu Musabal-Zarqawi, one of the leaders of al-Qaeda, shuttles between Iran and Iraq. This was designed to show that both countries, in spite of strained relations and conflict, support the same terrorists that were behind the September 11 attacks ("Gli uomini di Al Qaeda più di casa in Iran che a Baghdad," *Corriere della Sera*, February 7, 2003). The media campaign for aggression against Iran is underway. Nevertheless, after Baghdad, the American war machine, now at the border with Iran, could move against Teheran under propitious conditions, realizing thereby the strategic objectives shared by the Israeli-American tag team.

Iraq is a country proud of its independence. But, unlike Iran, it was left prostrate by a deadly embargo lasting some fifteen years, and subjected to UN inspections that imposed a unilateral disarmament on the regime. The "Food for Oil" program and the so-called "intelligent sanctions" devised and controlled by the US and the UK prevented the country from recovering from economic crisis and returning to the socio-economic and technological standards that it had previously achieved. The "Iraqi threat" against Israel was thus relatively minor.

As for US policy, its priorities towards Israel have been inverted. The aim of the US government (and oil companies) in occupying Iraq and invading Afghanistan was to achieve three objectives:

1. Penetration of almost all the republics of Central Asia allows the US to achieve a long-pursued strategic objective: to have military bases all around Russia and within the territories of the former Soviet Union.

2. Thanks to US power in Afghanistan and Pakistan, the oil and gas pipelines reaching from the republics of Central Asia to the Indian Ocean will bypass Russia and Iran. This will allow Washington and oil companies such as Unocal to realize their respective goals, while ditching the Taliban with whom they flirted in the past (Rashid 2001).
3. In Iran, conflict between the new generations and the Islamic theocracy could provoke an internal change without the US having to resort to military intervention. The presence of American bases and military personnel in Iraq, on the border with Iran, represents the "minimum deterrent" to achieve its objective.

"The Israeli military staff continuously updates its plans to attack Iran," writes *Limes*. But "the political decision-makers leave to the US the task of dissuading — either politically or militarily — Iran in the hope that the regime's moderate wing will get stronger" ("Dopo Saddam nel mirino di Sharon ci sono gli ayatollah," *Limes*, No.1, 2003). If this is true, contrary to the desires of the Israelis, the "punishment" of Iran in Bush's infinite war might have to be postponed. Another reason for postponing the inevitable is the Iraqi resistance, which continues to inflict severe losses, in human, economic and political terms, on the American military occupation. And Afghanistan has not been fully pacified, signifying further problems and unending costs for the US empire.

Conclusion

It is not possible to understand the world with notions such as "globalization," "development" or "Empire (without imperialism)." The imperialist states and the imperialist system are central facts of today's world, not to be dissolved in the political imagination of scholars ensconced in their offices and attuned to cyberspace and discourse analysis. The stakes are too high, the issues too serious.

Imperialism takes different forms. It uses both war and local development as the two extremes of a continuum of power relations. It also relies on very diverse forms of domination, subjecting peoples and states all over the world to the will and institutionalized practices of an interlocked political and economic elite — a transnational capitalist class.

In the contemporary context and current conjuncture, imperialism is used as a means to advance capitalism, a form of development based on economic exploitation and political oppression, a project designed to separate direct producers from their means of production and profit their new owners.

The US is at the centre of this constellation of economic and political power and coercive armed force, but it counts on a system of alliances with other states, mostly in Europe. This power is exercised and projected in various ways by diverse agencies and measures, including most particularly the state apparatus and its international adjuncts, the institutionality of the new world order, the international financial institutions and the guardians of the world economic order, the armed forces of the imperial state, the operating agents of the system (the MNCs) and even a broad swath of northern and southern NGOs that have been brought into the system.

Imperialism advances in diverse ways, through assaults on the negotiating capacity of organized labour; interventions and policies of the capitalist state; operations of the MNCs and the IFIs; the project of local development; repression of the anti-systemic social movements; and war.

But imperialism is also rife with internal contradictions and subject to forces that will eventually come into conflict, creating the objective and subjective conditions of its demise. On this historians generally agree. Notwithstanding the common projections of a long future and frequent claims by their promoters that the sun will not set on the empire, all empires bear the seeds of their own destruction. Nevertheless, we should not simply wait for this process to unfold. We must do what we can to hasten the end and help bring about the dawning of a new world.

12. REFLECTIONS ON EMPIRE AND IMPERIALISM

Hardt and Negri: A Theory in Search of Reality

HARDT AND NEGRI HAVE WRITTEN TWO BOOKS, *EMPIRE* (2000) AND *Multitude: War and Democracy in the Age of Empire* (2004), both highly acclaimed in most of the mass media. The second book is an attempt to rectify some of the more egregious theoretical, conceptual and empirical weaknesses of *Empire*. Hardt and Negri's original opus has the virtue of misunderstanding US history, writing an epitaph on imperialism at a moment when the US is engaged in three colonial wars and dissolving the class structure and class movements into an amorphous "multitude" despite major class uprisings in Argentina, Bolivia and Ecuador, and class polarization in Venezuela.

The US colonial wars in Yugoslavia, Afghanistan and Iraq and threats of future wars in at least sixty other potential "terrorist sanctuaries" speak to an empire based on imperialism. Almost 75 percent of the five hundred biggest MNCs are owned and based in the US and Europe, where the imperial state fights to open markets and impose favourable investment opportunities. Studies of the internal operations of the leading MNCs demonstrate that almost 80 percent of the strategic decisions on location, technology and research are made in home offices in the US and Europe. Yet Hardt and Negri claim that empire is dissociated from imperialism. The age of imperial war reflects a profound myopia, in which a vocation for abstract theorizing blinds the writers to everyday realities. Their notion of a world of stateless MNCs is bizarre — every day in every way the US and European governments through the WTO, the Doha Trade Rounds, and World Bank/IMF formulate rules and impose structures that favour their corporations.

The most significant conflicts today are national liberation struggles — in Venezuela, Iraq, Afghanistan, Bolivia and elsewhere. Despite Hardt and Negri's "analysis" to the contrary, neither the "nation" nor "nationalism" has disappeared or become irrelevant. Moreover, the growth of internationalism is directly related to the solidarity of worldwide movements with these national struggles. The case of Venezuela in this regard is striking. The US-backed referendum against Chavez elicited the opposition of personalities, parties and movements throughout Latin America, many of which expressed their active support for Chavez by their presence in Caracas.

Hardt and Negri's second book is an attempt to salvage the disastrous (theoretical and empirical) failings of *Empire* by improvising extenuating circumstances (the war) and by extending the time frame in which their "Empire" will exist without imperialism. Yet they cite no evidence that would justify these projections: the thrust of US politics is for greater military intervention and more military threats of "preventive wars" in Middle Eastern countries (e.g., Iran). The projections for imperialist wars are based on the structure of US-European-Asian capitalism, increasingly dependent on and competing for high-cost and scarce energy resources controlled by Third World countries. Today more than ever, European and US multinational banks receive a greater percentage of their profits and interest payments from their control of overseas markets and enterprises. The absence of any deep structural analysis of US, European and Asian economies and state policy by Hardt and Negri reduces their newest intellectual effort to an unsuccessful lawyer's brief for their earlier failure.

The conceptual locus of social and political action is not found in an amorphous "multitude" but in class, ethnic and national identities, and consciousness emerging from specific sets of political contests. To Hardt and Negri what is not an "industrial proletariat" is simply a "multitude"; classes disappear because in a particular conjuncture non-working classes happen to play a leading role. The tin miners in Bolivia continue to play a political role even as many of them become coca farmers and exhibit even greater protagonism. Unemployed manufacturing workers in Argentina were a leading force in recent major upheavals, but their unemployed status does not mean they have lost their class identity. Even if "multitude" refers to diverse groups acting collectively, diversity does not obliterate their class history, consciousness or social demands.

Hardt and Negri's discussion of the intellectual origins of the US independence revolution — they attribute a major influence to Spinoza rather than John Locke — has no scholarly basis. In the face of the UN secretary general's abject servility to US interests in Iraq and elsewhere, Hardt and Negri's call for an international regime modelled on the UN is nothing less than surreal. Given the authors' denial of imperialism and class conflict, the favourable reviews of their books in the mass weekly newsmagazines is understandable. What is incomprehensible is their readership among critical intellectuals. If Hardt and Negri's books can be summarized as *a theory in search of reality*, then the attention of left intellectuals to their books reflects *reality's desperate search for theory.*

How the Empire Works: A Multi-Track Strategy

US empire-building has largely focused on military conquest, threats of regional wars and a massive enlargement of clandestine military and intelligence operations. Particularly since the wars against and occupations of Afghanistan and Iraq and the failed coup in Venezuela, the military character of US policy has been foremost in public debate. But US policy to expand and consolidate imperial power operates on at least four tracks: *military, political-diplomatic, economic* and *local development*. On many of the crucial issues of the day, American diplomats, intelligence operatives and agency heads are intimidating, bribing and pressuring would-be adversaries into accepting and collaborating with US imperialism or at the least refraining from criticizing it. Numerous cases come to mind. To sabotage the International Court of Justice, which the US has always opposed, Washington diplomats have successfully pressured a number of countries into signing bilateral agreements providing impunity to US soldiers in their country. The list includes Romania, Argentina, Colombia, England and of course Israel, which jumped at the chance to gain impunity for its war criminals, and the list is lengthening. At the Johannesburg global meeting, US diplomats were able to prevent the EU and other member states from passing any significant resolutions on major problems, including fossil fuel targets, global warming or poverty reduction. In relation to adverse decisions by the WTO concerning US trade practices, US officials threatened European and other diplomats with dire consequences if they actually implement WTO-approved sanctions. The Europeans have refrained from implementing the rulings. It is clear that empire-building operates on two interrelated tracks: political and economic threats against subordinate allied competitors and clients, always backed by military force or threats against perceived adversaries.

Operations of the Diplomatic Channel

One of the principal aims of US political offices at its overseas embassies is to convert opposition political leaders into allies of Washington. Techniques include convincing them to turn from mass-based direct action (whether armed or civil) to electoral politics. The embassy offers these leaders legality in return for separation from mass struggles for basic socio-economic changes. With legality and institutional commitments, these opposition politicians are vulnerable to further embassy pressures to avoid direct attacks on US policy. In countering opposition, the embassy utilizes its local and overseas political "assets" to bolster the political position of Washington — thus avoiding direct confrontation and making it appear that the debate is between national or regional adversaries.

The process by which the diplomatic channel operates to silence or limit legal opposition is evident in a recent international conference organized to discuss and debate Plan Colombia and US policy and its implications for Latin America. The conference took place in El Salvador, July 20–22, 2001, and was sponsored by the Philosophy Department of the University of El Salvador.

The following case study of US diplomatic intervention shows how embassy officials combined several of the above-mentioned techniques to undermine the effectiveness of the conference. Contrary to its propaganda, Washington is more concerned with political manipulation to impose uniformity in support of its political line than in the free and open debate of ideas. This conclusion draws on an extended memorandum issued from the US embassy in El Salvador in July 2001, secured via the Freedom of Information Act.

The first point to make is that the embassy characterized the event as an organized propaganda exercise despite the academic setting and the presence of prominent Nobel Prize recipients (José Saromago and Adolfo Perez Esquivel), the president of the World Council of Churches (Bishop Pagura from Argentina), then-president of the Algerian Parliament (Ahmed Ben Bella) and two well-known professors from Mexico and the US (Heinz Dieterich and James Petras). The sponsors included Farabundo Marti National Liberation (FMLN), the main opposition party, and a host of local foundations and US NGOs.

According to the memo, an embassy political officer (Poloff) "spoke frankly and forcefully... to FMLN members that the press release [critical of the US] was inflammatory rhetoric and there would be two serious costs if the conference proceeded in this fashion." Among the serious costs to the FMLN, Poloff mentioned that the "FMLN would damage its own image, showing that it preferred outdated US-bashing to responsible discussion of serious issues." Putting the FMLN official (Eugenion Chicus, the FMLN advisor for the foreign affairs committee in the legislature) on the defensive, Poloff noted that the FMLN could not control what other participants said. Poloff insisted that "as an organizer the FMLN showed responsibility [for the views] expressed" and he went on to warn "if it did not distance itself from inflammatory rhetoric, it tacitly associated itself with those comments."

This memo raises several important issues. First, the embassy threatened a political party with reprisals ("serious costs"), which implies a reversion to illegality since the embassy official claims that its image (as a legal electoral party) was damaged by reverting to outdated US-bashing (a reference to the anti-imperialist politics of the FMLN when it represented the popular insurgency). The embassy's use of violent, hyperbolic rhetoric to refer to the dissenting views of the Nobel Prize winners, bishop and academics as a means of discrediting the conference is a technique designed to remind the FMLN that a condition for US tolerance is that it desist from systematic criticism of US empire-building.

US strategy was based on pressuring the FMLN to drop the critical orientation of the conference and to operate within the parameters dictated by the embassy. Washington's claim to favour a responsible discussion of serious issues was a simple propaganda ploy, appealing to the FMLN legislative advisers' non-confrontational style as a minority in the Salvadorian congress. In reality the embassy designed its own strategy to counter the conference and its coverage by the major news network. The embassy recruited "friendly" Colombian journalists and politicians to "ensure that the US point of view is articulated" (memo). The strategy was to find respectable Colombian journalists and a "reasonable voice from the left" in El Salvador to meet with US officials and writers from right-wing think-tanks, to provide them with the arguments, then presumably bring them back to El Salvador to counter the conference. Among the persons who would influence the respectable Colombian journalist, listed as Eduardo Torres (anchor on three television channels and columnist for the conservative Colombian daily *El Diario de Hoy*), was Francisco Santos, one of the owners of Bogota's largest daily newspaper, *El Tiempo*, who the US embassy assumed would present the US point of view. Whether Santos was an asset of US intelligence is not clear, but today he is the vice-president of Colombia under President Uribe — past and present organizer of paramilitary death squads.

The embassy's search for a "reasonable voice from the left" is a common ploy in which individuals with some background on the left and some mild criticisms of the existing order are co-opted to do the dirty work of discrediting prestigious critics like those invited to the conference. Using their self-proclaimed credentials as "human rights" activists, they spend most of their time attacking the left and praising the rhetorical concerns of Washington. Their views are amplified: as the memo states, "We could follow up with telepress conferences between journalists and public and private sector Colombian specialists. In addition Post [an embassy operative] will make sure that media and interested contacts" are informed.

The embassy was not successful in preventing the conference, but it did pressure the university to cancel the use of the university meeting hall at the last minute and to limit media coverage to the several hundred who attended the meeting.

The two-track strategy is evidently an important component of empire-building. In El Salvador, track one included the military intervention of the 1980s and the killing of over 75,000 Salvadorians. It was followed by track two, which was comprised of the so-called peace accords, the legalization of the FMLN and the pressure and co-optation tactics. The second track relies heavily on personal contacts, threats to rescind legal status and ambassadorial goodwill, and in some cases the co-optation of leftists who have access to the media and who can be used to discredit the left.

The challenge for the left is to focus its opposition on both tracks: to oppose militarization as well as diplomatic-political intimidation and co-optation. The left must reject the imperial rhetoric that labels anti-imperialism as outmoded, that speaks of reasonable concerns for human rights while engaging in a worldwide campaign to violate them. Empire-building is an integral process that combines violence and diplomacy, repression and co-optation. The diplomats and militarists work in tandem, promoting the same imperial goals. They are not on parallel tracks; the two tracks converge in a world where the voices of resistance are silenced by violence and "reasonable" voices from the left.

2003–2004: Diagnosis, Prognosis and Postmortem

Neither 2003 nor 2004 were years of historic victories or defeats. They were years of constantly shifting relations of power between imperialism and popular resistance movements, with US setbacks in Iraq and continued occupation disguised as a return of Iraqi sovereignty. The US empire and its Israeli colonial partners were able to conquer new countries and territories but were not able to consolidate rule in the face of mounting popular resistance. The US economy did not decline or collapse as some leftists had predicted, but expanded and gained momentum even as the economic fundamentals, particularly the deficit in current accounts and the budget, deteriorated. Both the left-wing and right-wing oracles were mistaken: the US experienced neither a terminal crisis nor permanent triumphs.

On the right, the prophets of successful colonial wars, beginning with Iraq and Palestine and then advancing to Iran, Syria and Lebanon, were quickly discredited. The heroic Palestinian resistance fighters' sacrifice and dedication blocked Sharon's totalitarian vision of an ethnically pure Jewish state. In Iraq, the massive popular resistance after the colonial conquest, inflicting thousands of injuries and more than a thousand deaths on the occupying power, put the lie to the Rumsfeld-Zionist "cabal" in the Pentagon, undermining its authority everywhere, even in parts of the Washington establishment.

There were no decisive military victories or successful political victories for the US. The major losers were the Zionists, like Wolfowitz, Perle and Feith, who projected a series of US wars to destroy or undermine all of Israel's adversaries in the Middle East and Europe. The high cost of the Bush-led, Blair-supported invasion and occupation of Iraq, the political isolation of "the coalition of the willing" and continued resistance in Iraq have imposed severe constraints on new US colonial invasions, putting a damper on plans to settle accounts with regimes in Iran and Korea — and Colombia, Cuba and Venezuela. In regards to the Middle East, imperialist "realists" like James Baker (former secretary of state under Bush the Senior), with links to conservative Arab oil interests, reject the Zionist ideologues within the US state who advocate US wars to impose pro-Israeli regime changes. The fraudulent claims emanating from Wolfowitz and other Sharon supporters regarding Iraq's weapons of mass destruction as a justification for war was the high point in the unprecedented power of the Zionist influence on US politics. However, the disgrace and the partial exposure of this self-styled "cabal" in the context of a bitter electoral contest between Republicans and Democrats led to at least a temporary decline in the credibility and public presence of this sector within the Bush administration. Support for the US empire is thus divided between ideologues with dual national loyalties and "realists" linked to US and Arab oil interests and European banks. Their differences are playing out and to some extent will shape foreign policy, determining whether the US will share imperial spoils with Europe, Russia and the Arab elite, or continue to pursue the politics of blind military colonialism.

In 2003 the dynamic Chinese economy emerged into the centre of world politics. With the third largest economy in the world, China has accumulated a huge trade surplus with the US and growing and powerful links with all the major and minor countries of Asia and Oceania. US imperialism cannot survive in Asia without coming to terms with China. Once again the imperial policymakers are divided. "Realists" propose a long-term strategy of accommodation and complementary and gradual assimilation, based on hundreds of billions of US dollar investments, exports and imports as well as large-scale Chinese purchases of US bonds. The "confrontationalists" are made up of the uncompetitive backward sectors of US industry, the trade-union bureaucracy and militarist ideologues who clothe their aggressive policies in the rhetoric of "human rights," "unfair trade" and "sweatshop labour." Apart from some pseudo-populist electoral rhetoric, the "realists" seem to be directing imperial relations with China, forcing the ideologues to focus on creating conflicts with North Korea and Taiwan.

As for Latin America, both the right- and left-wing oracles failed to recognize the deeper structural factors that influenced political events in 2003 and 2004. On the left, the elections of Lucio Gutiérrez in Ecuador, Inacio Lula da Silva in Brazil and Néstor Kirchner in Argentina, and the massive presence at the World Social Forum in Porto Alegre were described as major political turning points leading to the defeat of ALCA, the end of neo-liberalism and a rejection of the US empire. The extreme right in the US, particularly the Cuban émigrés in the Bush administration (especially Otto Reich) also predicted dire days ahead. However, it was only a few months into 2003 before Lucio Gutiérrez declared his total subservience to the IMF, ALCA and Plan Colombia, as well as support for price increases, salary reductions and the privatization of petroleum and electricity. Da Silva followed suit, applying IMF prescriptions to the extreme: appointing right-wing neo-liberal bankers, corporate executives and ideologues to all the key economic positions; and supporting a modified version of ALCA and establishing a non-functional Friends of Venezuela Committee dominated by Latin American presidents openly opposed to President Chavez. In Argentina, newly elected President Kirchner, under intense pressure from the mass social movements, combined progressive judiciary changes limiting immunity for human rights violators with a reduction in debt payments and political tactics to divide and weaken the militant unemployed workers' movements.

The left prophecies were not fulfilled. Relations between the US and Latin America at the state level did not change: ALCA moved forward with minor changes, neo-liberal economic policies continued to be applied, albeit with a whitewash effort to move beyond the "Washington Consensus" into a more humane form, and the region as a whole slipped further into the morass of slow growth, increasing debts and deepening poverty.

The major defeats of the US empire during 2003 and 2004 took place in Venezuela and Cuba. US support for an executive lock-out in Venezuela was defeated, and in Cuba, US-backed terrorists and paid propagandists were neutralized. In Latin America, imperial power continued to deteriorate, and anti-imperial resistance gained strength despite some political limitations. In Bolivia, US client Sánchez de Lozada was overthrown, and pro-privatization referenda in Uruguay and Colombia were decisively defeated. In Ecuador, congressional opposition and a massive popular march reminiscent of the uprising of 2000 succeeded in deposing Gutiérrez from office, while in Peru, Toledo was opposed by over 84 percent of the population and unlikely to finish his term of office. In August 2004, Chavez successfully fought off one more attempt by "democratic" opposition forces (the dominant class with a significant sector of the middle class) to oust him, this time via a recall referendum.

On the social movement front, the MST in Brazil, despite Da Silva's broken promises, has engaged in over 330 land occupations involving over 55,000 families. In Argentina, over 50,000 *piqueteros* marched to commemorate the December 19/20, 2001, uprising. Clearly the socio-political movements have not been paralyzed by the pro-imperialist reversals of the pseudo-populist presidents. But it is also clear that despite the power of these popular movements to defeat imperial clients, they have not been able to replace incumbent reactionaries with leaders from within their ranks. This was evident even in the case of the Bolivian insurrection of October 2003: the new president, Carlos Meza, was a lifelong neo-liberal who supported Sánchez de Lozado up to the last days in office. After taking office, Meza continued to attack and arrest coca farmers, expressed support for ALCA and took no initiative to change extant gas and oil agreements, except for ambiguous promises even in the aftermath of a referendum won by opponents of the government's plan to turn over the industry to foreign capital, hoping thereby to receive a few crumbs from the better managers of Bolivia's oil and gas reserves.

The year 2003 was one of mass mobilizations and a dress rehearsal for social revolutions to come. However, for that to happen, leaders of the social movements and what remains of the left need to become more aware of the pitfalls of the electoral and reformist road to political power pursued by popular leaders such as Evo Morales in Bolivia.

There has been no systematic rollback of US imperial power. While it loses in Venezuela with Chavez, it wins with Da Silva in Brazil. What it wins in defeating and capturing Saddam Hussein, it loses in the face of the costly and prolonged people's war during the occupation. International financial meetings are disrupted by the proponents of anti-globalization, but bilateral and regional free trade agreements are signed. Mass resistance, misconceived by Hardt and Negri as the response of "the multitude" to "Empire," increases the cost of conquest, but the empire and its mercenary satraps become more savage. US forces continue to occupy the country, notwithstanding Iraqi resistance and opposition; thousands of young men have been rounded up and herded into overcrowded prison camps to be interrogated and tortured. In occupied Palestine, Israel continues to build apartheid walls despite almost universal condemnation and continues its policy of assassinating leaders and activists in the resistance, under the benign protection of their "brothers" in the Pentagon. The superstructure of the empire — Bush, Cheney et al. — are challenged, but the foundations (military budgets, oil interests) are not questioned.

The economic crisis remains latent but does not explode. The US continues to borrow heavily on world markets and to consume large volumes of Asian capital to sustain massive imports. Dire predictions of decline or overextension ("imperial overreach") have been clearly exaggerated. Despite a failure to get its allies in the coalition of the willing to share the costs of military empire, Washington, with congressional support for additional funds ($80 billion in 2004 alone), is buying and training thousands of Iraqi mercenaries and is able to secure others from Eastern Europe and private security companies. US intellectual critics are more influential abroad than within the US. Despite the growing costs of empire (the military defence in Iraq alone costs the US $4 million a month, and the US military budget in 2004 was set at $401.3 billion), the dynamics for changing imperial politics is clearly abroad — in Iraq, Latin America and perhaps in parts of Europe.

The relationship between imperialism and popular resistance is too complex and contradictory to pigeonhole. What we can conclude is that the US empire is dangerously violent but by no means omnipotent; that popular movements can successfully challenge colonial rule and dump client regimes; and that the US economy can recover, however temporarily, even with its precarious foundations. Developments in 2003 and 2004 also suggest that the left would gain more from patient study of the complex and contradictory realities of class and national struggle than from grandiose global prophecies disengaged from popular movements.

Imperial War, Economic Crisis and Popular Uprisings

The political and social struggles over the past decade have once again demonstrated that the prophets of long cycles based on economic projections cannot understand the most profound contemporary events. It is not the "the forces of production" but the social and political relations of production, broadly understood as state power, productive systems and class relations, that are the driving forces of history. The system is not an amorphous "world capitalism" or "Empire" but a form of imperialism. The system is not controlled by a vacuous "centre" (versus "periphery") but by a US imperial state that has recolonized the Third World and subordinated imperial rivals in Europe and Asia. The imperial state is not merely a product of "market forces" but a result of military and political power dictated by the dominant classes in the leading imperial economies. The behaviour of the dominant classes is not a derivative of "long cycles" or other structural forces but is a result of their strategic policies and political alliances. To understand the momentous events of the past, present and future, we need to have a theory that is derived from clearly identified political forces acting in concrete circumstances and not long-term projections based on abstract formulations divorced from the principal political and social struggles.

There are four world-historic struggles in the imperialist system at present. The first is the struggle of US imperialism to conquer the world through wars (Iraq, Afghanistan), military presence (Colombia, Uzbekistan), economic blockades (Venezuela), threats with weapons of mass destruction (North Korea) and diplomatic blackmail (Europe and Japan). The second major struggle is found in national and social liberation movements, their resistance to imperialism and their ability to conquer political space — in the streets, countryside, jungles and parliaments throughout the world. The third great struggle is between the dominant classes in the metropolitan centres of the empire seeking to expand investment and trade and conquer markets throughout the world at the expense of the waged and unwaged workers, the employed and unemployed, and the exploited and socially excluded, who bear the brunt of the global economic restructuring process and deteriorating domestic economies. The fourth great conflict is between the imperialist regimes of war and conquest and the anti-imperialist, anti-war movements in Europe, the Middle East, Latin America, Asia, North Africa and North America. The outcomes of their struggle will have profound impact on the future of humanity.

In the short and medium terms, the US imperialist state is prepared to engage in a series of wars of conquest, beginning in Afghanistan and Iraq but possibly proceeding to Iran and other oil-rich countries in the Middle East, the Caspian region of Eurasia, Latin America (Venezuela), North Korea and other "rogue" states," not to speak of Cuba, forever a thorn in the US's backside. In this connection, George W. Bush and his minions, on his fence-mending visit to Canada in December 2004, rattled the sabre of possible intervention in Cuba should Fidel Castro survive Bush's second coming. The outcome of these moves and maneuvers is likely to strengthen the geo-political, geo-petroleum and military position of the US in the world economy. At the same time as these developments on the world stage, the domestic economy of the US is entering a deep recession, which threatens the financial and domestic foundations of its empire and will have a profoundly negative impact on the economies of the pro-imperialist regimes throughout the world that depend on US markets and investments.

The combined impact of imperialist wars of conquest and a world-wide recession will strengthen the advanced liberation movements in the Third World. The collapse of neo-liberalism, the breakdown of "free trade," and the weakening of pro-US client regimes will favour the extra-parliamentary left movements. Major uprisings are likely in the Arab world. Powerful movements in Latin America in the next few years could overthrow regimes in Argentina, Bolivia, Ecuador and elsewhere. Political pressure will increase for social transformations in Venezuela, Brazil, Uruguay and Peru. The combined effects of imperial war, economic crisis and powerful liberation movements will be a major stimulant to the growth of mass movements in Europe and to a lesser extent in Japan and North America. Significant struggles that challenge the complicity of regimes in US wars of conquest have emerged in Spain, France, Italy and elsewhere. Growing unemployment resulting from recession and cuts in wages and social welfare could radicalize these movements.

The political effects of imperial war, world recession and the growth of liberation and anti-imperialist movements will undoubtedly intrude on the internal politics of the US. However, terror propaganda in the mass media, large-scale police-state surveillance, a corrupt and impotent trade-union leadership and a two-party system tied to the imperialist state will limit the political influence of the anti-war/anti-globalization movement within the US and prevent it taking an anti-imperialist form. The politically important and possibly decisive movement against the system will not occur here, but the forces of anti-imperialism are building elsewhere — all over the world in fact.

The years 2003 and 2004 were decisive for shaping subsequent developments within the imperialist system. US imperialism was able to conquer Iraq, but in so doing it sowed some seeds of its own eventual destruction. For one thing, the short-term military success of the imperial state could not prevent recession at home. Indeed the mounting war costs exacerbated it. Rising oil prices, a declining dollar and ballooning deficits, both fiscal and on the country's trade account, will severely test the US economy in the years to come, as will the growing cost of providing security for the empire. Diverse and increasingly desperate efforts to secure global conditions of "good governance" (spreading the responsibility for and costs of maintaining "order") will fail; the hens will come home to roost in the US, the centre of the empire.

The transitional costs of securing and maintaining the empire and of imperial conquest will no doubt be passed on to the working class both within the US and more importantly in the Third World, especially Latin America. This will take the form of greater transfers of wealth and increased militarization, conditions that will entail high political and economic costs. Client regimes in Latin America will be forced to accept the rules of empire by means of ALCA and other such imperial devices. Washington will undoubtedly demand the privatization of the state oil resources in Ecuador, Venezuela and Mexico and prompt, full payments of debts as well as a further lowering of trade barriers in the region, facilitating thereby the process of neo-colonization — and a further denationalizing and pillaging of the region's productive resources.

The increasing cost of securing the empire is taking place at a moment when major socio-political confrontations are occurring in Colombia, Venezuela, Argentina and Bolivia and when the neo-liberal model is under attack or collapsing under the weight of its internal contradiction, under attack from forces of opposition and resistance generated by the system itself.

Under these conditions of widespread and mounting resistance, Washington will find it difficult to squeeze more economic resources from Latin America's impoverished but combative people. In the middle range, the clash between the military cost of empire and the declining domestic economy, rising liberation movements and the collapsing neo-liberal Latin American economies will put enormous pressure on center-left regimes attempting to navigate a "middle course" — combining international agreements with the empire and domestic social reforms. The chain of Washington's world empire has both its strongest and its weakest link in Latin America.

The unequal development of socio-political movements in Latin America, along with their fragmentation and lack of national leadership, is a serious strategic weakness of the left in the face of the centralized military and economic power of the US imperial state. While the World Social Forum is useful as a meeting ground for diverse debates, it does not provide the programmatic and strategic cohesion needed to defeat the advance of empire and weaken its client regimes. What can be expected is that profound changes will take place at the level of the nation-states, which in turn can serve as an "axis of virtue" to provide political support to the burgeoning liberation movements in other countries.

No one can predict the full consequences of the US imperial offensive in the Middle East and Latin America (on hold in Colombia and Cuba) because so much will depend on the strategic and political responses of people across the world — on the forces of resistance and the political capacity of diverse political organizations to mobilize them. Much will also depend on the answer to political questions such as the following:

- Will the military adventurers in the Middle East, moving from Afghanistan and Iraq to Iran and possibly Syria (depending on political developments related to the unresolved issue of Palestine and unequivocal US support for Israel), eventually precipitate an uprising in Saudi Arabia, leading to more US intervention and an escalation of conflict in the Gulf region?
- Will the IMF agreements with Brazil precipitate a major default, a crisis in the regime and a further radicalization?
- Can the European regimes continue their complicity in aggressive US actions in the face of a deepening economic crisis, rising mass movements and the possible cutting off of oil supplies?
- Can the US overcome the challenge presented to its hegemony from within the system — by a united Europe and intra- and inter-imperialist rivalry?
- Can the US empire come to terms with the challenge to its power presented by China and a resurgent Russia, which is consolidating its power base in Eurasia (within the fifteen republics formerly part of the USSR) by use of its energy reserves, $50-a-barrel oil lever and joint enterprises in selected high-tech sectors such as supersonic missiles and computer software with companies in India?[1]
- Can the empire consolidate access to and control over the strategic resources that it needs? It is argued and increasingly evident that US imperialism has "feet of clay" — that it could very well succumb to the same forces that have led to the demise of all previous forms of imperialism.
- Can the system sustain itself in the face of a propensity towards economic crisis and the increasing costs of empire?

Answers to these and other such questions cannot be deduced from abstract economic formulas about the "crisis of world capitalism." They are not to be found in books such as *Empire* and *Multitude*. On the contrary, such academic treatises are designed, intentionally or not, to elude even the questions themselves. Nor are the answers to be found in the inter-imperialist rivalries, although these rivalries and the economic competition and power struggles within the system will generate conditions that make anti-imperialist action possible. The answers to the above questions will be induced from the level of class and national consciousness expressed through direct political intervention. The answer to imperialism is in action — in the action of people all over the world no longer prepared to live its reality.

ENDNOTES

1: The Fragrance of Imperialism

1. In *Empire* the authors have replaced a class analysis of the groups and categories that make up the popular sector and popular movement — or, from a different theoretical perspective, an emerging "global civil society" — with the rather nebulous and analytically useless notion of "the multitude." In 2004, the "multitude," a concept that resurrects the nineteenth century sociological theory of "the masses" in conflict with the elite, becomes the central focus of their analysis of the dynamics associated with the "forces of resistance" building up within the Empire.
2. On an exposition and critique of postmodernism as a form of analysis, see Brass (1991) and Veltmeyer (1997 and 2002a).
3. All dollar figures in this book are in US dollars unless otherwise noted.
4. In the early 1970s Negri conceived and was part of "Autonomia," an intellectual and political movement defined by a search for a new way of doing politics without political parties. The context for this new way of thinking and doing politics — prefiguring what in the 1980s emerged as a "postmodern" form of politics (Holloway 2002) — was Italy, also the major object of Negri's political "practice" and reflections on the emerging world order.

3: The Imperial State

1. The Ramonet and Cassen citation is based on their speeches at the World Social Forum 2002 in Porto Alegre, Brazil. ATTAC (Association pour le Taxe Tobin pour l'Aide aux Citoyens) is an NGO and social movement against neo-liberal globalization, founded by Bernard Cassen. On its origins see Cassen (2003). For a more extended critique of globalization theory, see Petras and Veltmeyer (2001) and Petras (2000).
2. At a recent selection of the IMF head, the US tried to impose one of its own, but the Europeans eventually won out, but not before they were forced to alter their nominee.
3. As discussed below, this point relates to an academic debate on the relative power of the state (governments) and the MNCs (Wolfe 2002).

4: Spoils of Empire: The US in Latin America

1. At a global level, North-South FDI inflows accounted for 60 percent of all international resource flows in 2000 (versus 6 percent in 1980 and 25 percent in 1990) (UNCTAD 2002: 24). UNCTAD estimates that from 1987 to 2000, up to $4.6 trillion of FDI was deployed in mergers and acquisitions; which is to say, a large part of the capital assigned a productive function (which by some accounts as little as 5 percent of all the capital in circulation in world markets) is in fact "unproductive," used to acquire already established firms rather than to invest in new technology. This pattern holds for Latin America, where, it is estimated, up to 70 percent of all FDI is used in this unproductive fashion.

2. According to ECLAC (1998) no less than 50 percent — and more in the case of Brazil and Argentina — of all FDI in the 1990s ($97.2 billion from 1990 to 1997, and thus well over $100 billion over the decade) was used to purchase the assets of existing privatized firms without an productive investment in new technology to initiate what ECLAC views as a process of "productive transformation."

3. Based on figures presented and analyzed by Gabetta, Calcagno and Calcagno (2002), 42 percent of FDI in Argentina is European (25 percent Spanish). As with US capital, the bulk of this capital was used to buy up privatized enterprises rather than for productive investment.

4. As for financial corporations in Brazil, according to a Brazilian financial advisory firm, ABM Consulting, the ten largest banks in Brazil, including Citibank and Bank Boston, earned returns of 22 percent on their holdings in Brazil in 2001, compared to 12 percent on a global level. This is one reason why George Soros, a forward-thinking international financier with significant holdings in Brazil, declares: "The system has broken down," in that it "does not provide an adequate flow of capital to countries [like Brazil] that need it and qualify for it."

5. As for overseas development assistance (ODA), which also serves as a form of debt financing, overall flows in the region continue to lag well behind "private international resource flows," although, given the retreat of the private commercial banks and the slump in FDI, the major multilateral lenders such as the World Bank did increase their lending to developing countries in 2002. However, even this "inflow" of "international resources" in one form served as a means of securing an "outflow" in another. The relatively modest net inflow of $418 million from the World Bank in the first half of the year can be compared to a net loan repayment to the World Bank of $260 million (IMF 2002a: 6).

6. Using US export prices as a proxy, it has been found that even in the area of high-tech exports, exports from the developing countries are "subject to a higher degree of volatility... [with] steeper falls in prices after 1998 than the exports... of the same products traded among the developed countries" (UNCTAD 2002: 117); evidence related to terms of trade for developing countries is reviewed on pp. 197–99.

7. According to the *World Investment Report* (UNCTAD 2002), from 1991 to 2001 a majority of countries in the developing world liberalized their trade regimes and financial markets and "converg[ed] towards a more welcoming stance on FDI: in regard to 306 recorded regulatory changes, all but 75 were more favourable to FDI."

8. UNCTAD (2002: 70) estimates that at least $700 billion in export earnings could be generated for the LDCs if protection for labour-intensive activities in the industrialized countries was removed. In this connection, even Horst Kohler, managing director of the IMF, has said that "the true test of the credibility of wealthy nations'" efforts to combat poverty lies in their willingness to open up their markets and phase out trade-distorting subsidies in areas where the LDCs have a comparative advantage (Kohler 2002). Recent efforts at Doha in 2002 and Cancun in 2003 by the leading group of twenty-one developing countries to change this structure and its unevenly applied rules of trade, and to establish a "fair and [free] market oriented trading

system" on the basis of a "program of fundamental reforms" have foundered on the reef of collective resistance by the US and the EU. The collapse of negotiations at Cancun between the OECD countries and the developing countries reflects a similar failure of a generalized call by and within the UN some three decades earlier for a "new international economic order." At these negotiations the imperial powers are willing to negotiate anything and everything except their own fundamental economic interests.

9. Not only is the existing structure of international trade tilted severely against the developing countries, but these countries are expected to pay for reforms to this structure — reforms, such as TRIPS (trade-related intellectual property rights), that clearly favour the developed countries. In this connection, UNCTAD (2002: 59) has identified "significant costs" incurred by the developing countries in implementing or securing these TRIPS. UNCTAD estimates that the implementation costs of TRIPS would be, on average, $150 million, as much as the annual development budgets of some countries. Not only do these countries have to absorb the considerable administrative and implementation costs involved, but also the charges for the protected patent or intellectual property rights all go in one direction.

10. Nor does it take into account the indirect contribution of Mexican labour to capital formation via its depressant effect on the wages of employed workers in sectors in which they tend to be employed. One of the major offensives of capital against labour over the past three decades has been to challenge and reduce the share of labour in national income and thereby increase the income available as capital. The first battle in this offensive was to break the social contract that guaranteed the participation of labour in productivity gains (see Davis 1984 and Crouch and Pizzorno 1978). In subsequent years capital has found diverse ways of increasing the share of capital and reducing that of labour in national income, including the use of unemployment as a lever for lowering wages, the importing of cheaper forms of labour and the international relocation of production in areas with abundant supplies of cheap labour.

11. In this connection Delgado Wise (2004) points out that what Mexico essentially exports is its labour force — without it ever having to leave the country. The profitability of this labour process is reflected in the fact that US-based MNCs in the *maquilladora* sector account for a full third of all profits generated.

12. Delgado Wise points out that in contrast to the stereotype of the Mexican migrant, 40.7 percent of the core group of temporary or "circular" Mexican migrants have completed their secondary schooling or higher, a figure that rises to 55 percent of all Mexican-born US residents (versus 51.8 percent of the general population). In addition, over 250,000 Mexican residents have a university degree or some post-graduate qualification (2004: 10).

13. To establish the dimensions of Mexican labour's contribution to the US economy, Delgado Wise (2004: 2, 9) calculates that 8.5 million Mexicans, slightly more than one third "undocumented" (i.e., "illegal") reside and work in the US; "sojourners" (temporary migrants) account for between 800,000 and a million "sojourns" a year (Tuirán 2000); and each year around 370,000 Mexicans "settle" (establish a permanent residence) in the US, constituting a mass of 22.9 million (8.5 million immigrants born in Mexico — 27 percent of

all foreign-born immigrants in the US — plus 14.4 Americans of Mexican descent).

14. From a fiscal point of view, international migrants generally contribute more to the receiving economy than they receive in benefits and public services. Through their transfer of resources, migrants contribute to the mass of social capital available to the US state. According to data from the National Migration Forum (Delgado Wise 2004: 14), in 1997 the migrant population in the US contributed US$80 billion more than they received in the form of benefits. In this and other ways migrants are a major force for dynamizing the receiving economy.

15. Delgado Wise (2004: 14) points out that, unlike labour that is exported indirectly via the *maquilladores*, Mexican workers who emigrate and settle in the US consumed a significant part of their wages there, which means that the potential multiplying impact of their earnings is transferred to the US economy. This impact is over ten times greater than the impact of remittances on foreign-exchange earnings in Mexico and thus on the balance of payments.

5: The US Republic and the Weight of Empire

1. It is also possible to compare the economic power of the MNCs with that of the nation-states. UNCTAD (2003) compares the GNP of the biggest countries with the total annual sales of the biggest MNCs or, more accurately, with the value added in the process of their economic activities. By this disputed measure, fully one-half of the hundred biggest "economies" in the world are MNCs, raising questions about a presumed "weakening" of the nation-state under the impact of globalization — the internationalization and globalization of relations of economic and political power, decision-making vis-à-vis the (authoritative) allocation of society's productive resources presumably passing from the nation-state to a complex of international organizations. On this see, inter alia, Weiss (1998).

2. At a global level, FDI activity in 2001 was down considerably (51 percent for inflows, 55 percent for outflows) from the previous year — in the LDCs down from $238 billion to $205 billion. According to UNCTAD (2002) this was the result of two major factors: (1) a reduction in the frenzied pace of merger and acquisition activity, totalling $4.6 trillion from 1987 to 2001, and (2) a sharp decrease in the value of traded corporate stock — shares of stocks listed in the New York Stock Exchange fell by one-third in 2001. To these two factors could be added a slowdown in the privatization agenda, particularly in Latin America, where most of the leading public companies have already been sold off.

3. Ranked by foreign assets as opposed to market capitalization, US MNCs appear to be less dominant, accounting for only 22 percent of the top hundred, according to UNCTAD (2002). And measured by UNCTAD's index of "trans-nationalization," US-based MNCs appear to be even less dominant, yet all of them are ranked below several Swiss companies and a Canadian company (UNCTAD 2002: Table 4.1).

7: The Class Dynamics of Anti-imperialist Politics

1. On these criticisms and subsequent heated intellectual and political debates, see Petras (2002), who reported on the much-publicized signing by these progressive and leftist intellectuals of a letter of condemnation prepared by none other than Joanne Landry of the US Council on Foreign Relations, the major foreign policy forum for US administrations for over four decades.

8: Dynamics of Inter-imperialist Rivalry

1. These growing social inequalities, clearly related directly to the neo-liberal program of structural adjustments and the workings of "free markets" in the late 1980s and the 1990s generated considerable concern in policymaking and political circles. On the left the concern was with the gross inequity of the process, confirming their worst-case scenarios of capitalism in its neo-liberal form. On the right, the concern was that "excessive inequalities" would generate a politically destabilizing level of social discontent and a consequent "threat to global stability" (Kapstein 1995; Lewis 2004) or "governability" (Annan 1998; World Bank 1994). As for the World Bank and the IMF, the growth of social inequality did nothing to shake its faith in the neo-liberal medicine dished out to governments. What it did do is produce some disenchantment with the "Washington Consensus" on correct policy and increase the call for a new design of the structural adjustment program, giving the process a "human face" (Salop 1992). Economists at the Bank dusted off an old academic debate on the policy connection between "economic growth" and "social distribution" or "equity" (Birdsall, Ross and Sabot 1999; Kanbur and Lustig 1999). At the level of this debate the issue was whether an increase in social inequality was a precondition for growth or, as suggested by experience in Asia, an obstacle.

2. The 2002 IMPE (Indirizzi di massima per le politiche economiche) and the 2002–2006 draft stated that "the EU economy would inevitably and progressively consolidate itself and reach a growth rate near to or greater than the potential one in the middle of 2002, growing further in 2003" (Vasapollo 2003).

3. "Productivity" is defined by Lewis as the ratio of the value of goods and services provided consumers to the amount of time worked and capital used to produce them. As Lewis constructs it, labour productivity (output of goods and services per unit input on labour) might be higher in the EU, but the productivity of capital in both services and industry is higher in the US. The problem with this analysis, however, is that Lewis mixes up or confuses the contributions of capital and labour to productivity growth, attributing the differential to management and technology (supposedly functions of capital) as well as relative differences in market interference by the state and the cost of labour (too high in the EU because of minimum wage legislation, social benefits, etc.).

4. According to the studies conducted at the McKinsey Global Institute (Lewis 2004: 85), the US is the productivity leader in virtually every industry, with the exception of automotive, machine tools and consumer electronics in Japan, and retail banking in the Netherlands.

5. The McKinsey Global Institute, which has published a decade of studies on

the sources of productivity and wealth differentials between countries, has provided neo-liberal policymakers considerable grist for their mill against the welfare state. In the most recent work of "Bill" Lewis, the institute's "director emeritus," the institute takes aim at the "politics of poverty" practised by "populist" governments such as Inacio "Lula" da Silva's in Brazil, which spend what Lewis deems to be an inordinate percentage of government revenues (11.3 percent) on welfare and the government-run pension system for private and public sector employees (Lewis 2004: 275). He compares this to the 0.6 percent of GDP spent by the US government on welfare and pensions in 1913. Presumably, the low level of social expenditures (and the politics of poverty) in the US allowed it to accumulate sufficient capital to embark on a program of economic and social development denied to countries such as Brazil, mired as they are in non-market activity and public spending on welfare.

6.   Whether or not Europe is falling behind the US, as argued by Lewis and others, is a contentious issue. Articles in journals such as the *Economist* and the *New Republic*, which are highly respected by the intellectual and political right, have cited the widely published figures of the OECD on GDP and hours worked to conclude, contrary to Lewis, that productivity in France and Germany and a few other North European countries actually is higher than that in the US — by as much as 5 to 10 percent. They conclude from this that the US lead in GDP per capita, the basic indicator used to measure a country's standard of living, is explained primarily by more work per person in the US. This, in turn implies that a greater number of Europeans than Americans either prefer and choose leisure time over material standard of living or — as reflected in differences in the rate of unemployment (about twice as high in Europe than the US) — they cannot find work.

7.   The Centro Studi Trasformazioni Economico-Sociali (CESTES) and its journal *Proteo* (co-edited by Rappresentanze sindacali di Base [RdB], have been working for over three years on an analysis of these dynamics of global competition and its impact on Italy.

8.   Recall the interview by Alberto Negri of General Jackson (*Sole 214 Ore*, April 1999), who declared that the American and English military contingents were staying in the Balkans "to protect the strategic pipelines which run through this region."

9:   Russia and China in the Empire: Western Imperialism at Bay

1.   In the context of the rivalry between the US and the EU, it is important to recall that from 1992 to 1998 there was a fall in imports from and exports to the EU. While in 1992 the EU received 48 percent of Russian exports and accounted for 43 percent of its imports, in 1998 the figures had fallen to 31 percent and 36 percent respectively. The EU countries having the greatest trade relations with Russia in 1998 were Germany (35 percent of EU exports and 31 percent of EU imports), Italy (13 percent of exports and 14 percent of imports), France (8 percent of exports and 10 percent of imports) and the United Kingdom (6 percent of exports and 10 percent of imports).

2.   In China there are seven parties besides the Communist Party. One of them is

the Democratic Construction of the Fatherland, a party of private entrepreneurs with 700,000 members (*Affari e Finanza,* November 11, 2002).

10:Imperialism as Local Development

1. The IDRB was but one of three institutions of a new world economic order planned by representatives of the capitalist democracies that met at Bretton Woods in 1944. Other institutional pillars included the IMF, an institution designed to help out countries experiencing temporary balance-of-payment problems, and the ITO, an institution stillborn in the face of US protectionism, taking form as GATT until it finally was born as the WTO fifty years later.
2. On the motivations behind, and the uses and misuses of, foreign aid in this context see Maizels and Mssanke (1984) and Griffin and Evans (1970).
3. In this connection, the development practitioners associated with these NGOs often see themselves as partisan of grassroots organizations and in conflict with the donor organizations that fund them, to the point of disowning their connection to these organizations lest they be seen as their agents. From the perspective of the donor organizations, however, this does not normally present any problems — as long as the NGOs act within the parameters set for them. However, in the current context of the Bush administration the question of foreign aid has become controversial enough that the administration has placed pressures on the NGOs to own up to this connection. On this point there were various reports of Andrew Natsios, president of USAID, at a meeting on May 21, 2003, of Interaction, an umbrella group of 160 US NGOs, in which he explicitly warned the NGOs to do a better job of owning up to their connection to the government as private contractors or lose future funding from this source.
4. On the political dynamics of this assault — the opening gambit in a protracted class war of capital against labour — see Davis (1984) and Crouch and Pizzorno (1978) in regard to the European theatre of this war and Leiva and Petras (1994) in regard to Chile.
5. The literature on the role of these NGOs in the development process is voluminous but see, for example, Macdonald (1997) and Reilly (1989). For a highly critical view of these NGOs, conceptualized in the 1980s as part of the "third sector" (versus the public and the private sectors) and in the 1990s as parts of an emergent civil society, as agents of imperialism, see Petras and Veltmeyer (2001).
6. On the political dynamics of this "alternative development" project see, inter alia, Veltmeyer (2002a).
7. The structural and political conditions of this poverty have been well documented and analyzed from a variety of perspectives. See, for example, Morley (1995); World Bank (1989), UNDP (1996).
8. There is, in fact, an ongoing debate on this issue, with the economists of the World Bank assiduously avoiding or massaging the relevant evidence provided by a broad array of academic studies and internal assessments.

11:Imperialism as War: The Neo-cons Take Action

1. Curiously much of the intellectual and political left in Europe and the US have failed to support the war of resistance waged in Iraq notwithstanding a general condemnation of the war as totally illegitimate and based on false pretences. Thus, for example, a check of znet between May 2003 and October 2004 did not show a single article of support for the Iraq resistance authored by Albert, Chomsky, Wallerstein, Zinn and other leftist intellectuals who have generally lent their ideological support to resistance movements everywhere in the past and present.

12:Reflections on Empire and Imperialism

1. An example of this strategy is the deal struck by President Putin with the Indian government in his visit to New Delhi (*La Jornada*, 5 December 2004: 27) for a joint venture between the Russian parastatal (NPO) Mashinostroyenia and India's Research and Development Defence Organization for sharing military technology and the manufacture of a new generation of supersonic missiles. Other examples of Russia's strategy for recovering power and influence, particularly in Eurasia, is its recent takeover of Armenia's power-production facilities, part of a debt settlement, buying a controlling share in Estonia's biggest oil terminal, investments in several Lithuanian gas companies, purchase of a controlling interest in the Georgian capital's utility company and expansion of Russian investments in electrical production in the Ukraine.

BIBLIOGRAPHY

Aglietta, M. 1982. "World Capitalism in the 1980s." *New Left Review* 136 (November/December): 5–41.

Albright, Madeleine. 2003. "Interview: Medeleine Albright talks about her new book, 'Madam Secretary.'" *US News and World Report* NPR, September.

Amador, Robert González. 2003. "Más de dos billones de dólares: La sangría de América Latina en dos décadas." *La Jornada* November 29. <www.Argenpress.info>.

Amsden, A.H. 1989. *Asia's Next Giant: South Korea and Late Industrialization.* New York: Oxford University Press.

Anand, Sudhir, and Ravi Kanbur. 1993. "Inequality and Development: A Critique." *Journal of Development Economics* 41 (June).

Annan, Kofi. 1998. "The Quiet Revolution." *Global Governance* 4 (2): 123–38.

Aronson, Geoffrey. 2002. "A Sideshow to the Conquest of Iraq." *Le Monde Diplomatique* May.

Baily, Martin Neil. 2001. "US Economic Performance and the Challenge for Europe." Keynote address to the Brussels Economic Forum European Commission, May 3. <www.iie.com/publications>.

Becht, M. 1997. *Corporate Ownership and Control: The European Experience.* Brussels: ECGN.

Bello, W. 1994. *Dark Victory: United States, Structural Adjustment and Global Poverty.* London: Pluto Press.

_____. 1998. "VFA Will Make Washington's Foes Ours, Too." *PDI* August 31. <palaris-l@lists.best.com>.

Bienefeld, Manfred. 1988. "The NICS in the Development Debate." *Studies in Political Economy* 25 (Spring).

Birdsall, Nancy, David Ross and Richard Sabot. 1999. "Inequality and Growth Reconsidered: Lessons from East Asia." *World Bank Economic Observer* 9 (3).

Brass, T. 1991. "Moral Economists, Subalterns, New Social Movements and the (Re)Emergence of a (Post) Modernised (Middle) Peasant." *Journal of Peasant Studies* 18 (2).

Brenner, Robert. 1998. "The Economics of Global Turbulence." *New Left Review* 229 (May/June).

Brzezinski, Zbignieuw .1993. *Global Turmoil on the Eve of the Twenty-first Century.* New York: Scribner's.

_____. 1998. *La Grande Scacchiera.* Milan: Longanesi.

Bulmer-Thomas, Victor. 1996. *The New Economic Model in Latin America and its Impact on Income Distribution and Power.* New York: St. Martin's Press.

Burnside, Craig, and David Dollar. 1997. *Aid, Policies and Growth.* Washington, DC: World Bank.

Cassen, Bernard. 2003. "On the Attack." *New Left Review* 19 (January/February).

Castells, Manuel. 2000. *The Rise of the Network Society,* Vol. 1, Second edition. Oxford: Blackwell.

Chossudovsky, Michel. 2004. "Abandon the Battlefield." June 25. <www.globalresearch.ca>.

Clark, W. 2003. "Dollaro contro euro. Guerra di valute." *La Contraddizione* (August).

Cohen, B.J., et al. 1968. *American Foreign Policy: Essays and Comments.* New York: Harper and Row.

Collier, Paul. 1997. "The Failure of Conditionality." In Catherine Gwin and Joan Nelson (eds.), *Perspectives on Aid and Development.* Washington, DC: ODI; Baltimore, MD: Johns Hopkins University Press.

Collins, Chuck, Chris Hartman and Holly Sklar. 1999. "Divided Decade: Economic Disparity at the Century's Turn." In UFE *(United for a Fair Economy) Report,* December 15.

Cooper, Robert. 2000a. "The Post-Modern State, Reordering the World: The Long Term Implications of September 11." Foreign Policy Centre website <info@fpc.org.uk>.

_____. 2000b. "The New Liberal Imperialism." *The Guardian* April 7.

Crouch, C., and A. Pizzorno. 1978. *Resurgence of Class Conflict in Western Europe since 1968.* London: Holmes and Meier.

Davis, Mike. 1984. "The Political Economy of Late-Imperial America." *New Left Review* 143 (Jan/Feb).

Deaglio, Mario. 2001. *Le fine dell'euforia.* Milan: Feltrinelli.

Delgado Wise, Raúl. 2004. "Critical Dimension of Mexico-US Migration under the Aegis of Neoliberalism and NAFTA." *Canadian Journal of International Development Studies* 24 (4): 591–605.

Doremus, Paul, William Kelly, Louis Pauly and Simon Reich 1999. *The Myth of the Global Corporation.* Princeton, NJ: Princeton University Press.

ECLAC (United Nations Economic Commission for Ltin America and the Caribbean). 1990. *Productive Transformation with Equity.* Santiago: ECLAC.

_____. 1998. *Foreign Investment in Latin America and the Caribbean.* Santiago: ECLAC.

_____. 2000a. *Panorama Preliminar de las Economies de América y el Caríbe.* Santiago: ECLAC/CEPAL.

_____. 2000b, 2002. *Statistical Yearbook.* Santiago: ECLAC/CEPAL.

Feldstein, Martin. 1997. "EMU and International Conflict." *Foreign Affairs* (November/December).

Ferguson, Niall. 2001. "Clashing Civilizations or Mad Mullah: The United States Between Informal and Formal Empire." In Strobe Talbott and Nayan Chanda (eds.), *The Age of Terror: America and the World after September 11.* New York: Basic.

_____. 2003. *Empire: The Rise and Demise of the British World Order and the Lessons for Global Power.* New York: Basic.

_____. 2004. *Colossus: The Rise and Fall of the American Empire.* London: Allen Lane.

Financial Times. 2004. "*Global 500, Special Report,*" May 27.

Fitoussi J.P. 1997. *Il dibattito proibito.* Bologna: Il Mulino.

Franks, J., and C. Mayer. 1997. "Corporate Ownership and Control in the UK, Germany and France." *Journal of Applied Corporate Finance* 9 (4).

Friedmann, John 1992. *Empowerment: The Politics of Alternative Development.* Cambridge: Blackwell.

Fröbel, Folker, Jürgen Heinrichs and Otto Kreye. 1980. *The New International Division of Labour: Structural Unemployment in Industrial Countries and Industrialisation in Developing Countries.* Cambridge: Cambridge University Press.

1980.

Gabetta, Carlos, Alfredo Calcagno and Eric Calcagno. 2002. "Dossier: Attac Sevilla Debate." *Le Monde Diplomatique* Info-Diplo, March 9.

Gordon, Robert. 1999. "Has the New Economy Rendered the Productivity Slowdown Obsolete." June. <http://faculty-web.at.northwestern.edu/economics/gordon/334.html> (accessed August 2005).

Griffin, K.B., and J.L. Evans. 1970. "Foreign Assistance: Objectives and Consequences." *Economic Development and Cultural Change* 18 (3): 313–27.

Hardt, Michael, and Antonio Negri. 2000. *Empire*. Cambridge: Harvard University Press.

_____. 2004. *Multitude: War and Democracy in the Age of Empire*. New York: Penguin.

Hayter, Teresa 1971. *Aid as Imperialism*. Harmondsmouth, UK: Penguin.

Hobsbawm, E.J. 1987. *The Age of Empire: 1875–1984*. New York: Pantheon.

_____. 1999. *Intervista sul nuovo secolo*. Bari, Italy: Laterza Edizioni.

Holloway, John. 2002. *Cambiar el mundo sin tomar el poder*. Buenos Aires: Editor Andrés, Alfredo Méndez.

Huntington, P. Samuel. 1996. *The Clash of Civilisations and the Remaking of World Order*. New York: Simon and Schuster.

International Monetary Fund (IMF). 2002a. *Recent Trends in the Transfer of Resources to Developing Countries*. August 27.

_____. 2002b. *World Economic Outlook: Trade and Finance*. September. Washington, DC.

_____. 2004, 2005. *International Financial Statistics Yearbook*. Washington, DC.

Isenberg, Davis. 1999. "Imperial Overreach: Washington's Dubious Strategy to Overthrow Saddam Hussein." *Policy Analysis* 360 (November 17).

Judis, John B. 2004. "Imperial Amnesia." *Foreign Policy* (July/August).

Kanbur, Ravi, and Nora Lustig. 1999. "Why is Inequality Back on the Agenda?" Paper prepared for the Annual Bank Conference on Development Economics, World Bank, Washington, DC, April 28–30.

Kapstein, Ethan. 1996. "Workers and the World Economy." *Foreign Affairs* 75 (3).

Kennedy, Paul. 1989. *The Rise and Fall of the Great Powers: Economic Change and Military Conflict from 1500 to 2000*. New York: Vintage.

Knack, S. 1999. "Social Capital, Growth and Poverty: A Survey of Cross-Country Evidence." *Social Capital Initiative Working Paper* 7, World Bank, Social Development Department, Washington, DC.

Kohl, Helmut. 1996. Speech at the University of Leuven, Belgium, February. In L. Vasapollo (ed.), *Il piano inclinato del Capitale. Crisi, competizione globale e Guerra*. Rome: Jaca.

Krueger, Anne, C. Michalopoulos and V. Ruttan 1989. *Aid and Development*. Baltimore: Johns Hopkins University Press.

Krugman, P. 1995. *Geografia e commercio internazionale*. Italy: Garzanti. <www.garzanti.it>.

Leiva, Fernando, and James Petras. 1994. *Democracy and Poverty in Chile*. Boulder, CO: Westview.

Lenin, V.I. 1950. "Imperialism: The Highest Stage of Capitalism." *Selected Works*, Vol. I. Moscow: Foreign Languages Publishing House.

Levitt, Kari. 1985. "The State of Development Studies." *IDS Occasional Paper* no. 92.1, Saint Mary's University, Halifax, NS.

Lewis, William 2004. *The Power of Productivity: Wealth, Poverty and the Threat to Global Stability*. Chicago: University of Chicago Press.

Lipietz, Alain 1982. "Towards Global Fordism." *New Left Review* 132 (March/ April).

_____. 1987. *Mirages and Miracles: The Crisis in Global Fordism*. London: Verso.

Macdonald, Laura. 1997. *Supporting Civil Society: The Political Role of NGOs in Central America*. London, Macmillan.

Mackinder, Harold. 2005. "La Russia e.i. suoi vicini." *Rivista di Studi Geopolitici* 2.

Maizels, Alfred. 1970. *Industrial Growth and World Trade*. Cambridge: Cambridge University Press.

Maizels, A., and M.K. Mssanke. 1984. "Motivations for Aid to Developing Countries." *World Development* 100 (September): 879–901.

Marcos, Subcomandante. 1994. "A Tourist Guide to Chiapas." *Monthly Review* 46 (May): 8–18.

Marglin, Stephen, and Juliet Schor, eds. 1990. *The Golden Age of Capitalism: Reinterpreting the Post-War Experience*. Oxford: Clarendon.

Martufi, R., and L. Vasapollo. 2000. *Eurobang. La sfida del polo europeo nella competizione globale: Inchiesta su lavoro e capitale*. Rome: Mediaprint.

_____. 2003. *Vizi privati... senza pubbliche virtù. Lo stato delle privatizzazioni e il Reddito Sociale Minimo*. Rome: Mediaprint.

McQuaid, Linda. 2004. *It's the Crude, Dude: War, Big Oil and the Fight for the Planet*. Toronto: Doubleday Canada.

Mearsheimer, John. 2002. *Tragedy of Great Power Politics*. New York: W.W. Norton.

Mokhiber, Russel, and Robert Weissman. 2001. "Corporate Globalization and the Poor." August 6. <http://www.commondreams.org/views01/0807-01.htm>(accessed August 2005).

Montbrial, Tierry de. 2003. "Stati Uniti contro la potenza Europa." *Le Monde* August 5.

Morley, Samuel. 1995. "Structural Adjustment and Determinants of Poverty in Latin America." In Nora Lustig (ed.), *Coping with Austerity: Poverty and Inequality in Latin America*. Washington, DC: Brookings Institution.

Mosley, Paul. 1999. "Globalization, Economic Policy and Growth Performance." *International Monetary and Financial Issues for the 1990* 10: 157–74. New York and Geneva: United Nations.

Organisation for Economic Co-operation and Development. (OECD). 2003. *DAC Geographic Distribution of Flows*. Paris: OECD.

Patel, Surendra. 1998. "East Asia's Explosive Development and Its Relevance for Development Theory." IDS Working Paper, October, Saint Mary's University, Halifax, Canada.

Petras, James. 2000. *Globaloney*. Buenos Aires: Antidote.

Petras, James, and Henry Veltmeyer. 2001. *Globalization Unmasked: Imperialism in the 21st Century*. London: Zed; Halifax: Fernwood.

_____. 2003a. *System in Crisis: The Dynamics of Free Market Capitalism*. London: Zed; Halifax: Fernwood.

_____. 2003b. *Cardoso's Brazil: A Land for Sale*. Boulder, CO: Rowman and Littlefield.

Pomfret, John. 2001. "China Is Rising." *Washington Post National Weekly Edition* Oct. 29–Nov. 4.

Prodi, R. 1999. *Un'idea dell'Europa*. Bologna: Il Mulino.

Rahme, Alfredo. 2004. "Bajo la Lupa: Rusia y China eclipsan a EU." *La Jornada*

November 21.

Rashid, Ahmed. 2001. *Talibani. Islam, petrolio e il grande scontro in Asia Centrale.* Milan: Feltrinelli.

Reilly, Charles. 1989. *The Democratization of Development: Partnership at the Grassroots.* Annual report. Arlington: Inter-American Foundation.

Rodotà, Antonio. 2001. "Le grande sfida europea allo spazio." *Sole 24 Ore*, November 28.

Rodrik, Dani. 1995. "Why is there multilateral lending?" In Michael Bruno and Boris Pleskovic (eds.), *Annual World Bank Conference on Development Economics.* Washington, DC: World Bank.

Rogoff, Kenneth. 2004. "Europe's Quiet Leap Forward." *Foreign Policy* (July/August): 74–75.

Roy, Olivier. 1996. "Sharia e gasdotto, la ricetta dei Talebani." *Le Monde Diplomatique* November.

Ruiz Marrero, Carmelo. 2004. "Iraq, basurero de Estados Unidos." *Masiosare*, Sunday Supplement to *La Jornada*, December 5.

Sachs, Wolfgang, ed. 1992. *The Development Dictionary: A Guide to Knowledge and Power.* London: Zed.

Salbuchi, Adrian. 2000. *El cerebro del mundo: la cara oculta de la globalización.* Córdoba: Ediciones del Copista.

Salop, Joanne. 1992. "Reducing Poverty: Spreading the Word." *Finance & Development* 29 (4) (December).

Saxe-Fernández, John. 2002. *La compra-venta de México.* Mexico City: Plaza and Janés Editores.

Saxe-Fernández, John, and Omar Núñez. 2001. "Globalización e Imperialismo: La transferencia de Excedentes de América Latina." In Saxe-Fernández et al. (eds.), *Globalización, Imperialismo y Clase Social.* Buenos Aires/México: Editorial Lúmen.

Scott, James C. 1990. *Domination and the Arts of Resistance: Hidden Transcripts.* New Haven: Yale University Press.

Sinatti, Piero. 2001. "E nel gioco del petrolio Russia e USA sono alleati." *Il Sole 24 Ore* December 4.

Sklair, Leslie. 1997. "Social Movements for Global Capitalism: The Transnational Capitalist Class in Action." *Review of International Political Economy* 2 (3).

Solano, Javier. n.d. "Europe's Magic Bullet: Defence, Security and Control." GDS Infocentrre. <www.gdsinternational.com/infocentre>.

Soros, George. 2000. *Open Society: Reforming Global Capitalism.* New York: Public Affairs.

Stedile, Joao Pedro. 2003. *A Luta pela Terra No Brasil.* Sao Paulo: Scritta.

Strassman, Paul. 1999. *Information Productivity.* New Canaan, CT: Strassman Inc.

Summers, Lawrence. 2004. "America Overdrawn." *Foreign Policy* (July/August): 46–49.

Theuret, Patrice. 2002. "Dove va la Cina." *L'Ernesto* (November/December).

Thompson, G.F. 1992. *The Economic Emergence of a New Europe?* Cheltenham, UK: Edward Elgar.

Thurow, Lester C. 1992. *Head to Head: The Coming Battle among Japan, Europe and America.* New York: Morrow.

UNCTAD (United Nations Conference on Trade and Development), Division of Transnational Corporations. 1994, 1998, 2002, 2004. *World Investment Report: Transnational Corporations, Employment and the Workplace.* New York and Geneva: UN.

_____. 2003. *Trade and Development Report*. New York and Geneva: UN.

UNDP (United Nations Development Programme). 1996. "Good Governance and Sustainable Human Development." Governance Policy Paper. <http://magnet.undp.org/policy>.

US Census Bureau. 2002. *US Direct Investment Position Abroad on a Historical Cost Basis*. Washington, DC.

_____. 2003. *US Trade Balances*. <http://www.census.gov.foreign-trade/balance>.

US Department of Commerce. 1994, 1998 and 1999. *US Direct Investment Abroad*. Washington, DC.

US Senate, 106th Congress. 1999. *Private Banking and Money Laundering: A Case Study of Opportunities and Vulnerabilities Hearings before the Permanent Sub-Committee on Investigations of the Committee on Governmental Affairs*. Report, November 9–10.

US Senate, Permanent Subcommittee on Investigations. 2001. *A Gateway to Money Laundering*. Minority Staff Report on Correspondent Banking, February.

Vasapollo L. 2003. *Il piano inclinato del capitale. Crisi, competizione globale e Guerra*. Rome: Jaca.

Veltmeyer, Henry. 1997. "New Social Movements in Latin America: The Dynamics of Class and Identity." *Journal of Peasant Studies* 25 (1).

_____. 2002a. "The Politics of Language: Deconstructing the Discourse of Postdevelopment." *Canadian Journal of Development Studies* 22 (3): 597–624.

_____. 2002b. "Social exclusion and Rural Development on Latin America." *Canadian Journal of Latin American and Caribbean Studies* 23 (54).

Veltmeyer, Henry, and James Petras. 1997. *Economic Liberalism and Class Conflict in Latin America*. London: MacMillan.

Veltmeyer, Henry, James Petras and Steve Vieux. 2000. *The Dynamics of Social Change in Latin America*. London: Macmillan.

Wallerstein, I. 1976. *The Modern World System*. New York: Academic Press.

Weiss, Linda. 1998. *The Myth of the Powerless State: Governing the Economy in a Global Era*. Cambridge: Polity.

Wolf, Martin. 1999. "Not So New Economy." *Financial Times* August 1.

_____. 2002. "Countries Still Rule the World." *Financial Times* February 5.

Woolcock M., and D. Narayan. 2000. "Social Capital: Implications for Development Theory, Research and Policy." *World Bank Research Observer* 15 (2) (August).

World Bank. 1989. *Sub-Saharan Africa: From Crisis to Sustainable Growth*. Washington, DC.

_____. 1994. *Governance: The World Bank Experience*. Washington, DC: World Bank.

_____. 1997. *World Development Report*. New York: Oxford University Press.

_____. 2000, 2002. *Global Development Finance*. Washington, DC: World Bank.

_____. 2002. *Global Economic Prospects and the Developing Countries*. <www.worldbank.org>.

_____. 2003. *Global Development Finance, Statistical Appendix*. Washington, DC: World Bank.

_____. 2004. *Global Development Finance, Statistical Appendix*. Washington, DC: World Bank.

Young, I.M. 2003. "Europa provincia del mondo." *Il Manifesto* August 7.

INDEX

THE AUTHORS

JAMES PETRAS is Professor Emeritus in Sociology at Binghamton University, New York. He is the author of over sixty books and numerous other writings, including *Globaloney: El lenguaje imperial, los intelectuales y la izquierda* (2000), *Hegemonia dos Estados Unidos no Nova Milênio* (2001), *Globalization Unmasked* (2000), *Cardoso's Brazil: A Land for Sale* (2003) and *Social Movements and State Power* (2005).

HENRY VELTMEYER is Professor of International Development Studies at the Universidad Autónoma de Zacatecas (Zacatecas, México) and Saint Mary's University (Halifax, Canada). He has authored, coauthored and edited over thirty books on issues of global and Latin American development, including *Transcending Neoliberalism: Community Based Development in Latin America* (Kumarian, 2001), *Globalization/Antiglobalization* (Ashgate, 2004) and two books previously published by Fernwood Books/Zed Books – *Globalization Unmasked* (2000) and *System in Crisis* (2003).

LUCIANO VASAPOLLO is professor of statistical sciences at the University of Rome, Director of CESTES, a socioenomic research institute, and the journal of social scientific and world affairs. He has published numerous works, including *L'Europa vista dai Sud: Uno sguardo da Cuba* (2004), *La dolce maschera dell,Europa* (2004) and *Competizione globale*, with M. Casadio, J. Petras and H. Veltmeyer (2004).

MAURO CASADIO is Director of *Rete dei Comunisti*, a journal of independent socioeconomic research, and member of the Comitato Scientifico del Laboratorio per la Critica Sociale. He has contributed to numerous writings and books, including *No/Made Italy Eurobang: la multinazionale Italia e i lavoratori nella competizione globale* (2001), *Clash! Scontro tra potenze* (2004) and *Competizione globale* (2004).